THE ROTATION

THE ROTATION

A SEASON WITH THE PHILLIES AND ONE OF THE

GREATEST PITCHING STAFFS EVER ASSEMBLED

JIM SALISBURY AND TODD ZOLECKI

FOREWORD BY
GARY SMITH

RUNNING PRESS
PHILADELPHIA · LONDON

© 2012 by Jim Salisbury and Todd Zolecki

Cover and interior photography © Miles Kennedy

Published by Running Press,
A Member of the Perseus Books Group

Books published by Running Press are available at special discounts for bulk purchases in the United States by corporations, institutions, and other organizations. For more information, please contact the Special Markets Department at the Perseus Books Group, 2300 Chestnut Street, Suite 200, Philadelphia, PA 19103, or call (800) 810-4145, ext. 5000, or email special.markets@perseusbooks.com.

ISBN 978-0-7624-4400-7
Library of Congress Control Number: 2011925146

Ebook ISBN 978-0-7624-4491-5

9   8   7   6   5   4   3   2   1
Digit on the right indicates the number of this printing

Cover and interior designer: Josh McDonnell
Editor: Greg Jones
Typography: Akzidenz, Bembo, and City

Running Press Book Publishers
2300 Chestnut Street
Philadelphia, PA 19103-4371

Visit us on the web!
www.runningpress.com

To Mom, Dad and Ann, in appreciation of all your love and support.

—Jim Salisbury

To my late grandparents: Roy and Josie Vierzba and Art and Wanda Zolecki. My family's four aces.

—Todd Zolecki

CONTENTS

FOREWORD

Three decades had flown by since I'd stood inside the locker room of a professional sports team, waiting for athletes to emerge from mysterious hiding places, and with any luck at all—I *thought*—three decades more would fly, as well. I'd been liberated from that life by an offer to write for a magazine in 1982, and nothing could possibly un-liberate me . . . until something did.

The Rotation.

I watched my hand in surprise—a few weeks after the Phillies' December 2010 ambush acquisition of Cliff Lee—as it rose to volunteer me to write a series of stories for *Sports Illustrated* that would chronicle the team's historical starting pitching staff and their 2011 season. What would it be like, I wondered through that winter, for a team and a city to send four masters to the mound in succession, over and over again, for six—and surely seven—straight months?

The Four Aces, the Four Horsemen, the Fab Four: Every Philly writer worth his carpal tunnel had a nickname for them. Mine was The Legion of Arms, for it was a rotation that tickled the child inside an aging sports fan, a foursome that conjured memories of comic-book superheroes joining forces to quell their foes. And, yep, it was easy to feel like a 10-year-old on that February day when the Legion sat down shoulder to shoulder for its season-opening press conference.

But then came the reality of April and May, the hard fact that I'd have to spend long hours standing in a clubhouse, staring at vacant lockers or at players' backs. Back in my old life: back on a *beat*.

It's the perfect multilayered word, it occurred to me as I tried to hang in there with the two beat men who authored this book—Jim Salisbury of CSNPhilly.com and Todd Zolecki of MLB.com. *Beat*, as in the daily round that a cop makes, keeping tabs on the locals. *Beat*, as in the fear of getting beat by the competition that every daily reporter lives in, especially on a media-magnet story like this one. *Beat*, as in how a man feels trying to put in the ridiculous hours that Jim and Todd invested each day to capture this story and this book. *Beat*, as in the rhythmic tick of the clock as we waited for the

Four Aces to materialize and articulate what it feels like to mingle with co-masters and dominate the best hitters in the world.

And waited . . . and waited. . . . For the Legion of Arms, just like the superheroes they conjured, were a terse and tight-lipped crew, rationing out a few careful words in their speech bubbles and then hurrying off to ply their craft, to condition their bodies, to recover in their oxygen tent, to ice their arms, to study their foes on video, or to talk hunting and fishing in a back room.

This was a story, I quickly realized, that a writer would have to work at from the edges, widening his scope to teammates, pitching coaches, opponents, broadcasters, fans. Watching Jim and Todd work it relentlessly day after day for far more days than I—melding into the media pack around a player one moment and then slipping away the next, following their instincts to poke around alone on the margins—left me with a vast respect for what it took to work this beat.

And in the end, no matter how hard they worked it, they were always at the mercy of it. It could end, as it did, with catastrophic suddenness, leaving their audience frozen and wanting only to push the whole thing away.

But the secret of the master fan is not unlike that of the master pitcher—the secret that Doc Halladay took seven years to learn: It can't be only about outcome. It has to be about each moment along the way. "It's not so much about a distinct finish line," Doc said one day, when I finally got him to sit down. "I might not always finish everything, but it's the doing of it that matters. That became how I measured myself. It's not so much finishing as it is continually *beating at it*. I had to learn to be in the moment."

The moments. The ones that everyone saw and heard, and the ones that only guys like Salisbury and Zolecki saw and heard. The beating at it, every day of the best season in a Phillies fan's life—up 'til the last day. That's what this book offers. You weren't ready for it last November or December, with that last missed note in your ears, but now the thaw's coming fast, and what a shame to lose the beat of that summer song.

—Gary Smith, November 2011

INTRODUCTION

John Kruk has never been afraid to say what's on his mind. Plain. Simple. Organic. If the thought is rattling around the Krukker's brain, it's going to find its way to his tongue and someone else's ears. And if it makes you uncomfortable, well, *Here's Johnny*.

"It must be time to talk about my nuts," Kruk said at the start of a news conference in Clearwater, Florida, in March 1994.

A gaggle of baseball writers winced empathetically when Kruk, then the Phillies first baseman, spoke those words as he rejoined the team after starting treatment for testicular cancer that month.

Seventeen years later, in a news conference at Citizens Bank Park, Kruk was once again saying it like it is. Seated at a dais on the day it was announced that he'd been elected as the 2011 inductee to the team's Wall of Fame, Kruk couldn't resist giving Phillies President David Montgomery a little poke.

"If you had given us a hundred and how much million, we could have been a little better," Kruk said.

Montgomery smiled sheepishly.

"Things have changed, John," he said.

Have they ever.

Just ask Scott Rolen. When he played third base for the Phillies from 1996 to 2002, baseball seemed irrelevant in Philadelphia. The team had payrolls that ranked among the lowest in the game, it played in front of an ocean of empty seats at Veterans Stadium, and losing seasons piled up like snowdrifts.

Now?

In 2011, the Phillies' opening-day payroll exceeded $175 million and ranked second only to the payroll of the mighty New York Yankees. They won their fifth straight National League East title, and their streak of sellouts reached 204 regular-season games.

"It's a far cry from hot dog wrappers blowing around the turf at the Vet," Rolen said during a visit to Citizens Bank Park with the Cincinnati Reds in May 2011. "There were 6,000 people in the stands, we were 30 back, and headed toward 90-something losses. That's not really going on here anymore.

It seems to me the whole Phillies baseball culture has changed. The only similarity I see is the cheesesteaks."

Terry Francona has seen the change, too. He was just 37 when he was hired to manage the Phillies in 1997. It was his first big-league manager's job. Francona never kidded himself. He got the job because the Phillies had plummeted to the basement of the National League and getting out of it would be a long, arduous journey, the kind best suited for a young man.

"In those days, the expectation was if we played well, we'd get to .500," Francona said. "If they were ready to win, they wouldn't have hired me. They would have hired [Jim] Leyland or someone like that."

Francona was fired after four losing seasons and went on to win the World Series with the Boston Red Sox in 2004 and 2007.

He returned to Philadelphia with the Red Sox in the summer of 2008, and his daughter Alyssa joined him on the trip. She had attended high school in Bucks County when her father managed the Phillies and Padilla's Flotilla was as close as anyone could get to a parade in Philadelphia. Walking around Center City on that June day, Alyssa noticed a change. She felt the electricity that can light up a town when its baseball team is good.

"Dad, it's really different around here," Alyssa Francona told her father. "Everyone is wearing red."

And it's not just the fans that are wearing red. Roy Halladay wears red pinstripes now. So does Cliff Lee and Roy Oswalt and, of course, Cole Hamels. Now that, folks, is a starting pitching rotation, the best in baseball, one might say. Whereas Francona once had to send the immortal Calvin Maduro to the minors, and then recall him to be his No. 2 starter—all in the same week in 1997—Charlie Manuel can give the ball to a Cy Young winner, an ERA champ, or a World Series MVP on any given day.

That's why, entering the 2011 season, the Phillies were considered World Series favorites, right there with Francona's Red Sox and the ubiquitous Yankees, baseball's big boys.

It might not have worked out that way, with the Phillies and Red Sox playing in the World Series, but it sure was fun to fantasize about as the season approached.

"They've done a terrific job," Francona said of the Phils in March 2011. "They're in a different place now. They have the ballpark. They're a big market. And people are hungry for a good team. Those people deserve a team like that. It's good for baseball."

Francona paused that March day as images of the Phillies' rotation

Palmer said, "All Earl knows about big-league pitching is that he couldn't hit it." Palmer was wrong in some ways. Weaver actually knew plenty about pitching. He knew it was king in baseball. "The only thing that matters is what happens on that little hump in the middle of the field," Weaver once said. Amaro, a lifetime .235 hitter in 435 big-league games, knew the importance of pitching long before he started working for Gillick, but his commitment to it was made even stronger during his time under Gillick, a pitching-first guy. Not long after becoming GM, Amaro said, "Pitching rules the day." It became one of his favorite aphorisms. He didn't just say it. He lived it. He had an obsession with pitching, an obsession that led to The Rotation.

Trying to parlay Philadelphia's newfound status as a destination city for ballplayers—it's amazing how far the shine of one of those World Series rings can radiate—Amaro spent part of his first season as GM trying to make a trade for the best pitcher in baseball, Roy Halladay, the 2003 American League Cy Young Award winner. When that deal fell through, he landed Cliff Lee, the 2008 AL Cy Young winner.

Lee helped take the Phillies back to the World Series in 2009 and helped increase Philadelphia's luster as a destination city for top talent. Within the next nine months, Halladay and Roy Oswalt both waived no-trade clauses to come to the Phils. Philadelphia used to regularly appear on players' no-trade clauses. Now, to hell with those private jets, they'd hitchhike to town to be fitted for red pinstripes.

Of course, the lure all started with the winning.

Things have changed, John.

"I remember when I first came up," said Rollins, who debuted in 2000, when the team was still in Veterans Stadium and finished tied with the Chicago Cubs for the worst record in the game. "We'd have a meeting the first day of spring training and the GM would say our goal was to win the World Series. We'd kind of look around and think, 'Yeah, right.' But now we have that meeting and we all believe it."

——————— K ———————

To fully grasp what great baseball times these are in Philadelphia, you have to go back to a darker day when the Phils played in front of thousands of empty seats at the Vet.

During spring training in 1997, Curt Schilling practically pleaded for a contract extension. Three months later, before the deal even officially kicked in, he was raising his hand, offering to waive his no-trade clause. The Phillies went 4-22 in June of that year. During a three-game series at Camden Yards in that ugly season, President Bill Clinton came out to a game. Security rules dictated that all players be in uniform when Clinton came through the club-house for a pregame visit. Before Clinton arrived, a security force swept through the clubhouse. The room was packed as Clinton made the rounds.

The scene provided a perfect opportunity for the sharp-tongued Schilling.

"You'll have to excuse me if I seem a little nervous, Mr. President," Schilling said as he reached through a crowd to shake Clinton's hand. "I'm not used to being in my uniform in front of this many people."

There was no greater critic of the Phillies in the late 1990s than Schilling. Though he could often be self-serving, he pitched his ass off and there was never a doubt that he wanted to play for a winner. He'd often spoken of how great Philadelphia was in 1993 when he pitched for the surprise NL champions, but by 1996 those days were long gone, and by 2000, when Schilling finally forced a trade to Arizona . . . well, as he said a few years later, "We had fourteen big-league players on those teams."

The Phils' payrolls in the late 1990s were in the bottom third in the game, and Schilling took every opportunity to criticize ownership for not spending what it took to put a contender on the field. In 1999, the Phils opened the season with a $28-million payroll. In May of that year, before a game in Montreal, Schilling told reporters it was time for Phillies ownership to do more or sell the team. Schilling's stinging remarks were so calculated it was surprising that he didn't issue a script in French, just for the Montreal media.

Rolen got so fed up with the losing and the direction of the team that he turned down a long-term contract worth about $90 million from the Phils on his way to being traded to St. Louis.

In the late 1990s there was little for baseball fans to get excited about in Philadelphia, and when there was, the team occasionally went out of its way to reel in the excitement. In May 1998, Mike Piazza was traded from the Los Angeles Dodgers to the Florida Marlins. Florida was just a way station for Piazza. The Marlins made it known that they intended to quickly spin him off in another deal. Phillies fans began salivating. Piazza, one of the game's premier sluggers, had grown up in the Philadelphia suburbs. He idolized Mike Schmidt and made regular trips to Veterans Stadium as a kid. He was the perfect Phillie, except for one problem—there was no way in hell he was going to be a Phillie. Team officials put a quick end to any fairy-tale dreams. They preemptively reached out to reporters who covered the team to tell them that Piazza was "not a fit," which was code for the team's saying it didn't want to spend the money needed to extend his contract.

As sad days in franchise history go, it wasn't Black Friday, not even close, really. But the dousing of enthusiasm surrounding Mike Piazza's availability that spring was a sad reminder of how microscopic the Phillies had become on the baseball landscape.

Baseball was so grim in Philadelphia in the late 1990s that the people who ran radio station WIP for several years would not allow their hosts to talk about baseball. Imagine that—an all-sports radio station eliminating an entire major sport from its list of discussion topics.

It turned out that Phillies management had a plan. They could not compete with baseball's big boys while playing in Veterans Stadium. They needed one of those modern ballparks that people wanted to come to and, more importantly, spend oodles of money in. It probably wasn't right that for a good many years the baseball product became secondary while the team, along with the city and the state, figured out a way to get a new stadium, but those dark days gave birth to this Golden Age of Phillies baseball. David Montgomery always said that when the Phillies got their new stadium and their revenue streams improved, the club would have a payroll commensurate with its market size and be in the running for elite players.

He kept his promise.

But even as the doors to a new stadium opened in 2004, there were problems. Pitchers on both sides of the field complained about the stadium's cozy power alleys. John Smoltz ripped the place and David Wells ridiculed it. One rival coach called it "Williamsport." Jake Peavy said "that new park in Philly might be the worst in baseball." The Phillies will never attract an elite pitcher to that ballpark, the critics howled.

Baseball relevance did not automatically come with the new ballpark. Before spring training in 2005, in an effort to drum up some buzz for the coming season, the club invited media members to Citizens Bank Park to meet the team's new coaching staff. Meanwhile, on the same day 100 miles to the north, the Yankees were introducing the newest member of their starting pitching rotation, Randy Johnson.

Come meet our coaches!

Oh, yeah?

COME MEET OUR FIVE-TIME CY YOUNG WINNER!!

Something was still missing. The Phillies still weren't ready to be one of baseball's big boys.

Only winning would complete the transformation. Only winning would fill the seats and give the team the revenues it needed to be one of baseball's big boys.

They got to the doorstep in 2007. They broke the door down in 2008.

"I think we changed the culture and the feeling around here," said Pat Gillick, surveying the Phils' ascension in the spring of 2011. "It was always like Philly was behind New York and now I think that's changed. At least I think we're even with New York and maybe a little ahead."

In New York, they agree. After years of eating turkey on the card table in the den, the Phillies now sit at the adult table. Pass the cranberry sauce, Mr. Steinbrenner.

"I don't like that description because it sounds arrogant," said Brian Cashman, the Yankees GM. "I just look at it this way: Philly has graduated to a big-market team. They've jumped class. It shows what can happen if you go about your business the right way. They've done what the Red Sox did. Those red hats are all over the place. Red Sox Nation, Yankee Universe, Phillies Whatever. They're there. They've built a great brand, a great park, a packed park, and worldwide support. What they've done—you have to genuflect to it."

——————— K ———————

Things have changed, John.

But have they really?

Pitching has always, as Amaro likes to say, ruled the day in baseball. Oh, sure, there was Murderers' Row and the Big Red Machine, teams that pounded the baseball, but pitching has long been the consistent strength of winning teams, even if they had to pray for rain after using Spahn and Sain.

There would be no praying for rain with the 2011 Phillies. Hits and runs, maybe, but not rain. Many teams had one ace pitcher, some even had two, but the Phillies had depth, the ability to send an ace to the mound four out of five days, a tremendous strength in the daily test of endurance and skill that is the baseball season. Amaro had landed Halladay—or was it vice versa?—in a December 2009 trade, Oswalt in a July 2010 trade, and stunningly brought back Lee with a stealthy free-agent strike in December 2010. And not one of them blinked an eye at calling Citizens Bank Park home. Turns out that was a loser's lament.

"It's all about making pitches," Halladay says in almost every postgame interview. Effective pitching can win anywhere. Greg Maddux, the great former Atlanta Braves Cy Young winner, used to say that hitters don't hit home runs, pitchers give them up. Halladay, Lee, and Oswalt weren't ones to blame a cozy power alley for their leaving a 3-1 fastball over the heart of the plate. This veteran threesome joined homegrown Cole Hamels, twice an MVP in the run to the 2008 World Series title, in, dare we say, the best rotation ever assembled.

Entering 2011, this foursome owned 10 top-five finishes in Cy Young voting, three Cy Young Awards, 13 All-Star selections, a half dozen 20-win seasons, three postseason MVP Awards, and a 20-8 postseason record. In 2010, all four had finished in the top 21 in the majors in ERA. Halladay (.662), Oswalt (.643), and Lee (.625) came into the season ranked, respectively, first, fifth, and eighth in career winning percentage among active pitchers with at least 100 decisions. The last team to enter a season with three winning percentages that good was the 1957 Dodgers with Sal Maglie, Don Newcombe, and Carl Erskine.

"This is a great staff," a rival scout marveled the morning after waking up and learning the Phillies had signed Lee. "There will be a lot of hitters looking at 0 for 16 when you face them in a four-game series."

"Hands down, the best rotation in baseball, maybe one of the best ever," said another envious scout from a rival club.

Before even throwing a pitch as teammates in 2011, The Rotation was being compared to some of the best staffs ever: the 1954 Indians; the Dodgers of the mid-1960s; The Giants in 1962; the Mets in 1986; the Diamondbacks in 2001; the Athletics of the early 2000s; and others.

But on some of those staffs, the greatness went just two deep.

The Phillies go four deep, and with Joe Blanton, Vance Worley, and Kyle Kendrick in the mix, the No. 5 spot figured to be in capable hands.

On paper, the Phillies staff compared favorably to two of the best and deepest of the modern era—the 1971 Orioles and the Braves of the 1990s. The '71 Orioles had a foursome of 20-game winners. The Braves had three sure-bet Hall of Famers.

"When it's all said and done, this Phillies staff potentially could be in the argument with the best all-time," broadcaster and baseball historian Bob Costas said.

Time, health, and the great test of a season that can last seven months, ultimately, would have its say on The Rotation. But if what Earl Weaver said was true, if the only thing that matters is what happens on that little hump in the middle of the field, then the 2011 Phillies had every reason to report to spring training with the highest of hopes.

Meet The Rotation and Its Supporting Cast.

COLE HAMELS

On a cool autumn night in October 2008, 24-year-old Cole Hamels stood on the field at Citizens Bank Park and cradled the World Series MVP trophy in his left arm.

Magic filled that left arm, just as his mom and dad had suspected a decade earlier. Back home in San Diego, Amanda Hamels would watch her son throw balls in the yard and be amazed how he could pick out a target and "ping it," from any distance. Gary Hamels saw the magic, too. Young Cole would often pitch to his dad until one day, when the boy was about 13, Gary went in the house and told his wife, "I don't think I can catch this kid anymore."

Mark Furtak saw the magic early in 2000 when Hamels threw for him in the bullpen at Rancho Bernardo High School in San Diego.

"I think I can make the JV team," the gangly sophomore excitedly told the pitching coach.

To hell with that, Furtak thought to himself.

"I want you to think varsity," Furtak told the kid. "From this day on, I want you to act like a varsity guy."

Hamels did just that.

"He started off the season as our Number Three pitcher and by the end was our Number Two," Furtak said. "Our Number One was a first-round draft pick and by the end of the season Cole was keeping right up with him."

Scouts always flock to Rancho Bernardo because it has a tremendous baseball program that always turns out great talent. Former All-Star third baseman Hank Blalock came out of the program in 1999. In the spring of 2000, scouts came to watch pitcher Matt Wheatland, a first-round pick of the Detroit Tigers, and catcher Scott Heard, a first-round pick of the Texas Rangers.

When they were done watching Wheatland and Heard, they stuck around to see Cole Hamels.

"He was dominant—even as a sophomore," said Jim Fregosi Jr., who in those days was one of the Phillies' top West Coast scouts.

The Hamels kid had a nice, loose, easy-working arm, a beautiful delivery, and a tall, angular, projectable frame. His fastball was only in the mid-80s his sophomore year, but it would improve, no doubt, when Mother Nature did her work on that body.

What made scouts' jaws drop was that changeup, a baffling pitch that made hitters flail at air. Scouts scribbled Hamels' name in their notebooks. This kid had first-rounder written all over him. He'd be worth following the next two years.

———————— K ————————

Cole Hamels is the only member of The Rotation that is homegrown. Roy Halladay, Roy Oswalt, and Joe Blanton came in trades, Cliff Lee as a free agent. The Phillies got Hamels with the 17th overall pick in the 2002 draft.

Being drafted in the first round is the realization of a dream, a reward for hard work and talent, for any ballplayer.

For Hamels, and everyone close to him, it was extra special because his selection came less than two years after he wondered if he'd ever throw a baseball again.

Furtak is a middle school physical education teacher and a former pitcher at the University of Hawaii. He will enter his 23rd season as Rancho Bernardo's pitching coach in 2012.

He easily recalls his most difficult day on the job.

"I still remember hearing the pop," he said.

Hamels had just finished an impressive sophomore season and was pitching in a "coaches' league" in the summer of 2000. The league is designed to give coaches a look at younger players who will be moving up in coming seasons. Furtak recalled being excited before one of Hamels' starts that July. He always got a little rush when the lefty took the mound.

"I remember it like it was yesterday," he said in the fall of 2011. "It was at Grossmont High School. We were playing Poway."

Furtak paused.

"It was the worst thing I've ever gone through as a coach," he said.

Early in that game, Hamels threw a pitch and collapsed to the ground in pain. Furtak recalled seeing the ball hit halfway up the backstop as he sprinted the mound to tend to Hamels.

The young pitcher's face was white.

"My whole body hurts," he told Furtak.

Hamels clutched the upper part of his left arm. Furtak knew from the pop that something was dreadfully wrong. He had been in the stands on May 9, 1994, the night Cincinnati Reds pitcher Tom Browning suffered a broken left humerus while throwing a pitch in a game in San Diego. The injury effectively ended Browning's career.

"I was at the Browning game," he said. "It was like hearing a tree branch snap. This was the same thing."

Silence fell over the field as Hamels was tended to. Finally, with the help of others, the young pitcher rose to his feet, and made it to his mother's car for a race to the hospital.

"It was pure devastation," said Hamels, recalling the ride to the hospital. "I never cried so hard in my life. I thought it was over. I thought I'd have to take up soccer again."

Furtak stayed at the game, but his thoughts were elsewhere. He thought he had just witnessed the last pitch Cole Hamels would ever throw. He really did.

When the game was over, Furtak and Head Coach Sam Blalock went to the hospital.

"This is not a normal arm," Furtak plaintively told one of the doctors. "You need to do something special."

———————— K ————————

Hamels was diagnosed with a complete fracture of the humerus bone. Doctors believe he initially weakened the bone, or suffered a stress reaction or microfracture, running into a parked car while playing touch football the day before. The force of throwing a pitch caused the weakened bone to snap.

A day after the injury, Hamels visited Jan Fronek, a highly regarded San Diego orthopedic surgeon who was also the San Diego Padres team physician.

"I remember Dr. Fronek telling me he wasn't sure I'd ever throw a baseball again," Hamels said. "He said you might want to pick a different position."

Four days after the injury, Fronek performed surgery on Hamels and inserted two rods into the humerus.

Everyone crossed their fingers.

The rehab moved in baby steps. Hamels did not pitch during his junior year at Rancho Bernardo. He pinch-hit occasionally, but spent most of his time shagging balls in the outfield during batting practice. After having the rods removed in January 2001, he started tossing with Furtak at a distance of 10 feet. By April, he started throwing lightly in the bullpen. The intensity of the bullpen sessions increased until nearly a year had passed since the injury. The Broncos were playing a coaches' league game in July 2001. Furtak asked Hamels if he wanted to pitch an inning. Hamels got up on the mound. His arm stayed in one piece. If surgical procedures were measured like a pitcher's starts, Fronek would have been credited with a perfect game.

Getting on the mound a year after the injury helped Hamels clear an important physical and psychological hurdle, but he was far from ready to turn it loose for scouts. He was slow coming out of the gate in workouts before his senior season. He had felt some soreness in the arm and was still very tentative. The Rancho Bernardo coaching staff went slow with Hamels, letting the pitcher dictate his own pace. As the season began to unfold, Furtak believed Hamels was physically ready to let it all out. It was time for a pep talk.

"Cole, you've got about a two-month window here to show these guys how good you are," Furtak told Hamels. "You're ready."

Hamels made his senior-season debut on March 30, 2002. Furtak recalls seeing one scout, Darrell Conner of the Phillies, at the game.

"How's Cole doing?" Conner asked Furtak before the game.

"You're going to like this," Furtak told Conner. "You're going to really like this. He might be better than Wheatland."

Conner's report from that game showed how much he liked Hamels.

"The ball jumped out of his hand with very little effort," the report read. "Fastball gets on hitters quickly. Power kind of curveball with late 12-6 break. Changeup has good arm speed and fade. Threw it for strikes."

In the summary of his report, Conner mentioned this was Hamels' first start of the season and he was on a strict pitch count.

"A very pleasant surprise," Conner wrote. "I don't know what the medical will say, but if he's cleared, this young man profiles as an Eric Milton-type starter. I loved what I saw."

So did every other Phillies scout who stopped by that spring.

A report filed after Hamels' start on April 12, 2002, said: "See him as a Number One starter on a major-league club. Has impact-type stuff. Will move quickly through a system. Mound presence and professional approach stand out."

On May 3, another Phillies scouting report read: "A definite consideration at number seventeen."

Hamels got better and better that season. In his year away from the mound, he had gotten bigger and stronger physically, and it showed in his fastball.

"I had never seriously trained, so I think the rehab helped me," he said. "I went from 6-1, 140 to 6-3, 170. My fastball went from 85 to 91–92. I was like, 'Wow, this is pretty sweet.' "

Conner stayed on Hamels and all the Phillies' big scouts popped in for a look-see. Marti Wolever, who had taken over as scouting director when Mike Arbuckle moved up in the front office the previous year, watched one of Hamels' starts and told Conner, "That's our guy. Don't miss another start." Arbuckle made a trip to San Diego and was impressed with the kid's demeanor.

"He had a way about him that said, *I've got this under control*," Arbuckle recalled.

Less than two years after he had worried about Hamels' pitching days being over before they really started, Furtak enjoyed every pitch the left-hander threw that season. With each passing start, he saw Hamels' confidence and competitiveness grow. The kid was healthy—and really good.

"One time we were playing Torrey Pines," Furtak said. "Cole had a no-hitter going and a guy tried to bunt on him. He was pissed."

Hamels sought retribution. He threw at the code-breaking hitter twice, missing him both times. Hamels looked into the dugout where Furtak motioned for him to calm down. Furtak motioned for a fastball and Hamels blew the hitter away with two of them.

In another game, Furtak went to the mound and instructed Hamels to walk a batter.

"Can't I just hit him?" Hamels asked.

"Look," Furtak said. "Walk this guy, throw the next guy three straight curveballs and you're out of the inning."

Bingo, bango, bongo. Hamels was out of the inning.

The game Furtak remembers most was Hamels' last one.

"It was at Montgomery High School," he said. "Cole seemed a little out of sorts in the bullpen. He was bouncing his curveball ten feet in front of the plate. It was right before the draft and there must have been forty scouts standing there watching him warm up. Every time he bounced a curveball, they'd write something down."

In the dugout after warm-ups, Furtak tried to calm Hamels' nerves.

"Dude, you're going to be fine," he said. "You'll be awesome."

When Hamels took the mound, Furtak instructed the catcher to call a first-pitch curveball.

"It was a beauty," Furtak said.

Hamels gave the scouts plenty to write about that day. He pitched so brilliantly that the opposing coach asked him to sign a ball after the game.

"That kid is going to be something special," the coach told Furtak.

———————————— K ————————————

Even as Hamels dazzled during his senior season at Rancho Bernardo, there were skeptics in the scouting community. Conner remembers hearing his brethren from other clubs wonder how Hamels would react once he got to Double-A and was having a bad night, or a bad stretch of games. Was he tough enough to handle that adversity? Was he tough enough to make the climb to the majors?

Conner had no doubt.

"For me, coming back from that injury spoke volumes," Conner said. "He could have went to school and I believe been a success in whatever he did. He could have ridden off into the sunset, but he fought back. The toughness question never crossed my mind. It was never a concern for me."

The 2002 draft was a deep one. First-rounders that year included B. J. Upton, Zack Greinke, Prince Fielder, Jeff Francis, Joe Saunders, Khalil Greene, Scott Kazmir, Nick Swisher, Jeff Francoeur, Joe Blanton, and Matt Cain.

The Phillies had long liked Greinke, a shortstop-pitcher from the Orlando area who went on to win an American League Cy Young Award with Kansas City in 2009. In the spring of 2002, some folks in the Phillies organization favored using the 17th pick on Greinke—if he was still there. Interestingly, the Phillies liked Greinke as an infielder. The team had come to realize that Scott Rolen's time in Philadelphia was coming to an end and some in the organization leaned toward selecting Greinke and converting him to a third baseman. In the end, it was a moot point. Greinke went off the board at No. 6.

During the time they spent evaluating Greinke at Apopka High School, Phillies scouts noticed a teammate, a young outfielder named Michael Taylor. The Phils kept an eye on Taylor throughout his college days at Stanford, drafted him in 2007, and ultimately used him as part of the package to get Roy Halladay from Toronto in 2009.

Wolever never wavered in the spring of 2002. Though he looked at many others, Hamels was the guy he wanted in the first round. But Wolever had to do some convincing before Cole Hamels could be fitted for red pinstripes. Signing bonuses had skyrocketed by 2002 and it would take an investment of at least $2 million to get Hamels out of his commitment to the University of San Diego. The case was turned over to team physician Michael Ciccotti, who was charged with reviewing Hamels' health history and deciding if he'd be a wise investment.

Ciccotti spent hours on the case. He reviewed x-rays, MRIs, and surgical reports. He spoke frequently with Fronek.

"What are you thinking?" Wolever asked Ciccotti a few days before the draft.

"I think this guy's potential upside is worth the medical risk," Ciccotti told Wolever.

Wolever was thrilled to hear that.

Ciccotti felt comfortable making the call for a number of reasons. He and Fronek are old friends—their sons, Matt Ciccotti and Jeff Fronek, were classmates at Penn—in the fraternity of baseball team physicians and his trust for the San Diego surgeon and his work is immense. The injury, though serious, was not to the labrum or rotator cuff in the shoulder or the ulna collateral ligament in the elbow. Those are dreaded pitching injuries. This was a broken bone, in the middle of the shaft. Hamels was young and otherwise healthy. Those were all pluses in Ciccotti's mind.

The final piece of evidence that Ciccotti used in giving Hamels the thumbs-up was the pitcher's work during his senior season at Rancho Bernardo. The kid had healed, done his rehab, and come back better than ever. That was enough for Ciccotti to make the call that other teams weren't willing to make.

"The two guys most responsible for Cole being a Phillie are Marti Wolever and Dr. Ciccotti," said Mike Arbuckle, who moved on to Kansas City's front office in 2009. "Marti really pushed for him and Dr. Ciccotti gave him the OK after a whole bunch of teams red-flagged him. Dr. Ciccotti knew Cole's doctor and knew how he was handled. He said, 'It's not going to be an issue,' and we were comfortable with it."

The consensus around baseball: Hamels would have gone in the top 10, maybe the top 5, if he didn't have the medical concern.

Hamels' medical condition actually led Phillies scouts to engage in some high-stakes cat-and-mouse games before the draft. In the days before a draft, it is not uncommon for a scout from one club to call a scout from a rival club to get a feel for what that club might do with its first pick. When opposing teams asked Phillies scouts about Hamels, the Phillies scouts told strategic white lies.

"We can't take that risk," one Phillies scout told a rival club that was considering taking Hamels before the 17th pick.

On June 4, the 2002 draft began. In a basement conference room at Veterans Stadium, the Phillies scouting staff listened via conference call as the names began coming off the board. Sixteen picks were made and now there was elation in the room. Wolever cleared his throat and said, "The Philadelphia Phillies select left-handed pitcher Hamels, Colbert Hamels, from Rancho Bernardo High School, San Diego, California."

Conner, the Southern California-based area scout who had been on Hamels all along, was at home, getting ready to go check out some players for the next year's draft when he got the news. He was elated. All those visits to the Hamels' home, all those phone calls to the pitcher the night before starts, all those days behind the backstop . . . they were worth it.

"The way the draft works, there's a lot of chance and luck that goes into it," said Conner, still with the club as a West Coast cross-checker. "But when you get the one you want at Number One, it's pretty special. That was a very rewarding day."

Eight pitchers went before Hamels in the draft. Only Greinke's success rivals that of Hamels. Four left-handers—Adam Loewen, Francis, Saunders, and Kazmir—went ahead of Hamels. Kazmir was selected by the Mets two picks before Hamels at 17.

The two matched up against each other in Game 1 of the 2008 World Series when Kazmir was with Tampa Bay. Hamels went seven innings and allowed just two runs. Kazmir went six innings and allowed three. It was Hamels' fourth win of that postseason and when it was over, Rob Holiday, the Phillies' assistant director of scouting, looked at his boss, Wolever, as if to say, "We got the right one."

One of the 16 teams that passed on Hamels that June was his hometown Padres, who selected Greene, a shortstop out of Clemson with the 13th pick.

In the spring of 2011, Hamels said the Padres passed on him because he was too expensive. He received a $2 million bonus and the Padres paid Greene $1.5 million.

Bill Gayton, San Diego's scouting director in 2002, disputed Hamels' claim that he was too expensive for the Padres. Gayton said his team extensively scouted Hamels, liked him, and, of course, had no medical concerns given that their team physician was the pitcher's personal doctor.

"I took our whole draft room over to watch his last start and he was impressive," Gayton said.

According to Gayton, the Padres' decision to take Greene reflected an organizational desire to get a middle-of-the-diamond position player that could rise to the majors and make a quick impact. Greene, who was college baseball's Player of the Year in 2002, became the first position player from the 2002 draft to reach the majors when he made it to San Diego late in the 2003 season. He started at shortstop for the Padres for five seasons, but hasn't played since 2009.

As a kid, Hamels was a big Padres fan. He was angry when the Padres traded Fred McGriff. He liked watching Ken Caminiti and Steve Finley with the 1998 World Series team. And, of course, he loved watching Trevor Hoffman throw that changeup. It was his inspiration for learning the pitch. But a decade into his pro career, Hamels said he was glad that the Padres passed on him in the 2002 draft. He believes there would have been too many distractions pitching for his hometown team. And besides, he likes the passion of the East Coast.

"Now I know there is nothing better than pitching in Philadelphia in front of sellout crowds," Hamels said in April 2011. "There aren't too may sellouts on the West Coast. There's just so much to do out there. The East Coast is the ultimate baseball experience."

---------------- K ----------------

Brett Myers was a second-year major-leaguer on his way to making 32 starts for the Phillies when he started hearing about Cole Hamels in 2003.

"I was like, *Holy shit! This guy is striking out everyone,*" Myers recalled in April of 2011.

A year out of high school, Hamels looked like what scouts call a fast-tracker. He overmatched hitters in the South Atlantic League, going 6-1 with an 0.84 ERA in 13 starts. Out of curiosity, Phils officials brought Hamels, then just 19, to Cooperstown, New York, for the annual Hall of Fame exhibition game that June. Hamels dazzled everyone with his poise and control, striking out nine Tampa Bay Rays in five innings. He moved up to the Florida State League and held his own against hitters several years older. In all, Hamels struck out 147 batters in 101 innings his first year in pro ball. He was becoming an overnight phenom and his star was about to become even brighter.

The Phillies invited Hamels to big-league spring training camp in 2004. Though the pitcher had no chance of making the big club after just 100 pro innings in the low minors, club officials were eager to get a look at the 20-year-old prospect. On March 5, just before Hamels was about to be sent to minor-league camp, the Phillies brass decided to give him a start against the New York Yankees in Tampa. Two years earlier, Hamels had been playing catch with Mark Furtak as he rehabbed his broken arm. Now, he was about to pitch two innings against a Yankees lineup that had played in the World Series the year before. This would be the day that every sports fan in Philadelphia—not just the hard-core baseball fans, but every sports fan, from leather-lunged E-A-G-L-E-S backers to the orange-clad Flyers rooters—would learn the name Cole Hamels.

In his second inning of work, Hamels faced Derek Jeter, Alex Rodriguez, and Tony Clark. He struck out all three of them. In one inning, he went from prospect to mega-prospect, becoming probably the most ballyhooed minor-leaguer in franchise history.

It was no surprise that Hamels went to his changeup against the famed Yankee hitters. Major leaguers are wired to hit fastballs, and a good changeup—one that looks like a fastball until it dies at the plate—can reduce even the best hitter to a pile of frustration. As a youngster, Hamels watched Trevor Hoffman close games for the Padres throwing almost nothing but changeups. "I need that pitch," he said to himself. When Furtak got a look at Hamels as a sophomore in high school, he agreed. Hamels needed that pitch.

"He didn't have enough fastball to get it by hitters," Furtak said.

Furtak had no doubt the fastball would come as Hamels got stronger, but in the meantime, he decided to teach him the changeup and have him pitch backward—i.e., throw changeups in counts where hitters usually expect to see fastballs.

Furtak showed Hamels the changeup grip and told him to throw it.

"He threw it right into the ground," Furtak said with a laugh.

Hamels kept throwing the pitch and picked it up quickly. He had nice movement and fade on the pitch. He had the confidence to throw it in games because he had a first-round draft pick behind the plate. No matter where Hamels' changeup went, Scott Heard was going to catch it. Four years later, Derek Jeter and Alex Rodriguez couldn't hit it.

Phillies officials left that game in Tampa thinking that Hamels was riding in the high-speed lane to the majors. But it turned out that Hamels was pitching with a secret that day. His elbow hurt even before he took the mound, but he was so excited about the opportunity to pitch in a big-league game against the Yankees that he said nothing about it. It would be the first of several mistakes that Hamels made early in his pro career, the first of several mistakes that the young pitcher turned into the learning experiences that helped him become one of the top pitchers in the game.

Hamels made just 10 starts in 2004 and 2005. Ten. There were times when the same people who believed he would be a fast-tracker to the majors wondered if he was going to be an injury-plagued washout, just another great talent that never got out of Double-A. Hamels was slowed significantly by an elbow strain in 2004, and in 2005 by a lower-back condition that he learned would require almost constant maintenance.

In between the elbow strain and the back issue, Hamels broke a bone in his pitching hand throwing not a changeup, but a punch, in a fight outside a Clearwater barroom called Razzel's Lounge. A group of Phillies and Toronto Blue Jays minor leaguers were finishing up a night on the town on January 29, 2005. Words were exchanged between some of the ballplayers and some of the locals at the bar. Hamels said he acted in self-defense when he popped one of the locals. Clearwater police said he and the ballplayers were the aggressors, with Hamels, then 21, getting out of a car to throw that punch. No charges were filed, but Hamels was punished in more ways than one. The organization revoked his invite to big-league spring-training camp. And the broken hand required surgery and another trip to that prison known as injury rehab.

While the Phillies' big leaguers worked out of the major-league complex that February, Hamels reported to the minor-league complex for rehab workouts every afternoon, long after the big leaguers had left.

"I wish I was there," he said one day that February, his voice filled with regret.

There would be more regret later that season. Hamels' hand healed and he went 4-0 with a 2.19 ERA in six starts at Single A Clearwater and Double-A Reading. Phillies officials were starting to think that Hamels might be able to help the big club late in the season when lower back soreness ended his season in late July.

Back to rehab prison.

Hamels saw back specialists and was diagnosed with a disc problem. He had always been a kid that could grab a baseball and ring up a dozen strike-outs with ease. But now, in his early twenties, he had grown to 6-4 and it would take work to keep his long frame strong and aligned. It would take work to compete at the levels Hamels wanted to reach. Would he be willing to do it?

"I took a lot of things for granted," said Hamels, reflecting in 2006 on the hurdles he'd encountered early in his pro career. "I was a player who got by year after year on talent. But talent only takes you so far. The fact of the matter is you actually have to work at this game to be successful. I've learned that the hard way. But sometimes, to be a better person and player, you have to learn things the hard way.

"When you see an opportunity in front of you dwindling and dimin-ishing because of the way you go about your business—it's not a good feeling. I got offtrack that first big-league camp. I hurt my elbow and didn't tell anyone. Then I got in the fight. I made a mistake. I learned to walk the other way. It was a wake-up call. Everything."

Hamels echoed a lot of those remarks during spring training in 2011.

"You think you're invincible," he said. "I thought I was invincible. But then you learn. You learn that you have to take advantage of your opportu-nities because they disappear fast."

Razzel's is still there in Clearwater, on Gulf to Bay Boulevard, just a couple of miles from the Phillies' training facility. It is strictly off-limits to the Phillies' minor-leaguers. Call it *The Cole Hamels Rule*. The fight is still brought up to Phillies officials from time to time. Six years after it occurred, one long-time club official said that once he was sure Hamels' hand would heal, he actually didn't mind that the pitcher had the little dustup.

"Cole came from a perfect, almost *Leave It to Beaver* background," said the official, asking not to be named. "It showed he had some 'nads."

Married with two young sons, Hamels barely recognizes the guy that threw that punch outside of the bar in January 2005.

"Values change," he said during the spring of 2011.

Hamels laughed.

"The funny thing is that place is a shithole," he said. "There were so many better spots."

———————— K ————————

When measured against the new generation of big-league stadia, Great American Ball Park in Cincinnati is hardly an eye-catcher. There is no panorama of the city skyline because the diamond faces away from downtown. On the outside, the place looks to be encased in poured concrete. The Ohio River flows languidly beyond the right-field wall, bringing with it driftwood, barges, and the occasional passing recreational boat.

Despite its lack of aesthetic charm, Great American Ball Park has been almost a personal field of dreams for Cole Hamels. After enduring long hours in Clearwater rehabbing injuries to his elbow, hand, and back, he finally made it to the major leagues and debuted in Cincinnati on May 12, 2006. He was nervous. You could see that in the five walks that he allowed in five innings. But there was also magic in that left arm. You could see that in the zero hits he allowed until his final inning and in the seven strikeouts he rang up.

Hamels had an aura about him as he took the mound that night.

"You heard about him all the time when he was in the minors," said Brett Myers, who had been the team's No. 1 pick in 1999, three years before Hamels. "There was nobody else doing what he was doing. I didn't do it. Gavin Floyd [another former No. 1 pick] didn't do it. He was making hitters look stupid. It was like, 'What does he have that makes him so good?' When he got here he showed us. He had great command and a great changeup. He was polished as hell. And he had heart and attitude."

Though he'd mix in an occasional curveball, Hamels was working mostly with two pitches—fastball and changeup—in those days. He would eventually learn, painfully, that he'd have to broaden his repertoire, but that was enough for a rookie pitcher who had the benefit of being unfamiliar to big-league hitters.

Hamels went 9-8 with a 4.08 in 23 starts that first season. He was just 22 years old. The next season, he established himself as a mainstay in the rotation, going 15-5 with a 3.39 ERA in 28 starts. One of those starts—made in Cincinnati—figured importantly in the Phillies' rise to top of the National League.

It was April 21, 2007. The Phillies were off to a dreadful 4-11 start and heat was building on third-year manager Charlie Manuel. When the Phillies arrived at Great American Ball Park for their game against the Reds that night, the beleaguered Manuel called a team meeting. It lasted 80 minutes, so long that batting practice was cancelled. Manuel spoke in the meeting. So did coaches Jimy Williams and Davey Lopes. Veteran pitcher Jamie Moyer was one of several players to speak his mind, telling his teammates they were playing like "a bunch of pussies."

As the meeting went on, Hamels, just 23, sat and listened. This wasn't the perfect environment for that night's starter to prepare for a game, but things were a little desperate, so he had to deal with it. In talking about the meeting a few days later, Chase Utley said it was very beneficial in helping the team come together. But the best thing that happened for the Phillies' unity—and possibly Manuel's job status—that night was the performance that Hamels turned in when he took the mound. He pitched the first complete game of his career and struck out 15 in a 4-1 victory that started the five-game win streak that helped the Phillies extricate themselves from their early-season hole. Six months later, the Phils snapped a 14-year playoff drought and won their first of five straight NL East titles.

The Phils were a quick out in the 2007 postseason, but 2008 was a different story. Armed with a little October experience, a ripened lineup, a terrific bullpen, and a white-hot pitcher named Cole Hamels, the Phillies won the World Series that year. Still pitching with mostly fastballs and changeups, and the occasional curveball, Hamels went 5-2 with a 2.35 ERA in his final eight regular-season starts. He then won three Game 1s in the postseason and started the NLCS and World Series clinchers. He went 4-0 with a 1.80 ERA in five starts that October and won two series MVP Awards.

Not bad for a 24-year-old.

But that was just the thing. Hamels was just 24. He was young and on top of the baseball world and he didn't handle it well.

After brushing the confetti from his shoulders and telling the adoring crowd that he looked forward to winning the World Series "again and again and again," Hamels bathed a little too deeply in the spoils of success that off-season. He chatted with David Letterman and Ellen DeGeneres on TV. He and his wife, Heidi Strobel, a former contestant on the television reality show *Survivor*, moved into a penthouse at Liberty Place in Center City Philadelphia. He did autograph shows. In February, he appeared on the cover of *Sports Illustrated* with the headline: "The Fabulous New Life of Cole Hamels." The only problem was this new life wasn't so fabulous. While taking his victory lap around America, Hamels forgot what earned him the tour—his magic left arm. He neglected his off-season workouts and came to spring training in 2009 in less than peak condition. He was to be the Phillies' Opening Day starter that season, but was knocked from the assignment when he experienced elbow soreness in spring training. That soreness was a result of not coming into camp in pitching shape. He had tried to catch up in a hurry and tweaked the elbow.

Hamels opened that season with a poor showing—allowing 11 hits and seven runs in 3⅔ innings—in Denver, then failed to lock down a 7-1 lead against the Padres in an 8-7 loss at home on April 17. After the game, he said he was embarrassed. A few days later, he admitted he lost focus of what was important over the winter and did a poor job preparing for the season.

"If it comes down to the end of the year and we lose the division by one game, I can easily raise my hand and say I screwed up," he said. "I should be ready and by not being ready I'm jeopardizing the team. I pretty much didn't fulfill my end of the bargain and get ready the way I should have. This has been a big learning step. I didn't want to learn it, but I have."

Hamels was never able to recover from his slow start that season. Oh, he had good games. He had too much talent not to. But he was not able to take the next step toward the greatness that was predicted for him after October 2008. He went 10-11 with a 4.32 ERA in 32 starts in 2009 and struggled in four postseason starts as the Phillies lost the World Series to the New York Yankees. Following a poor start in Game 3 of the World Series, Hamels reflected on what had been a difficult, mentally draining season for him and mentioned how eager he was to put it behind him. That didn't mean he was giving up on the season or didn't want to pitch again. In fact, he publicly wished that Charlie Manuel would give him the ball if the series went to a seventh game. He was simply trying to say he was eager to put the learning experience of 2009 behind him, but the words didn't come out smoothly. In many circles, Hamels' comments were construed as if he couldn't wait for the Phillies' postseason ride to be over. It caused quite a stir and didn't win Hamels any points with the fans who had cheered him wildly just a year earlier.

At 25 years old, Cole Hamels had some work to do to get his career back on track, and in the winter that followed his latest learning experience, he did it.

———————— K ————————

Six weeks after losing to the Yankees in the World Series, the Phillies said hello to Roy Halladay and good-bye (temporarily) to Cliff Lee. Halladay came to the Phillies with the reputation of being the best pitcher in baseball, and Phillies officials were banking on a rebound season from Hamels as they tried to build a pitching staff that would take them back to the World Series in 2010.

Much of the early focus in spring training surrounded Halladay, but it soon shifted to Hamels. Lee was gone. The Phillies needed Hamels to be the pitcher he was in 2008, not the pitcher he was in 2009, if they were going to be the club they wanted to be in 2010.

Right from the beginning, it was clear that Hamels had reported to camp in better physical shape than the year before. He went underground during the off-season and stayed away from the spotlight. He worked on his body. He threw all winter. He worked on sharpening his curveball and adding a cutter after hitters started teeing off on his two-pitch repertoire. On the first day of camp, he smiled easily as he threw his new cutter on flat ground while playing catch. Hamels didn't work only on his body and pitching skills that winter. He also spent hours working on the mental side of the game. He just wasn't ready to tell anyone about it.

In the opinion of Pitching Coach Rich Dubee, Hamels' mental makeover was much needed. Throughout the spring of 2010, Dubee frequently mentioned that Hamels had been his own worst enemy in 2009.

"He pitched with a lot of anger," Dubee said. "He was easily frustrated when things didn't go well. His body language wasn't good. He wasn't nearly as focused as he was the previous two years."

Why the change?

"Cole got good too fast," Dubee said. "When he first came up he didn't have a World Series MVP. Now, all of a sudden, expectations of the public and the media are that much higher. When he wasn't able to tame those expectations, he got mad at himself."

Dubee didn't mince words as he laid it all on the line for Hamels.

"The success won't come back until the demeanor changes," he said.

Slowly but surely, the demeanor changed. Hamels had seemingly grown up in front of everyone in the Phillies organization, but now, at 26, after high times and low times, he was ready to really grow up.

He fixed his curveball. He added that cutter. Added strength gave his fastball more crackle than ever. And, of course, he had the great changeup that he learned from Mark Furtak way back when. Hamels went 12-11 with a 3.06 ERA in 2010. His 2.23 ERA after the All-Star break was the fifth-best in the majors, and better than the ERA of any other pitcher on the Phillies' staff. After the break, he struck out 104, second most in the majors.

Late that season, Hamels talked about how he turned things around. First and foremost, he said, he had learned that baseball was his job and required year-round focus and commitment. After the 2009 season, Hamels began carrying an equipment bag with him, and whether he's visiting family in San Diego or vacationing in Tahoe, he finds time to condition his body for two hours a day. Hamels said the cutter helped him immensely and gave him another weapon, making him a four-pitch guy. And finally, late in the 2010 season, he admitted to taking a suggestion from his younger brother, Mitchell, and reaching out to Jim Brogan, a San Diego-based performance specialist who helps athletes sharpen the mental side of their games.

Brogan, who played two seasons in the NBA, recalled the first time Hamels called him.

"OK," Brogan said. "Meet me at six in the morning."

"Six in the morning?" Hamels asked, incredulously.

"What are others doing at six in the morning?" Brogan asked Hamels.

"Sleeping," the pitcher said.

"That's just my point," Brogan said.

Brogan convinced Hamels that his failures were actually opportunities for improvement.

"You'll never be great if you worry about what just happened," Brogan told the pitcher. "Look forward. If you're successful at everything, if you're not failing every once in a while, you're probably not doing what you're supposed to be doing. You grow from failure."

Brogan taught Hamels that frustration was poison and oxygen was gold. Relax. Breathe. Perform. Excel. In 18 sessions that winter, and in text messages before every start in 2010, Hamels took in everything Brogan taught him.

"I have a better idea of how to succeed for a full season now," Hamels said late in the 2010 season. "I've learned that you can always start over. Throw a bad pitch—start over. I've learned you can't let your emotions distract you from what you're trying to do. That will drag you down. I don't stress anymore."

Why would a young man with so much talent stress in the first place?

"Expectations," Hamels said. "When you've been there, done that, and you get there again and don't have the results you're supposed to, you stress. You press instead of breathing. I can calm myself now."

In October 2010, Hamels found himself in the postseason for the fourth-straight year. He was back in Great American Ball Park in Cincinnati, a place where he always seemed to shine. It was Game 3 of the National League Division Series and Hamels was never better. He struck out nine and walked none in a brilliant shutout that propelled the Phillies to a third-straight National League Championship Series.

As he blew a 94-mph fastball by Scott Rolen to end that game, Hamels pumped his left arm in triumph.

The magic never went out of that left arm. It just veered off course a time or two. Back in the fast lane and all grown up, Cole Hamels was ready for his best season yet in 2011.

ROY HALLADAY

In June 1995, the Phillies had a chance to get Roy Halladay. They passed. Of course, Roy Halladay wasn't *Roy Halladay* then. At least he wasn't the guy you see now. In 1995, he was a tall, lanky schoolboy. He threw straight over the top and blew through high school competition around Denver, Colorado, on raw talent. He'd fire a couple fastballs by an overmatched hitter, and then drop a curveball on him, and . . . good morning, good afternoon, good night.

Phillies scouts spent a lot of time watching Halladay that spring and seriously considered taking him with the 14th pick in the first round of that year's draft. In fact, Halladay was still available when it was time for the Phils to make their selection.

The Angels opened that draft by selecting University of Nebraska outfielder Darin Erstad and the Padres followed by taking Ben Davis, a high school catcher from suburban Philadelphia. Anticipation in the Phillies' war room at Veterans Stadium grew as the Twins made University of Oklahoma pitcher Mark Redman the 13th pick.

A hush fell over the room. Mike Arbuckle, then the team's scouting director, announced to the Commissioner's Office via a conference call that with the 14th pick the Phillies would take Reggie Taylor, a high-upside high-school outfielder from Newberry, South Carolina.

"Our room was split in half," recalled Marti Wolever, the Phillies' No. 2 man in scouting at the time. "Reggie was a legit, five-tool guy. He had everything you were looking for. He could run, throw, he hit for power—he could do everything. We had genuine concerns about Roy. His arm action was a concern to us. It was a little long in back. We had questions. Was there deception in his delivery? We weren't sure about his plane to the plate. Could he get the ball down? There were concerns about his breaking ball.

"Some of our guys were on board with Roy, some weren't. But everyone was on board with Reggie. We chose Reggie based on the information we had. Mike made the right decision at the time."

The decision to take Taylor over Halladay illustrates the imperfect science that is scouting. Scouts look at an 18-year-old piece of clay and try to project if it can be molded into artwork by the time it's 22. It's not easy. If it were easy, Albert Pujols wouldn't have been the 402nd player taken in the 1999 draft—he would have been first. Taylor never developed into the player Phillies officials envisioned. He hit just .231 with 14 homers and 58 RBIs in 260 career games with three clubs. Halladay, taken by Toronto three picks later, blossomed into someone widely hailed as the best pitcher in baseball for his excellence over a long period.

Though Phillies officials often look back at that 1995 draft and wonder what might have been, they may indeed have made the right call in passing on Halladay. Turns out the Blue Jays had the same concerns about Halladay's delivery and arm action. Those concerns just didn't come to the fore until six years later. Halladay could have been on his way to becoming a journeyman, a fringe big-leaguer just like Taylor, if the Jays hadn't done something radical in spring training in 2001.

On pure talent, Halladay had risen to the big leagues quickly. Juan Samuel saw it. The Phillies third-base coach in 2011, Samuel finished up his playing career as a utility man with the Blue Jays in 1998. On the second-to-last day of the season, Samuel was in the clubhouse getting a head start on packing his belongings when someone said, "Hey, the kid is pitching a no-hitter." Samuel headed down to the dugout and, sure enough, saw a string of zeroes on the scoreboard. In just his second big-league start, Halladay was throwing a no-hitter against the Detroit Tigers. He lost the no-hit bid on a pinch-hit two-out homer by Bobby Higginson in the ninth. As tough as it was to see the 21-year-old kid lose his no-hitter with one out to go, Jays officials loved what they saw. Maybe that over-the-top delivery and straight fastball would play in the big leagues. Maybe they made the right call taking Halladay with the 17th pick in the 1995 draft.

Halladay continued to break into the majors in 1999 but by 2000 was veering badly offtrack. He had an ERA bigger than a big baby's birth weight that season and things weren't much better the following spring.

"He was getting his ass kicked," said Buck Martinez, the Jays manager in 2001.

Halladay was dazed and confused and he didn't know which way to turn. As a youth in Denver and on his way up the minor-league ladder, he'd always been the best pitcher on his team, a pitcher destined for greatness. Now, in the big leagues, the place he'd always dreamed of being, he was awful. He couldn't get people out. He was as confused and scared as a 16-year-old on a learner's permit trying to navigate rush-hour traffic. He was down in the dumps, his confidence in tatters.

"The one thing I knew is when I went out there I wasn't sure what was going to happen," Halladay recalled in the summer of 2011. "I was tentative. I wasn't aggressive. I didn't have a good approach.

"Pitching always seemed easy and even when it wasn't easy, I still always managed to get through things. I really didn't need the mental part of the game. I'd throw and get through it. I think you can do that to a certain point, but when things get bad they snowball on you, especially if you don't have that good mental approach, and there's no way to correct it. It continues to breed bad thoughts."

Big-league hitters are hungry lions that can sense when a pitcher is tentative, when his confidence is down, when he is vulnerable. Halladay had become a skittish impala by the spring of 2001 and there was no way the Jays could let him loose in the jungle, not with all those hungry lions in the American League East.

Halladay was the dominant topic of conversation in Jays' organizational meetings that spring.

"There was a lot of internal conversation about trading him," recalled Gord Ash, then the Jays' general manager. "Some quarters even called for him to be released."

Halladay's ERA in 2000 was 10.64, the highest single-season mark for a pitcher with 50 or more big-league innings. Ash knew he wasn't going to get great value for Halladay in a trade after a season like that, and he damn well knew he wasn't going to release a 23-year-old with an arm like that, even if scouts sometimes derisively referred to Halladay as "Iron Mike" because his upright stance, over-the-top delivery and straight fastball resembled one of those old metal-armed pitching machines that hitters used for batting practice.

"I believed in Roy, but I also believed if we were going to make it work, he had to go back to square one and start over," Ash said. "He needed to be rebuilt."

Major League Baseball is no place for a rebuilding job, at least not for the total makeover that Halladay needed. Jays officials decided that he would go back—way back—to the minor leagues. The guy who nearly pitched a no-hitter in his second big-league start was sent all the way to the low minors—the Jays' Class A affiliate in Dunedin, Florida—at the start of the 2001 season.

Demotions are usually handled by the GM and manager of a ball club.

The Jays knew that Halladay would be humiliated by the decision, so they had Tim Hewes, their in-house counselor and player-assistance provider, deliver the news. The baseball people followed up with Halladay afterward.

"It was a very emotional time for Roy," Ash said. "There was a heavy burden on him and we wanted to make sure it was handled in a professional way."

Halladay was not completely blindsided by the news. Martinez, the manager, had previously called him aside on the field and given him a heads-up.

"Before that I had no clue it was coming," Halladay said. "I was surprised. I thought it was pretty radical. Leading up to it, I never heard, 'We think you need a lot of changes.' I struggled the year before, but I never really got the feeling, 'We think you're way off.' "

But that's just what Jays officials were thinking.

"We'd watch him throw and say, 'How in the hell is he getting hit like this?' " said Martinez, a former major-league catcher. "Finally, we kind of broke it down. He stood tall and was easy to see. He was over the top. His fastball was 97 but straight as a string. He had a big curveball but nobody swung at it.

"We just said, 'You know, he's 6-6, has a great arm, he's young, he's too good of a talent. There's got to be a way to figure this out.' We just thought going back to square one was the best thing for him in the long haul."

Halladay did not fight the Jays' decision.

"He couldn't," Martinez said. "He was struggling to make the team."

Turns out, the demotion was the best thing that ever happened to Halladay's career. In body and mind, he became a different pitcher, the pitcher he'd always dreamed of becoming.

———————— K ————————

All Harry Leroy Halladay III ever wanted to be was a pitcher. Well, he wanted to be a pilot, too, like his dad, but pitching was definitely first on his list. When Halladay was in fifth grade, the family moved into a new house in the Denver area. His parents made sure the basement was at least 61 feet long so their only son—Roy has two sisters—could throw and hit balls into a mattress throughout the cold Colorado winter. When young Roy was about 10, his father took him to a pitching clinic hosted by a legendary Denver-area pitching coach named Bus Campbell.

"We'd really love to work with you," the elder Halladay told Campbell, who heard things like that all the time. Campbell knew the Halladays were serious when they tracked him down a second time. It was the start of a close teacher-pupil relationship that lasted until Campbell's death in 2008.

"Bus was this soft-spoken guy who could stand behind you and watch you throw twenty pitches and completely analyze everything you were doing," recalled Brad Lidge, another Denver-area pitcher who worked with Campbell. "I remember the first time I worked with him. He was so quiet, I had to say, 'What?' about ten times because he was so soft-spoken. But he was really good at relating to pitchers and helping them with their deliveries. I don't know if all the pitchers in the Denver area worked with him, but the lucky ones did."

Campbell's prized pupil was another quiet guy—Halladay. In time, Campbell became a scout for Toronto, the team that picked Halladay in the first round of the 1995 draft. Halladay listened and followed through on everything Campbell told him. Before Halladay's senior year at Arvada West High School, Campbell suggested that the pitcher join the cross-country team to build endurance and leg strength, two keys for a pitcher. Halladay, who still logs the miles of a cross-country runner between starts, laughs when he recalls his first race.

"I was in first place after a mile and ended up coming in about two-hundredth," he said. "I was dead-sprint for the first mile then hit a wall. After that, I learned."

Halladay ended the season as the No. 2 man on his team and had a couple of fourth-place finishes in sectional meets.

If cross-country was conditioning for pitching, then basketball was Halladay's escape from baseball and the expectations that had engulfed him as he had become a pitching prodigy. He played center on his high school team.

"I loved playing basketball," he said. "Sometimes I had more fun playing it in high school than baseball. I just wasn't very good. I could go out and if I was terrible, I didn't know any better. I expected to be terrible. So when I had a good game it was kind of fun. It was recreation."

By the spring, it was showtime for Halladay. No more conditioning. No more recreation. It was time to produce, and he did that. College and pro scouts flocked to his games at Arvada West. He had decided to attend the University of Arizona, but the lure of pro ball, of making the majors, was too strong and he signed with the Jays after the draft. No one in the Denver area was surprised that Halladay signed. Few first-rounders don't. And besides,

Halladay had practically been raised to be a major-leaguer. It's all he ever wanted. Pitching was his identity.

And that's why his poor season in 2000 and his demotion from the majors to the low minors the following spring was so jarring to him. That's why he was so happy that he and his wife, Brandy, had moved their residence from the Denver area to Florida that winter.

"The hard part for me was the thought of going home and telling people in my town," he said. "Jeez, I just got sent to A ball. I might never get out of A ball. It's awful hard when you grow up and are known as a baseball player from the time you're six and now you have to tell people in that hometown that you failed. Moving to Florida took a lot of pressure off me. It was a fresh start. Baseball wasn't my identity there. I could go out and try to be as good as I could be. I didn't have to do it for anyone else. It made it easier for me to put my heart into it and not feel like if I don't do this, I'm disappointing all these people."

When the Jays departed Dunedin for the regular season in 2001, Halladay stayed behind.

He was a minor-leaguer. He didn't know if he'd ever get back to the majors—never mind pitch a perfect game and a playoff no-hitter nine years later for the team that once passed on him—and he was crushed.

———————— K ————————

Talk to Roy Halladay for a few minutes and you soon realize that his favorite pronoun is "we." When he joined the Phillies in December 2009, he sat in a packed news conference and spoke of Philadelphia as the place "we" wanted to be. He was referring to the woman sitting in the front row at the news conference, his wife, Brandy. The couple began dating in Colorado in 1996 and married in 1998. Brandy Halladay was there for her husband's ascension to the majors and his fall back to the minors.

Only closers get saves in baseball, but Brandy Halladay deserved one in the spring of 2001. Her husband, just 23 at the time, was confused and dejected. His career was going the wrong way and he didn't know which way to turn. Brandy headed to a bookstore near Dunedin and purchased a handful of self-help books. On a whim, she breezed through an aisle of sports books and came across *The Mental ABCs of Pitching* by noted sports psychologist

Harvey Dorfman. She bought it, thinking there might be something in there to help restore her husband's bruised confidence.

Within those pages was Roy Halladay's road map to stardom.

Halladay devoured the book, ate up everything Dorfman had to say about concentration, having a plan, focusing on one pitch at a time, and learning from failure. From pitchers such as Greg Maddux and Jamie Moyer, to players such as Raul Ibanez, Dorfman had helped a number of major-leaguers enhance their physical performances with a sharper, stronger mind-set. No player was more affected by Dorfman than Halladay. He read the book—lived it—and with the help of Jays officials, eventually became close to Dorfman through a decade's worth of phone calls, emails, and personal meetings.

After first reading Dorfman's book, Halladay said he realized "the talent was there, but a lot was missing."

"I was very distracted by the big picture," he said. "I'd go out and think about having to go seven innings with three runs or less, who I was facing, and all this other stuff. It was never simple. There was just too much going on. I was never worried about executing the pitch. I was worried about everything else. I was very distracted. That's the best way to put it."

More than a decade after reading the book, Halladay still thumbs through it nights before he pitches. In the winter before the 2011 season, he addressed a group of about a dozen Phillies pitching prospects at a minicamp in Clearwater. He gave each pitcher a copy of the book.

On the morning of March 1, 2011, during spring training, Halladay got a call from Phillies General Manager Ruben Amaro Jr. Dorfman had died in North Carolina after an illness. He was 75.

When Halladay won the 2003 AL Cy Young Award, he singled out Dorfman as a reason for his success. Eight years later, and four months after winning the NL Cy Young as a Phillie, Halladay continued to credit Dorfman.

"I'm certain I would never have had the success I've had if it weren't for the time I spent with him and the things I learned from him," Halladay said. "He helped me turn the corner—professionally and personally. He made all the difference."

Geoff Baker observed the difference that Dorfman made in Halladay from a reporter's perspective in Toronto. Before Dorfman, Halladay tried to accommodate every person who pulled on him. After Dorfman, Halladay started to politely say no. His day became so structured and his mind so focused that the only time reporters were able to get to him was after a start. A one-on-one interview would require an appointment that wouldn't interfere with Halladay's daily routine. Halladay even turned down opportunities to do commercials in Toronto. Nothing would break the concentration that he learned from Dorfman. And if something did . . . *Zap*.

"Roy doesn't have a bad bone in his body," Baker said. "He was saying yes to everybody. Dorfman convinced him he had to start saying no or he wasn't going to make it. He had to concentrate on himself."

Halladay confirmed that. He was a pleaser and if he kept it up he was going to be a pleaser in another profession.

"I always felt like I had to try to please everybody—coaches, family, media—everybody," he said. "I wanted them to not only be proud of me but to think good things of me. I think everybody naturally wants that. Harvey helped a lot with that. He'd tell me, 'The ultimate reason you're here is to pitch. You have to be able to do this for yourself. Know what you need and what you don't need.'

"One of the best things he ever told me was, 'Stick with your routine. Stick with your way of thinking. Don't let people change that.' "

There were others who helped in Roy Halladay's transition from near washout to the best pitcher in baseball. Halladay found himself talking about another person of impact when Mel Queen died in May 2011, less than three months after Dorfman had passed away.

While Dorfman had helped Halladay build the right mind-set to succeed in the majors, Queen had helped him build a delivery and pitch repertoire that would work.

Queen, who pitched in the majors from 1964–72, was a longtime Jays' pitching instructor. He got hold of Halladay when the Jays sent him from Dunedin to Double-A Knoxville early in the 2001 season. The first thing Queen did was berate Halladay. He told the pitcher he was soft. He called him a wimp. He gave him the old you're-too-good-for-this lecture while questioning his manhood the whole way.

"He kicked me in the ass," Halladay said after Queen's death. "He challenged me. I think sometimes you need that. You need the honesty."

Once Queen got the old-school, drill-sergeant stuff out of the way, he went to work on the delivery. He killed Iron Mike, that straight-up-and-down delivery that allowed hitters a good look at the ball. He taught Halladay to start his delivery with a slight step back from the rubber to create some north-south momentum toward home plate. He junked the over-the-top release point and lowered Halladay's arm angle to about three-quarters. That and a couple of new grips added movement—sinking and cutting action—to

Halladay's straight fastball, making it more difficult to hit. A little shoulder tuck was added to hide the ball.

Halladay worked on these adjustments for two weeks in the bullpen, with Queen often breathing fire down his neck.

"After fifteen days I was able to take it all out in a game," Halladay said. "It was night and day."

The deaths of Dorfman and Queen, and Campbell three years earlier, touched Halladay deeply.

"This makes you step back and realize how many influential people you've had in your career, and how many people you really owe a lot of credit and gratitude to," he said in May 2011. "You obviously can't do it by yourself. Things like that kind of bring that to the forefront."

It's typical of Halladay to share credit. Heck, this is the guy who didn't leave out anyone, not even the batboy, when he bought $4,000 gift watches for his teammates and others after his May 2010 perfect game. But everyone from Gord Ash, the man who came up with the plan for Halladay to start over at square one, to Buck Martinez, Toronto's manager at the time, say the credit begins and ends with one person—Roy Halladay.

"Roy did the work," Martinez said. "He deserves all the credit. He could have flipped us off and told us to go to hell. He could have said, 'I'll go down, but I'm not going to do anything.' But to his credit, he made a commitment. He went from being a borderline failure, Number One pick, maybe out of the game, getting his brains beaten out, to the best pitcher in baseball. I remember catching him in the bullpen when he came back. It was pretty special."

———————————— K ————————————

A new pitcher with a new mind-set, Halladay climbed his way back to the majors in July 2001. Slowly, he established himself as the best in the game. He won 19 games and had a 2.93 ERA in 2002. He won the Cy Young Award a year later.

There are stages to a ballplayer's career: 1. Establish yourself as a major leaguer; 2. Make a lot of money; 3. Get a ring. Over the years, Halladay reached the first two stages, but by 2009 it was pretty clear to him that he was going to have difficulty reaching the third stage in Toronto. The Jays played in a tough division with the high-powered and deep-pocketed Boston

Red Sox and New York Yankees. At 32 years old, Halladay didn't see how the rebuilding Jays were going to catch those two clubs, at least not while he still had bullets left in his right arm.

Halladay was due to become a free agent at the end of the 2010 season and he had made it clear to Jays officials that he would sign elsewhere, with a contender, when his deal expired. During the first half of the 2009 season, he quietly asked the Jays to consider trading him to a contender. Jays officials were under no obligation to deal Halladay, but they were open to it, provided they could get top value, such as multiple blue-chip prospects, in return. Dealing Halladay with a year and a half left on his contract would fetch the Jays a higher price than hanging on to him for another year, and it would be better than risking just draft-pick compensation if he walked away to free agency after the 2010 season.

In 2009, Ruben Amaro Jr. was in his first year as Phillies general manager. The Phils were coming off a World Series championship in 2008 and had the lineup to get back to the World Series in 2009, but the starting pitching was suspect. Cole Hamels was having trouble duplicating his great work from the previous October and Brett Myers had been injured. The team scouted and eventually signed veteran Pedro Martinez, but he wasn't the guy Amaro really wanted. Amaro had long ago become obsessed with the tall right-handed ace of the Toronto Blue Jays. The Phillies and Jays train just five miles apart in neighboring Florida towns. Amaro had seen enough of Roy Halladay to know if he ever had the chance to get him, he would go for it.

"As far back as '08, they were eyeing Halladay," one team insider said of Amaro and his predecessor, Pat Gillick. "They knew he was going to be a free agent after 2010. For a long time, Roy was Ruben's white whale."

J. P. Ricciardi knew this. He was Toronto's GM from late 2001 to 2009, and a smart, young, wisecracking baseball executive, much like Amaro. Early in the 2009 season, Amaro told Ricciardi, "If you ever do anything with Doc. . . ."

"I'll let you know," Ricciardi said.

On July 6, 2009, Ricciardi called Amaro and said he was ready to start taking offers for Halladay.

A day later, Ricciardi told Ken Rosenthal of FOX Sports that Halladay was available—for the right price. Rosenthal posted a story on FOX's Website. He nearly broke the Internet.

Ricciardi was contacted by a Philadelphia writer asking what it would take for the Phillies to get Halladay.

"The type of talent that makes you stand up and take notice," Ricciardi said. "All the clubs that have contacted us understand that."

Ricciardi added that if no team met his steep price, he'd hang on to the best pitcher in baseball.

"It's going to take a lot," he said. "Someone is going to have to have the stomach for this and I'm not sure anyone does."

On the executive level of Citizens Bank Park, Amaro went into action. Advisers Gillick and Dallas Green urged him to go get Halladay.

"Ruben has a chance to make history in this town if he gets this guy," Green said at the time.

All the usual contenders—the Yankees, Red Sox, Rangers, and Angels—called Ricciardi about Halladay.

"I tried to get in it," Yankees GM Brian Cashman said. "But Toronto told us to trade him in the division, it would have been twice the sticker price."

In many ways, Ricciardi's talks with clubs other than the Phillies were hollow because Halladay had a no-trade clause and Philadelphia was the place he—and his family—wanted to go. Halladay admired the team's roster and liked that it didn't seem filled with egos. He believed the Phils knew how to win and could keep doing it.

"There was just something about the Phillies for all of us," Halladay said.

Even the pitcher's oldest son, Braden, wanted his dad to be a Phillie.

"He didn't like New York or Boston because we always got beat up by them," Halladay said with a laugh in the summer of 2011. "So I think that turned him off a little."

Focusing on the Phillies as the July 31, 2009 trade deadline approached, Ricciardi sent his most trusted aides to watch the Phils' top minor-league prospects.

Finally, as Halladay prepared for what many thought would be his final start as a Blue Jay in Toronto on July 24, Ricciardi prepared his wish list. He wanted outfield prospects Domonic Brown and Anthony Gose, pitching prospect Kyle Drabek, and left-hander J. A. Happ.

Amaro almost gagged on that price tag.

"I couldn't give up my top position prospect [Brown] and my top pitching prospect [Drabek]," he said later.

Halladay made that start on July 24 in Toronto. "We love you, Roy," shouted one fan, sensing that Halladay would soon be dealt. Phillies scout Charley Kerfeld popped in for the game just to make sure Halladay got on and off the mound healthy. The talks went on with the Phillies trying to build a deal around a package that included catcher Lou Marson, infielder Jason Donald, pitcher Jason Knapp, and Happ. In some variations of the deal, the Phils may have been willing to include Drabek, but the Jays wanted more. Ricciardi's job was on the line and he needed to make a big score for Halladay.

"To quote Sonny Corleone, 'I've got to come out of this with more than just my you-know-what in my hand,'" Ricciardi said the day after Halladay's July 24 start in Toronto.

Ricciardi used his best sales pitch on Amaro.

"Ruben," Ricciardi told Amaro over the phone. "You make this deal and you'll be like Caesar riding through the streets of Philly after he just conquered the Gauls."

In another conversation, Ricciardi mentioned a famous Clearwater eatery in his appeal for the Phillies' top prospects.

"Ruben, we're talking about prospects here," he said. "In three years, they'll be serving me my breakfast at Lenny's."

Even as he pursued his obsession, Amaro kept other options open. He needed starting pitching and he couldn't limit his focus to one guy. In Cleveland, the Indians had put a "for sale" sign on Cliff Lee, and though he didn't wear the "best pitcher in baseball" label, he had won a Cy Young Award and Phillies officials liked him. The Phillies' front office juggled two pursuits—Halladay and Lee—as the deadline approached. On the morning of July 29, Halladay rose in his Seattle hotel room, thinking that this indeed might be the day he made his last start for the Jays. Talks between the Phillies and Jays had reached a point where the deal was going to get done or it wasn't.

"We're going to get one of them," a Phillies official said that morning, referring to Halladay or Lee.

A short while later, reporters who had followed the Jays to Seattle in anticipation of a Halladay trade, read Internet reports that Cliff Lee was hugging Cleveland teammates in the visiting dugout in Anaheim. He had been traded to the Phillies. Halladay was crestfallen. He knew he was stuck in Toronto. He knew another postseason would go on without him. His biological clock was ticking and he wondered if he'd ever get to pitch in a postseason. On top of it all, he had to go out and pitch a game against the Mariners. In one of the most difficult starts of his life, he lost, 3-2, in unusually stifling Seattle heat. After the game, Halladay appeared drained and anguished. He disappeared to a back room in the clubhouse for a while. Most of his teammates had already boarded a bus for the airport when he emerged to speak with reporters.

"When all was said and done it had to be the right situation for Toronto," Halladay said that day. "That wasn't the case. I'm a Blue Jay and I'm happy to be one."

Only half of that last statement was true.

"I liked being where I was, but I was ready to go somewhere where we had a chance," said Halladay, looking back at that day two years later. "Going through that month with nothing happening—it kind of sucks it all out of you. It was disappointing, but at the same time, a weight was gone."

Halladay finished speaking with reporters that day in Seattle and headed for the bus. Possibly the worst part of his day was about to come. The Jays were headed for a series against the A's in Oakland. They would be staying at the Westin St. Francis in San Francisco, the same hotel where the Phillies were staying for a concurrent series with the Giants. Down the street, in an equipment trunk in the visiting clubhouse at AT&T Park, was a Phillies jersey with Halladay's name and No. 34 on it. It stayed buried at the bottom of the trunk. Lee showed up and was issued No. 34. Halladay's long July drama was over. All he wanted to do when he got to the St. Francis was lock his door and get away from it all.

———————— K ————————

During his dozen years in Toronto, Halladay had five top-five seasons in both ERA and AL Cy Young voting (winning the award once). He had a pair of 20-win seasons and three times led the league in innings. Once a skittish impala in a land of lions, he had become the king of the jungle with an assassin's mentality that matched a razor-sharp arsenal of pitches.

"He understands the dynamics of pitching," Buck Martinez said. "He puts pressure on the hitter and makes them uncomfortable from the first pitch of the game because he throws strikes. But he's not throwing it over the middle of the plate. He knows what inch he wants to hit. He cuts the ball and sinks the ball and changes speeds. There are guys with better stuff, but Halladay's strength is he's got his foot on your throat the whole game. Body language means so much and his says, *I'm better than you.*"

Of course, Halladay would never verbalize that. Others have to say it.

"I'll tell you what, he's the best pitcher I've ever faced," said Jerry Hairston Jr., who finished his fourteenth big-league season in 2011. "And I've faced a lot of guys. As a hitter, you hate to give a guy credit like that. But it's true. You just never know what he's going to throw."

Halladay never reached the postseason in 12 seasons in Toronto. Each October, he'd go home and watch other teams try to get to the World Series. With each passing year, Halladay's desperation to reach the Series grew stronger. He thought he might have a chance to get there in 2009, but instead watched Cliff Lee get there—wearing the No. 34 Phillies uniform that had once been reserved for him.

"Turn that darn TV off!" Brandy Halladay told her husband as he watched the Phillies and Yankees play in the 2009 World Series.

"I had to turn my face," Brandy added a couple of months later. "It was tough to watch."

But as difficult as it was to watch another World Series without her husband even getting a smell of it, July 2009 was tougher on the Halladays.

"We had never been the subject of trade discussion before and all of a sudden it was everywhere," Brandy said. "You figured, 'It's got to happen.' When it didn't, it was very disappointing. It was hard for Roy to go back and do his job. That uproar taxed us. It was difficult."

Brandy Halladay said her husband wasn't just disappointed that another pennant race would go by without him. He was disappointed that he wasn't going to be a Phillie.

"It was one hundred and ten percent about the Phillies," she said. "We really thought we were coming here. This is where we wanted to be."

The Phillies lost that World Series in six games to the Yankees. A week later, Amaro packed his suitcase for the annual general managers' meetings in Chicago. It was time to start building the 2010 Phillies.

Even though he had landed Lee in July, Amaro's lust for Halladay had not dulled. Alex Anthopoulos had moved up from an assistant's post and replaced J. P. Ricciardi as Toronto's GM. Amaro was headed up to his room at the O'Hare Hilton when he and Anthopoulos crossed paths near an elevator bank.

"We'd still like to talk about Halladay if you're going to move him," Amaro told Anthopoulos, who was all ears and eager to talk.

The next morning, a story in the *Philadelphia Inquirer* proclaimed that the Phillies were still angling to get Halladay. Later that afternoon, Amaro shot down the report, even though he knew it was true.

A month later, Amaro and his lieutenants headed for the winter meetings in Indianapolis. They were juggling two pretty big balls in the air, talking with Lee's representative about a contract extension—the pitcher's deal was set to expire after 2010—and with the Jays (secretly) about a trade for Halladay. While talks of an extension with Lee proved difficult, dealings with the Jays were smooth. The Jays had resolved to give Halladay his wish, and the Phillies, encouraged by the development of some of their young right-handed pitching prospects, were ready to include Drabek in the deal. The Phillies would not do the deal without signing Halladay to a contract extension. They also required a physical exam with their own doctors.

A few days after the winter meetings, Greg Landry, Halladay's agent, was home in Louisiana shopping for goodies for his son Cooper's third birthday party when his cell phone rang. It was Anthopoulos. The Jays and Phillies had reached a tentative agreement on a trade.

"We were having twenty-five kids over that day," Landry recalled. "I got the call and rushed home and told my wife, 'Roy just got traded. We're getting seventy-two hours to negotiate a deal. I have to go to Philly.' "

Landry's wife was OK with his missing the birthday party. Halladay felt horrible about it. He and Landry had been together since Halladay was drafted. Their families are close.

"Roy," Landry told his client. "Don't worry about it. When my son is older he'll say my dad couldn't stay for my third birthday because he had to help Roy Halladay negotiate a deal with the Phillies. Trust me, Roy, this is a good thing."

It was a real good thing. Halladay passed his physical and agreed to a long-term extension. Amaro netted his white whale. And Phillies fans rejoiced—at least briefly. They were dumbfounded when the Phillies announced that they had dealt Lee to Seattle in a companion move. It was a trade the Phillies ultimately regretted. By mid-season 2010 they were trying to get Lee back from Seattle. The Phils never regretted getting Halladay. He couldn't stop beaming at his introductory news conference on December 16, 2009.

"This is the place I want to be," said Halladay, finally pulling on the No. 34 jersey that Lee had kept warm. "I was holding out hope and trying to be as optimistic as possible that I'd end up here, and it happened."

Halladay's first season with the Phillies was almost storybook. He pitched the 20th perfect game in major-league history in May. In September, he wiped champagne from his eyes after pitching a shutout to clinch the NL East title and ensure his first-ever trip to the postseason. Eight days later, he pitched the first postseason no-hitter in 54 years, blanking the Cincinnati Reds in front of a delirious crowd at Citizens Bank Park.

Martinez, the guy who all those years earlier had tipped off Halladay about the Blue Jays' plans to send him to the minors, watched that game on television.

"I was so happy for him," Martinez said. "That no-hitter was everything Roy had pined for—a good team, the postseason, the big stage, and excellence."

Actually, it wasn't everything that Halladay had pined for. The 2010 Phillies lost to San Francisco in the NL Championship Series. Halladay reported to spring training in 2011 still looking to fulfill his biggest career desire, the goal that drove him to Philadelphia in the first place—a World Series championship.

ROY OSWALT

The HomePlate Fish & Steakhouse just outside of rural Weir, Mississippi, served a popular fish buffet and a 44-ounce steak in honor of its owner. It sat on land Roy Oswalt purchased from a timber company and personally cleared with his Caterpillar D6N XL, a $230,000 bulldozer he received as a gift from Houston Astros owner Drayton McLane for winning Game 6 of the 2005 National League Championship Series. Oswalt used the 35,000-pound yellow monster to move earth and timber because he wanted people in Weir (pronounced "where") to have a place to eat on the weekends.

"I built it for the community," he said.

Folks had to drive at least 20 miles to the nearest restaurant before HomePlate opened in November 2009. But being the only restaurant in town hardly guaranteed success. There are only 550 people in Weir, where Oswalt grew up, and less than 9,000 in Choctaw County, where Weir is located. Restaurants had come and gone because folks trying to make a living running them could not make ends meet. Oswalt hoped to do just enough business to keep the place open.

HomePlate had wood paneling, fluorescent lighting, and baseball memorabilia on the walls. There was no wine list or beer selection. (Choctaw County is a dry county, which was fine with Oswalt because he lived down the road and did not want to worry about drunk drivers so close to home.) The food was affordable and business was good. It served dinner from 4 P.M. to 9 P.M. on Fridays and Saturdays—folks in Weir eat at home during the week, so it was closed weeknights—and fared well enough early on to eventually open for lunch on Thursdays, Fridays, and Saturdays.

But as the economy soured, the restaurant struggled.

HomePlate closed in the summer of 2011.

"I don't know what I'm going to do," Oswalt said. "I may reopen it. I don't know. It's kind of sad."

Professional baseball players often relocate to Florida, Arizona, or California once they get a few bucks in their pockets because of the weather and training opportunities in the off-season. But Oswalt never dreamed of leaving Mississippi. It is where he grew up, it is where he will retire, and it is where he will be buried.

"It's home," he said. "Everyone knows you as you, not for what you do. That's what I like about it. Every once in awhile somebody gets excited about what I do, but most everybody is like, 'That's Roy. He's on his tractor, pushing something. He's no big deal.'"

Oswalt has a deep connection with Weir, where he learned about life, work ethic, and baseball. His grandfather, Houston Oswalt, was a logger, until he retired at 78. But retirement means different things to different people and Houston did not retire to the golf course or front porch to play backgammon with the neighbors.

He started a 20-acre watermelon farm.

"He did it for us more than anything to make us work," Oswalt said.

Houston had Roy and Roy's older brother, Brian, get to work every morning at dawn. The two boys always thought they would finish in time to go fishing, but that rarely happened. They instead spent the entire day fertilizing and hoeing the fields. One day Roy and Brian decided to sleep in. At around 7:30 A.M. their grandfather rolled up to the house and rustled them out of bed.

"Hurry up and get your clothes on," Houston said. "You're all late. We're going to have to make up the difference."

The boys got to sleep in a little, but also had their workday extended by an hour and a half.

"It'd always take all day," Oswalt said. "But that's how we made our money to buy school clothes for the next year. It makes you appreciate the money part of [baseball] because we'd work all week for $300."

Eventually, Roy and Brian started working for their father, Billy, who ran a logging business. Brian ran the skidder, which grabbed the trees and dragged them onto a ramp. Once on the ramp, Roy cut off the limbs and then worked the knuckleboom loader, which picked up the trees to be loaded onto the trucks. They started at five in the morning—fixing and sharpening the saws—and finished at five in the evening, although some days lasted longer as they drove two to three hours to the job site. And just like their days in the watermelon fields, they always imagined they would have enough energy to hang out with their friends afterward. But when Friday night came they were too tired to leave the house. They settled for Saturday nights out instead.

"That's when I decided I didn't want to do logging," Oswalt said. "It's a lot of hours. It's a lot of work."

Older brother Brian agreed. It was hard work, but they were fun times.

"You wouldn't say you miss it," Brian said in the summer of 2011. "But me and Roy are both kind of like, 'Life is going by real quick and you look back at things and miss certain things or aspects of it.' It was slower then."

Roy always loved baseball and had the passion to play it. As a youngster he even pitched against his future wife, Nicole, in a youth-league game. Nicole went on to play college softball. Roy doesn't remember what happened in that long ago at-bat, but the story still brings a smile to his face. As a teenager, Roy would finish work during the summer and jump onto the log truck for a ride home. Well, close to home. He would have to walk or hitch-hike the remaining three miles. But once he got home he had plenty of energy for baseball. He would hop in his truck and make the drive wherever he was scheduled to pitch.

"Are you ready to go?" his coach would ask him.

"I'm ready," he would reply.

He pitched seven innings every time.

Oswalt attended high school at Weir Attendance Center, which had no baseball team when he was a freshman. Billy Oswalt wanted to change that. He had watched his sons play baseball with success and petitioned the school board to add a baseball program. It said, sure, raise the money and build the field. The Oswalts and others raised the money needed to start the program. And on one Saturday, Billy and a couple of his employees at the logging company cleared about 60 trees for the field. It took him another couple days to flatten the land. His boys pitched in. The trees cleared were sold to raise money to complete the construction of the field.

There were 31 kids in Oswalt's class and roughly 130 kids in the entire high school, so he had his teammates recruit kids to field a full team. Roy, a sophomore, pitched. Brian, a senior, played second base. The Lions played 40 games in three seasons. Roy pitched 38 of them.

"There was no such thing as a bullpen," he said. "You started and finished."

The school had an established football program. Oswalt played four years as wide receiver and defensive back for the team, which produced NFL players such as Alvin McKinley (Panthers, Browns, and Broncos defensive lineman, 2000–07) and Dennis McKinley (Cardinals fullback, 1999–2002). He enjoyed the sport, but he wasn't big enough to keep playing it. Some thought he wasn't big enough to keep playing baseball, either. He was just 5-10, 155 pounds as a senior, so nobody thought a whole lot about him as a major-league prospect.

Baltimore Orioles part-time scout Kenny Dupont seemed to be the lone exception. He watched Roy pitch five or six times in high school and liked what he saw. In fact, he filed a report with the Orioles about the small right-hander from middle-of-nowhere Mississippi. He told Baltimore to give Oswalt a look, despite the fact he hit only 86–88 mph on the radar gun.

"They actually laughed at me," Dupont said. "They said he was too small. They said he had bad mechanics. They said there would be too much wear and tear. They did not project him to be a 90-plus guy. They told me I was crazy."

The Orioles could feel comfortable in their evaluation of Oswalt because nobody else considered him a prospect, including Division I colleges. Having nowhere to go, but wanting to play baseball, Oswalt enrolled at Holmes Community College in Goodman, Mississippi, about 50 miles from Weir.

Dupont, who coincidentally became the pitching coach at Holmes, always believed Oswalt would throw harder once he started concentrating on baseball, which is exactly what happened. Oswalt dedicated himself to the game. He would walk to one side of the field with a five-gallon bucket of baseballs. He would long toss to the other side of the field, collect the balls in the bucket, and throw them back to the other side. Even in the rain.

"He was the hardest-working guy I've ever coached," Dupont said in the summer of 2011.

Oswalt cleaned up his mechanics and started to throw 90–92 mph as a freshman. The Houston Astros selected him in the 23rd round of the 1996 draft and offered him $50,000 to sign. He did not immediately sign. The Astros maintained rights to Oswalt until two weeks before the 1997 draft. In the interim, the little right-hander's fastball had jumped to 95 mph. Houston increased its offer to $500,000. Roy signed.

He was on his way.

Or so it seemed.

———————————— K ————————————

Oswalt developed calcium deposits in his shoulder in 1999, which forced him to miss the first month of the season with Class A Michigan. He rehabbed the shoulder, rejoined the team, and felt great before feeling pain in a different part of the shoulder later in the season. The Astros had tried to change his pitching mechanics, which could have had something to do with it. But the pain got worse and worse and he started taking painkillers to handle it. He figured he could finish the season, rest in the off-season and be ready for spring training. But the shoulder hurt like hell every time he threw a pitch. He could barely raise his right arm over his head, and even when he returned to Mississippi in the off-season, simple tasks like reaching the top shelf at the grocery store became difficult.

He figured he needed shoulder surgery.

Before he made the call to the Astros medical staff he had some work to finish on the used Ford F150 he used for hunting. Oswalt knew trucks and cars. His neighbors down the road used to race, so they were always building engines. Oswalt spent enough time there to learn a few things and felt pretty confident he could fix the hiss he heard coming from his engine. It was running when he reached for a bare spark plug wire with his right hand.

Zzzzzzzzzzzzzzzzap!

Electricity shot through Oswalt's body. His hand gripped the wire tighter and tighter. He couldn't let go, so he did the only thing he thought he could do. He jumped backward. It jarred the wire from his hand and he tumbled to safety.

Shaken from the shock, he noticed something.

His shoulder felt better.

"The next day I couldn't feel it at all," he said.

Oswalt told the Astros about his spark-plug miracle, but they were skeptical. A country boy from Mississippi had just called, telling them he had just electrocuted himself, and magically healed his shoulder.

Sure, Roy.

They told Oswalt that time and rest had probably healed it.

"I'm telling you it wasn't time," he told them. "It was to the point when I was about to call you to tell you to cut me open and look in there."

The spark-plug incident provided the jolt to a remarkable career. Oswalt went 15-7 with a 2.21 ERA in Single A Kissimmee and Double-A Round Rock the following season. He went 14-3 with a 2.73 ERA his rookie season with the Astros in 2001, finishing second to Albert Pujols for National League Rookie of the Year. He won 20 games twice, made the All-Star team three times, and finished in the top five in Cy Young voting five times.

He also won the 2005 NLCS MVP Award, which was how he got the bulldozer. He was talking to McLane one day, when the Astros owner casually mentioned he owned a bulldozer and was cleaning up 500 acres of land he owned in Texas.

"When you're finished with it I wouldn't mind buying it from you at a discount," Oswalt told McLane.

They went back and forth about it, but hadn't finalized anything when McLane ran into Oswalt before Game 6 of the NLCS at Busch Stadium in St. Louis. Oswalt was watching film of Cardinals hitters when McLane approached. The Astros had never reached the World Series before and McLane wanted it more than anything.

"If you win this game I'll buy you a new bulldozer," he said.

Those words got Oswalt to look away from the screen in front of him. He shot up from his chair and shook McLane's hand.

Deal.

Oswalt won the game. He allowed three hits, one run, one walk, and struck out six in seven innings to send Houston to its first World Series. Oswalt walked off the mound after the seventh inning and looked at McLane, who was sitting by the visitors' dugout.

"You better call me in the off-season," he thought to himself.

McLane called.

"Hey, come pick it up," he told Oswalt over the phone. "We got you one."

───────────── K ─────────────

Oswalt drove home to Mississippi just hours after the Chicago White Sox swept the Astros in the 2005 World Series.

It made no sense to stick around.

He always feels the tug back home. He loves it there. When he is not with his family in the off-season, he is spending free time where he spent much of his childhood—outdoors. Except he no longer has to hoe the watermelon fields or run the knuckleboom. He gets to make up for those countless times when he ran out of daylight and couldn't go hunting or fishing. At any moment in the off-season Oswalt might be hunting or working land he owns in Mississippi, Missouri, or Illinois.

"Nothing really has changed a whole lot for him," Brian Oswalt said. "Outside, being around the same things."

Oswalt owns the Double 4 Ranch near his home in Kosciusko, Mississippi, which boasts 1,000 acres, whitetail deer, gemsboks, blackbuck antelope, and mouflon sheep. Billy Oswalt and Robbie Hall, a cousin, serve as guides for patron hunters. According to Oswalt, a city slicker with almost no hunting experience would have "about a ninety percent" chance of killing something on his reserve.

But that isn't how Oswalt hunts. He is a little more methodical. A little more deliberate. He selects an animal—not just a buck, but a specific buck—and begins his pursuit.

"It makes it more of a challenge than just a deer coming out to eat and shooting it," he said.

That's how he got Eight Ball.

He spent the entire three-month season in 2004 hunting a deer he nicknamed Eight Ball because of its eight-point rack. He never took a shot at anything else, even deer that were bigger and better than his target. Eight Ball became Oswalt's Moby Dick. He had photographic evidence of his existence from the night-vision cameras he has on his property. Deer, like most animals, stay in a particular area, but Eight Ball hadn't revealed himself when Oswalt had been in position to take a shot. And time was running out. It was the last day of deer season and Oswalt was sitting in his stand just before dark. Something told him to get out of the stand and walk to the edge of a ridge.

"I never do that," he said. "I always stay in the stand until dark. Just something told me to go over the ridge."

Eight Ball was 15 steps away.

"I could have killed him with a rock," Oswalt said.

Eight Ball was with a doe. Startled at hearing the hunter, the doe ran away. She passed Eight Ball, blocking the buck's view. Oswalt raised his rifle and looked through his scope.

He was so close the scope only showed the animal's neck.

Got him.

"It's the challenge," the pitcher/hunter said. "You always have the chance of killing something that's unbelievable or extraordinary. And I can't just sit around my house. I talk to guys and they sit around the house for three or four months during the off-season. I'm just not that type."

So he will climb into his stand and sit there for hours in the off-season.

Waiting.

Watching.

"It's just the peace and quiet I like about it more than anything," he said. "It's you. It's just you out there. Plus, you're waiting for that next adrenaline rush. You never know when that adrenaline rush is going to hit."

—————————— K ——————————

The land has given Oswalt's family plenty over the years, but nature took something back when thunderstorms and tornadoes tore through Mississippi on April 24, 2010. As the rain fell and the wind howled, Oswalt's mother, Jean, grabbed her Yorkie, Sweetie, and ducked into a closet in the back of her home.

It would be the last time she saw her house in one piece.

Inside the closet she heard what sounded like explosions as a tornado touched down. Her home was being shredded into pieces and tossed like kindling by 200-mph winds. When the storm passed and she emerged, she noticed her husband Billy's Bible—Billy was on a hunting trip in Missouri when the storm struck—a few feet from her. It was unmarked.

She considered it a sign. Seven people died from the storm, but she survived. A few strong beams around the frame of the closet stood tall and saved her from injury or worse.

Oswalt was with the Astros when he heard the news. He immediately gathered his wife and two daughters and drove eight hours from Houston to Weir.

"Prepare yourself," Oswalt's brother Brian told him during the drive. "There's nothing left."

The childhood home of Brian, Roy, and Patricia Oswalt, their older sister, had been destroyed in a blink of an eye. Trees had vanished. The landscape had totally changed.

"It looked like a bomb went off," Roy said.

The loss crushed him. He took pictures of the destruction on his cell phone, which he flipped through nearly a year later in the Phillies' spring training clubhouse. One picture showed a friend's banged-up pickup truck, which had been tossed the way a child might throw a Tonka truck from one side of the sandbox to the other.

Oswalt, whose own home roughly a mile away was untouched, immediately got to work. He used the bulldozer McLane gave him to clean up the rubble of his childhood home.

"That was pretty rough," he said.

Priceless mementos had been destroyed. There were pictures and home movies, some with Roy pitching as a youngster. Gone. Oswalt had given his parents his 2005 National League Championship Series MVP trophy. Gone.

"I actually pushed up pieces of it with the bulldozer," he said.

The Astros made a duplicate NLCS MVP trophy for Oswalt. The local photography studio that had taken high school portraits of all three Oswalt children still had the negatives on file and made reprints after the originals, which had hung on the wall.

"In a small town, everyone tries to help each other," said Oswalt, who also used his bulldozer to help neighbors clear rubble. "People have a way of picking right back up. There's a good spirit in our town."

—————————— K ——————————

Oswalt didn't feel the spirit in Houston. The Astros had not made the playoffs since 2005, had not finished better than third in the National League Central since 2006, and had not enjoyed a winning season since 2008. He knew he wouldn't pitch forever and he knew he wouldn't win in Houston, so he requested a trade during the 2010 season. He made his desires known privately before eventually taking them public.

"He wanted a chance to win before his contract was up and he took it back to the farm," Houston General Manager Ed Wade said.

Agent Bob Garber told the Astros that Oswalt wanted to be traded to Texas or St. Louis because of their proximity to his home. Wade told Garber he would try to find a match with the Rangers or Cardinals, but he also made it clear he would not force a deal to those teams. Wade had been down that road when he was the Phillies' GM. Curt Schilling demanded a trade in 2000 and told the Phillies he only would accept a trade to Arizona. Wade sent his ace to the Diamondbacks for the uninspiring package of Omar Daal, Nelson Figueroa, Travis Lee, and Vicente Padilla.

"Lesson learned," Wade recalled in 2011. "OK, you don't want to go where we want you to go? Then stay here."

Oswalt didn't have as much leverage as he might have thought.

Wade started making calls around the same time the Phillies started making calls. The Phillies were looking for a starter or a reliever, depending on what made the most sense. But they also were struggling, falling seven games behind the Atlanta Braves and a half game behind the New York Mets in the National League East on July 20. So they were making calls about possibly trading Jayson Werth, too.

Phillies General Manager Ruben Amaro Jr. made one of his first calls to Seattle Mariners General Manager Jack Zduriencik, who was trying to trade

Cliff Lee. The Phillies had traded Lee to the Mariners in December 2009, but Seattle's plans to compete in the American League West had imploded and there seemed to be no reason to keep him because he was not going to re-sign with the Mariners once he became a free agent.

"What would it take to bring back Cliff?" Amaro asked Zduriencik.

"It would have to start with Domonic Brown."

"Can't do it, Jack," Amaro replied.

Brown was the organization's top prospect and the Phillies projected him to be one of their everyday outfielders, potentially as early as 2011. If the Phillies did not trade Brown to get Lee from Cleveland in July 2009 or Halladay from the Blue Jays in December 2009, they were not going to trade him to Seattle, knowing Lee could sign with another team in a few months.

The Phillies and Astros started to talk.

There were multiple reports that Oswalt would not go anywhere other than St. Louis or Texas, which had teams wondering if they might be wasting their time. Those teams asked Wade about Oswalt's willingness to play else-where, and he told them he didn't know.

"You just need to proceed," Wade told clubs. "If there's something that makes sense, then we'll be in a position of presenting it to him."

Wade had a feeling much of Oswalt's demands were acts of gamesman-ship. While he might have preferred St. Louis or Texas, based on what had been expressed privately, Oswalt would not kill a deal if it meant staying in Houston. He wanted out.

"He was very vocal about it," Wade said.

Wade read Oswalt correctly. As Texas and St. Louis faded from the pic-ture and the July 31 trade deadline approached, Wade got a sense from Garber that Oswalt was open to exploring other opportunities, "particularly Philadelphia."

The Astros needed somebody to replace Oswalt's arm in the rotation, so the Phillies agreed to send them left-hander J. A. Happ. They also included outfielder Anthony Gose and shortstop Jonathan Villar, a pair of minor-league prospects. The Astros did not need Gose because they figured they had enough outfield depth in their system. They needed a corner infielder and they targeted Brett Wallace from the Toronto Blue Jays. The Phillies tried to include the Blue Jays in the deal, trying to make it a three-team swap. But Wade, who was talking with Blue Jays General Manager Alex Anthopoulos on other trade matters, took over those discussions and agreed to swap Wallace for Gose separately.

The Phillies believed Happ, Gose, and Villar were expendable because they had comparable players elsewhere in the system. They had more than a season of Oswalt, who would replace Happ. They had Tyson Gillies in Double-A Reading. He made up for the loss of Gose. They knew Villar had a lot of talent, but he was years away from the big leagues and Freddy Galvis could step in earlier.

The Phillies and Astros had agreed on the talent, but they also needed to agree on the money. Oswalt was owed $7 million for the rest of the season, plus $16 million in 2011 and a possible $16 million in a mutual option in 2012. The option included a buyout: $2 million if the Phillies declined their side of the option or $1 million if Oswalt declined his side of the option.

In addition to Oswalt, the Phillies received $11 million from Houston in the deal. That raised some eyebrows around the game, but it was the price rebuilding Houston had to pay to move a veteran who didn't want to be there, add some young talent, and gain some salary relief.

"It shows you what the market was like," Wade said. "We took money back on (Lance) Berkman, too. We traded two iconic players and, in order to make the deals work, we had to take back money on both of them."

That is the price for acquiring young, controllable talent, even when that team is giving up an ace in return. The Astros got Happ, who finished second in the 2009 National League Rookie of the Year voting. They got Wallace, who would be Houston's first baseman, and Villar, who could be Houston's shortstop of the future. The Phillies needed some money in return to offset their 2010 and 2011 budgets. They wanted payroll flexibility.

Houston presented the offer to Oswalt and Garber, who then spoke with Philadelphia. There had been multiple reports Oswalt would not accept a trade to Philadelphia unless the Phillies picked up his $16 million option for 2012. It turned out to be bad information. The Phillies did not pick up the option, but instead added $1 million to Oswalt's side of the buyout, making it $2 million either way.

Oswalt took roughly 24 hours to think about it. He finally accepted.

"There was definite talk about the option," Garber said. "But to get to a team like Philadelphia that has a chance to win a World Series, I think that was more important to Roy than the money."

Oswalt was headed to Philadelphia, which was further from home than St. Louis or Texas.

But Weir would never be far from his heart or mind.

CLIFF LEE

S cott Proefrock hung up the phone in his office and looked at his boss, David Montgomery, the leader of the Phillies empire, who sat quietly on his couch a few feet away.

It was December 13, 2010, and team officials had reached the end of the line with Cliff Lee. They had talked on the phone and exchanged countless emails and text messages with his agent, Darek Braunecker, over the past 120 hours, but remained agonizingly short of an agreement that would return Lee to Philadelphia to form one of the greatest rotations in baseball history. Proefrock, Montgomery, and other Phillies officials had been at Citizens Bank Park that Monday night for the annual Phillies Charities dinner when Proefrock returned to his office to talk to Braunecker on the phone. Braunecker was pissed. He had better offers on the table from the New York Yankees and Texas Rangers, but had kept them in limbo for days while he tried to finalize the last-minute, cloak-and-dagger negotiations with the Phillies, the team his client so badly wanted to join. And now, just inches from the goal line, the deal was falling apart over a few million dollars.

Contracts crumble in baseball every day, but feelings had entered the equation as the two sides talked money, club options, and performance bonuses.

This had become personal.

"You broke my heart once, Ruben," Lee's wife, Kristen, told Ruben Amaro Jr. in a conference call a day earlier. "Don't break it again."

But on that Monday night in December, heartbreak hung in the air as Braunecker expressed his frustrations to Proefrock.

"I can't believe you're going to allow this thing to slip through your fingers over a few million dollars!" he said. "We knew this would happen!"

"Look, Darek," Proefrock said calmly. "You've got two very competitive people and they're each trying to play last hit. Don't fly off the handle. It's not going to help."

Montgomery listened as Proefrock tried to soothe the agent's nerves. The two parties had painstakingly rebuilt their relationship following bad blood that developed when the Phillies traded Lee to Seattle in December 2009. Nobody wanted things to fall apart again. Not now. Not when they were so close to performing a baseball miracle.

Proefrock hung up the phone. Montgomery sighed.

The gravity of the situation had weighed on him. The Phillies were astoundingly close to bringing a fantasy rotation into the real world, and Montgomery knew he had the power to make it happen. He just had to say yes. But Montgomery, a Roxborough native who had risen from the ticket office to the club presidency, also had to think about the long-term viability of the franchise he had run since 1997. He had to consider the risks, which were considerable, of handing a 32-year-old pitcher a five-year contract worth $120 million. As his inner businessman weighed the wisdom of the deal, the lifelong Phillies fan inside him said: *Do it. Make history happen.*

He looked at Proefrock.

"I can feel the waves crashing over me," he said with resignation.

———————— K ————————

Clifton Phifer Lee—Clifton is his maternal grandfather's name; Phifer is his mother's maiden name—had made a fine Plan B.

Ruben Amaro Jr. had doggedly pursued Roy Halladay for weeks, but as the July 31, 2009 trade deadline approached he could not part with Domonic Brown, Kyle Drabek, and other prospects to bring him to Philadelphia, when he could get Lee, who had won the American League Cy Young a year earlier, for considerably less. So instead of catching his Moby Dick, Amaro caught the next biggest fish in the ocean on July 29, when he sent prospects Carlos Carrasco, Jason Donald, Lou Marson, and Jason Knapp to the Cleveland Indians for Lee and outfielder Ben Francisco.

In a fairy-tale debut, Lee threw a complete game July 31 against the San Francisco Giants at AT&T Park. He went 5-0 with a 0.68 ERA in his first five starts and 4-0 with a 1.56 ERA in five postseason starts—including a complete game, 10-strikeout victory in Game 1 of the World Series against the New York Yankees at Yankee Stadium—to solidify his rock-star status in Philadelphia. Fans embraced Lee like they had Jim Thome when he'd arrived as a free agent before the 2003 season. They might have liked him more. He was talented. He was cool. He was theirs. In a column on the eve of the 2011 regular season, the *Philadelphia Inquirer*'s Maria Panaritis, described the city's love affair with Lee this way:

"Cliff Lee love isn't about box scores, ERAs, or innings pitched. You won't

*understand it by dissecting interview transcripts, psychoanalyzing his heart. . . .
It is about animal instinct. It is about being a Marlboro Man in a Metrosexual
World. And it begins and ends with Game 1 of the 2009 World Series, when in
one of those rare moments of superhero shine, a less-is-more ace incinerated the
almighty Yankees the way Indiana Jones crushed the Germans with little more
than a whip, a sneer, and a few good Hollywood one-liners."*

The iconic Lee moment for many Phillies fans came in the sixth inning
in Game 1 against the Yankees, when Johnny Damon hit a broken-bat pop-
up to the mound. Lee did not move as the ball fell toward him. Just before it
reached him, he nonchalantly stuck out his glove to the side, opened it, and
caught it.

Whatever.

Lee gets asked about that catch occasionally. He said he actually was
thinking about dropping the ball and throwing to first to get the runner on
first in a rundown. But then he realized Damon was running to first too fast
and he wouldn't have time to pick up the ball and make the play. So at the
last second, he just decided to catch it.

"I wouldn't make a catch like that just totally nonchalant without some-
what of a reason," he said. "That's definitely why I did that. It didn't come
across looking good for me."

It looked like Lee, in the biggest game of his life, was playing catch in the
backyard with his son, Jaxon.

"Nothing ruffles his feathers," Kristen Lee said. "He's just kind of the
same, even keel, no matter what. When he comes home, if I didn't know if
we won or lost, I wouldn't be able to tell by the way he was acting. He
doesn't bring anything home. That's a blessing for me."

Lee had been a bit of a wild man in high school. Some might have called
him immature.

"Weren't we all?" Kristen said, laughing.

But Lee's outlook on life changed profoundly when Kristen and Jaxon,
who was four months old at the time, visited him during the final weekend
of his 2001 season when he was a minor-leaguer with Class A Jupiter in
Florida. Jaxon developed a fever and started vomiting and had to be taken to
the emergency room. After extensive testing, doctors gave Cliff and Kristen
the terrible news their son might have leukemia. Further testing confirmed
he had acute myelogenous leukemia and he had a 30 percent chance to live.

Jaxon received chemotherapy and radiation treatments. The treatments started to work, but he suffered a relapse. He received a stem-cell blood transplant, which turned around his recovery. A year later, Jaxon had beaten leukemia.

"That definitely affected Cliff in a huge way," Kristen said. "That's pretty much one of the most traumatic things that you can go through as a parent, and it puts everything in perspective. It changes everything about you. It definitely has affected him on the mound."

The effect has been positive. Because when you have gone through what the Lees went through, there's no such thing as a bad game, no such thing as a bad season. Jaxon responded well to treatments a decade ago and has been healthy since.

Lee had three pretty good seasons with the Cleveland Indians from 2004 to 2006, winning 46 games, but he had an awful 2007. He suffered an abdominal injury in spring training and never recovered. He was 5-8 with a 6.38 ERA when the Indians demoted him to Triple-A Buffalo in July. They brought him back when rosters expanded on September 1, but he did not make the postseason roster. His struggles motivated him. He worked hard in the off-season, learned the importance of living in the moment, and started to take Adderall to treat attention deficit disorder. He improved the command of his pitches and had a career-year in 2008, starting the All-Star Game for the American League and finishing 22-3 with a 2.54 ERA to win the AL Cy Young Award.

"I started focusing more on controlling what I could control, focusing on my routine and my preparation," he said. "Don't leave anything to chance with that. And if I do that, there's no reason to be anything other than confident and expect to win. I've really been more conscious of that since then."

Lee had his mojo back, and he was on his way to becoming one of the most coveted pitchers in baseball.

———————————— K ————————————

Poof.

Gone.

Nobody imagined the Phillies would trade their Marlboro Man to the Seattle Mariners the same day they acquired Roy Halladay from the Toronto Blue Jays on December 16, 2009. He would make only $9 million in 2010, which was a steal for a pitcher of his caliber. And who wouldn't want

Halladay and Lee in the same rotation? But the relationship between the Phillies and Lee, who could become a free agent following the 2010 season, became strained as the two sides talked about a contract extension.

As a player traded in the middle of a multiyear deal, Lee had the right to demand a trade within 15 days of the last game of the World Series. If he made that request and the Phillies did not trade him by March 15, he would become a free agent. Of course, that right came with a significant catch. Major League Baseball's Basic Agreement said if Lee requested a trade, the team that acquired him would retain his rights for three seasons. So instead of Lee becoming a free agent following the 2010 season when he was 32, he would became a free agent following the 2012 season when he was 34. Postponing free agency two more years would cost Lee millions, so the possibility of exercising his rights seemed remote. But Darek Braunecker used the clause to leverage the Phillies to pay Lee for not invoking it.

"Let's have a discussion about what value that has to the organization," Braunecker told team officials.

This was not unprecedented. Harold Baines used his trade rights in 1989 to add an additional year to his contract with the Texas Rangers. He wasn't the only one. Although Braunecker never threatened to demand a trade, he pressured the Phillies into adding $1 million of incentives to Lee's 2010 deal. The Phillies took the request as an aggressive act, threatening them without threatening them.

We won't shoot you, but we have a gun and we can, so hand over your wallet.

It indicated to the Phillies that negotiations could prove difficult in the future.

Less than a month later on December 3, Amaro and Scott Proefrock visited Braunecker at his hotel at the winter meetings in Indianapolis. There the Phillies offered Lee a three-year contract extension worth $18 million per season. The offer included a fourth-year option. The dollars were well received, but the Phillies fell short on the years. Braunecker told them he believed he could find a six- or seven-year contract if Lee became a free agent the following off-season. There had been speculation Lee would settle for nothing less than a monster payday, which was a concern for the Phillies. Lee told the *Cleveland Plain Dealer* in spring training of 2009 that signing a contract extension less than one year from free agency made no sense "when I just watched what CC did." He was referring to former Indians teammate CC Sabathia, who had just received a seven-year, $161 million contract from the New York Yankees.

"I never indicated to them that he was intent on testing free agency," Braunecker said in 2011. "But I was clear on the length of a deal I thought we could get in free agency. I felt like there was going to be a six-to-seven-year market. Their policy was three years. What I needed a commitment from them on was would they be willing to deviate from their policy? We couldn't sacrifice four years of guaranteed income. That was it. Ruben said, 'That is our policy, but it's not a hard-and-fast policy. That's our comfort zone. There is an exception to every rule and this guy is probably worthy of the exception.' OK, well, good enough. Let's keep the dialogue going. Let's stay in touch. You guys let me know. When we left that meeting, I'll take it to my grave, I was under the assumption, based on our conversations and what they communicated to me, that they were open."

In fact, Amaro and Proefrock left the meeting in Indianapolis believing they could re-sign Lee. But an interesting thing happened when they returned to their hotel suite to tell the rest of the front-office brain trust what they had offered. Everybody else in the room believed they had offered way too much for Lee, who just two years before had been toiling in the minor leagues. That got Amaro thinking maybe he could spend his money better elsewhere. Even after failing to get Halladay in July 2009, Amaro never really stopped talking with the Blue Jays. So in this high-stakes quest for an ace, he circled back and intensified his discussions with Toronto. Amaro might have fallen short in his pursuit of Halladay in July, but the right-hander remained his obsession and the Blue Jays remained under pressure to deal him. The framework for a trade between the Phillies and Blue Jays for Halladay was coming together by the end of the winter meetings. That weekend FOX Sports' Ken Rosenthal floated a story that seemed so out-of-the-blue it had to be true, so detailed that it read like a trial balloon floated by the Phillies front office. Rosenthal speculated the Phillies might trade Lee on their way to acquiring Halladay, even mentioning the Mariners as a potential destination for Lee. Braunecker was alarmed by Rosenthal's story. He called both Amaro and Proefrock the next morning, but neither picked up the phone, which he considered suspicious. He fired off text messages to Amaro and Proefrock.

Proefrock stared at the text message from Braunecker. The Phillies' assistant GM was in an impossibly difficult position. He could not confirm anything to Braunecker because nothing with Halladay had been finalized. He couldn't say, "Yes, it's true. If we agree to an extension with Roy, we're trading Cliff." He couldn't say that because if the Halladay deal fell apart they would still have Lee, except Lee would know the Phillies were trying to trade him. That could have catastrophic consequences in their negotiations.

Finally, Proefrock hit the reply button.

"Don't believe everything you read," he told Braunecker in a text.

Proefrock's non-denial denial to Braunecker proved prescient Monday, December 14, when the trade with Halladay fell apart. And at that moment, Proefrock suggested Amaro call Braunecker and ask for a counteroffer. It had been 11 days since the Phillies made their three-year offer in Indianapolis and Braunecker had never formally responded. The Phillies hoped Braunecker's concerns about Halladay's arrival might lower his request for more years. But Braunecker could not panic and lowball his client. He countered with a six-year request, which in his mind was nothing more than the first counteroffer in standard contract negotiations. Amaro took the counteroffer as confirmation Lee would be difficult to keep, although it would not be wrong to suggest Amaro used it as motivation to get the man he had wanted all along.

Halladay saved the day. He personally called Amaro later that Monday night and the two agreed on an extension.

News quickly spread. Lee was thrilled to learn Halladay was joining the team, but his excitement wouldn't last.

The Phillies had been talking with Seattle about Lee at the same time they were talking with Toronto about Halladay. The moment Halladay passed his physical on December 16, Amaro called Lee, who was leaving for a deer-hunting trip, and told him he had been traded to Seattle for three prospects: right-handers Phillippe Aumont and J. C. Ramirez, and outfielder Tyson Gillies.

Lee was crushed.

"I thought we were working out an extension with the Phillies," Lee said. "I thought I would spend the rest of my career there."

Critics of the deal said the Phillies traded Lee because they had to shed Lee's $9 million salary. Amaro was adamant he made the trade to restock a depleted farm system, but critics killed him for that, too.

Amaro wanted to keep Lee, but David Montgomery insisted he replenish the farm system if he planned to send more prospects to Toronto. Losing seven prospects in less than five months—four for Lee in July and three for Halladay in December—was a substantial drain on the organization. And while the Phillies wanted to win a World Series, they didn't want to find themselves with an aging roster and nobody left to replace them. They needed some talent coming through the pipeline.

Amaro was never told he needed to trade Lee, but he had no other option. Lee easily was the most attractive player on his roster. He also was the only player that could bring back comparable talent to satisfy his boss.

Amaro took a beating for it. First, the Phillies sacrificed a popular, known quantity in Lee, who was making just $9 million, for three prospects who had never played above Double-A. Second, even the people who understood the Phillies' predicament thought Amaro rushed into the deal.

"If I made a mistake in that process, it was that I didn't take the time to really maximize," said Amaro, looking back.

The Mariners wanted Lee because they already had Felix Hernandez and Erik Bedard in the rotation and had just signed Chone Figgins as a free agent. They expected to be contenders in the American League West and believed Lee could push them over the top. The Phillies felt Seattle was the perfect trade partner. They had intimate knowledge of the Mariners' farm system; Phillies Assistant General Manager Benny Looper spent 22 years with the Mariners before joining the Phillies in November 2008. Former Phillies General Manager Pat Gillick worked in Seattle before joining the Phillies in November 2005, and Special Assistant to the General Manager Charley Kerfeld lived just outside of Seattle and knew Seattle's organization well.

"There were some other teams," Amaro said. "There was some talent that we liked, but we didn't think we were going to get a similar package. We wanted to get an older package, but as far as ceiling was concerned we really liked the ceiling on these three guys."

Amaro could have waited to trade Lee to get a bigger and better deal, except he couldn't.

"Tough message to send," he said. "We just got Halladay and now we're going to wait three weeks and have him sit there and have the fans go, 'What? What are you doing?' And I knew I had to move him. I knew I had to move him and I knew I had to move him in a fairly efficient way. It's just kind of a tough message to send to the fans, 'Oh, we have these two aces right now and, oh, by the way, right around Christmastime you're going to lose one.' But we were moving so much talent we had to get some talent back. I mean, we were nude."

Nude or not, Amaro would never hear the end of it.

———————— K ————————

The relationship between the Phillies and Cliff Lee had soured, perhaps irrevocably.

"If you want to do business that way that's your prerogative," Darek Braunecker told Ruben Amaro Jr. in a heated telephone conversation after the trade. "It's not the way I do things and Cliff deserves better than that. You guys have made a colossal mistake. And you know what? We're going to end up doing business together again, but I can promise you this: the way I do business with you from this point forward is going to be a lot different than it's been to this point."

Braunecker had let Lee read the emails and text messages and listen to the voice mails from the Phillies. He wanted to let Lee know he had not misinterpreted anything or missed any signals that Lee's time in Philadelphia had come to an end.

"Cliff knew exactly what was being said and what they were telling us," Braunecker said. "And then when Ruben called him and informed him, he said why would you guys continue to tell Darek this didn't affect me and there was no truth to this when clearly there was? Why wouldn't you have just been honest with us? Ruben said we had to do what we had to do in this situation."

Braunecker and Lee had reasons to be upset, while the Phillies had reasons to move onto Halladay. Halladay represented a guarantee. They *knew* they would have him in uniform beyond 2010, if they traded for him. Despite the fact the Phillies felt good about their conversation with Braunecker in Indianapolis, Lee wasn't a sure thing. Knowing he could only have one, Amaro took the guarantee.

After banishing him to the Northwest, the Phillies tried to make amends with Lee almost immediately. Not because they dreamed they would ever bring him back, but because it seemed like the right thing to do. So when Braunecker asked the Phillies to reimburse the Lees for the deposit they made on their spring-training housing in Clearwater, Florida, for 2010, they obliged. The reparations continued April 30, 2010, when Scott Proefrock, on a whim, emailed Braunecker and asked him to pass along his well wishes to Lee, who was coming off the disabled list to make his first start for Seattle. Braunecker said he would.

Braunecker noted how the Phillies signed Ryan Howard to a five-year, $125 million contract extension a few days earlier.

"I wish we could have applied some of that money to keep Cliff in Philly," he told Proefrock in a return email.

With no hidden agendas, the lines of communication had reopened between the two sides, and that made Proefrock happy.

Braunecker and Proefrock know each other well. Proefrock's family lives outside Baltimore, about a mile from New York Yankees right-hander A. J. Burnett, another Braunecker client. Proefrock's son, John, is the best friend of Burnett's son, also named A. J. Proefrock and Braunecker attended parties at Burnett's house long before Lee joined the Phillies.

Their familiarity helped ease any bitterness and hurt feelings.

"It wasn't personal," Proefrock said. "It was business. Over the course of time everybody came to understand that."

Proefrock, the man who rebuilt the Phillies' relationship with Cliff Lee, was born April 7, 1960, in Dayton, Ohio, but spent the majority of his youth in Massachusetts, where he became a die-hard Boston Red Sox fan. He and his friends often made the drive from Cape Cod to Fenway Park to watch Carl Yastrzemski. Proefrock later graduated from William & Mary and spent his first four years out of college working as an accountant in Richmond, Virginia.

He hated it.

Some of his friends had attended the sports management program at the University of Massachusetts, and one got a job with the New York Mets in 1986 when they won the World Series. That sounded pretty good to him, so Proefrock quit his job to enroll at UMass. He volunteered at the Cape Cod League and connected with one of his college professors, Bernie Mullin, who left UMass to become vice president of business operations with the Pittsburgh Pirates. Mullin asked him to work with the Pirates as a marketing intern. Proefrock, who was paid $150 a week, did a good enough job to inspire the Pirates to hire him as their director of marketing information systems three months later in November 1987.

Proefrock's knowledge of computers from his accounting days served him well. He created databases for everything from potential ticket buyers to player highlights for the scoreboard operator. He got to know Jim Bowden, who was working for Pirates General Manager Syd Thrift. He helped Bowden create databases on the baseball side. Thrift left the organization in 1988 and Bowden soon followed. Larry Doughty replaced Thrift. He brought in Cam Bonifay and Chuck LaMar to work underneath him, which worked out well for Proefrock. He was the only one with intimate knowledge of the databases Bowden had been compiling, so the Pirates hired Proefrock as scouting and player development assistant in December 1989.

Proefrock got his first taste of baseball ops and loved it. He attended the winter meetings in Nashville and still remembers being in a room with Milwaukee Brewers General Manager Harry Dalton, Brewers Manager Tom Trebelhorn, Pirates Manager Jim Leyland, and Doughty. The Brewers were talking about their headaches with Gary Sheffield, while the Pirates were talking about their headaches with Barry Bonds.

"I was just a fly on the wall," Proefrock said.

He enjoyed his time in Pittsburgh, but realized there were greener pastures in Atlanta. The Pirates were on the brink of losing Barry Bonds, Bobby Bonilla, and Doug Drabek in free agency, while the Braves had an incredible amount of talent coming up through their system. So when LaMar left for the Braves a year later, Proefrock joined him. He still remembers telling Doughty his decision, and Doughty calling Pirates president Carl Barger to tell him the news. Barger walked into Doughty's office, looked at Proefrock, shook his head, and said, "There's no loyalty in baseball anymore." He turned around and left. Proefrock felt awful, but something stuck with him about his departure from Pittsburgh. (And it wasn't that Barger left a year later for the Florida Marlins.) The Pirates organization gave full-time employees holiday bonuses every December, but Proefrock did not receive one for his apparent lack of loyalty, despite working with the organization the entire year. It was a disheartening end to an otherwise good experience with the Pirates.

Not long after, Proefrock received a Christmas card from Doughty. Inside was a personal check for the amount of his holiday bonus.

That seemed like a pretty good way to treat people. Proefrock always remembered that.

Proefrock worked with the Braves for five years before following LaMar to the Tampa Bay Devil Rays. He met his wife, K. K., in Atlanta in 1991. He was in charge of setting up the Braves' postseason organizational meetings that year. He picked the Atlanta Marriott as the venue. K. K. worked at the Marriott and was the liaison between the hotel and the Braves.

"I was taken immediately with her," Proefrock said. "We talked, but I don't remember anything."

When he returned to his office at the ballpark, he ran into Paul Egins, who now works in the Colorado Rockies front office.

"I met the girl I'm going to marry today," Proefrock told Egins.

They married two years later, and after their time in Atlanta and Tampa Bay had ended they moved to Baltimore in 2006, when Proefrock got a job with the Orioles. He worked there for three seasons before joining the Phillies as assistant general manager in November 2008.

Proefrock is a genial man who attends Mass every Sunday. He spends as much time as possible with his wife and five children, which isn't always easy. The family has been unable to sell its Baltimore-area home, which means

Proefrock often spends weeknights at his in-laws in Wilmington, Delaware, returning home to Maryland for the weekends.

"It's hardest on my wife," Proefrock said. "A lot of times I feel like I create more problems when I'm home. She says, 'Great, now I have six kids I have to take care of.' She's a trooper. But the good thing is she knew what she was getting herself into. She knew I was in baseball."

Proefrock's easygoing demeanor and good nature makes him a good fit as Phillies assistant general manager. He deals regularly with agents and general managers and assistant general managers from other teams. A good part of his job is building and maintaining relationships with people. Arrogance and short fuses can kill a deal. Holding grudges helps nobody. That temperament served him well as he tried to rebuild the relationship with Braunecker.

"It's a lesson for everybody," Proefrock said. "There were no bridges burned. And there could have been. It was not a pleasant situation, discussion, the whole aspect of it."

It eventually became a distant memory.

———————————— K ————————————

Roy Halladay was living up to the hype in the summer of 2010, but Philadelphians still had Cliff Lee on their minds.

Seriously, Ruben, why did you trade Cliff?

The questions picked up during the summer. Jamie Moyer blew out his elbow on July 20, ending his season and possibly his career. Joe Blanton had a 6.03 ERA after losing a game in St. Louis on July 21, putting the Phillies seven games behind the Atlanta Braves in the National League East. Charlie Manuel fired Hitting Coach Milt Thompson on July 22, which looked like an act of desperation on a sinking team with a little more than two months to play.

The Phillies needed help, and a stud left-hander like Lee certainly could help. Ruben Amaro Jr. started fantasizing about reuniting with Lee. He called Mariners General Manager Jack Zduriencik to see what it would take to get Lee back. Zduriencik started with outfielder Domonic Brown, whom *Baseball America* considered the top prospect in baseball.

"Can't do it, Jack," Amaro replied.

After kicking around a few other possibilities, the talks ended.

"I completely understood," Amaro said. "That's exactly who I would be asking for if I were them. But for our purposes and for our future there are pieces we have to hold and he was one of them. Our biggest issue is the longevity of the guys that are on the field playing every day. We have to protect the position players. In this day and age position players are *tough* to come by. So tough."

The Phillies would not reacquire Lee, but once again they would get a hell of a Plan B. They turned their attention to Houston. Amaro sent J. A. Happ and prospects Anthony Gose and Jonathan Villar to the Houston Astros for Roy Oswalt.

The Phillies figured Lee was gone forever. Amaro believed whatever team got Lee at the trade deadline would lock him up to a multiyear contract. The Yankees had been close, but in a move that would turn out to be a break for the Phillies, the Mariners sent Lee to Texas when the Rangers sweetened their pot at the last second and included first baseman Justin Smoak.

"The perfect storm," Amaro said. "My feeling was that if he had gone to New York, had that deal gone though, Cliff would have been a New Yorker for several years."

Lee went on to pitch for Texas in the World Series before becoming a free agent. Meanwhile, Proefrock, the relationship builder, kept in touch with Braunecker.

"Let us know if you're interested in coming our way," he emailed him after the World Series.

—————————— K ——————————

Ruben Amaro Jr. knew the Phillies could have only one, but even one seemed impossible and he knew it. Still, he asked.

Jayson Werth or Cliff Lee?

Amaro and his top lieutenants had gathered in a conference room at Citizens Bank Park shortly after the Phillies lost to the San Francisco Giants in the 2010 National League Championship Series. The Phillies had hoped to become the first team to win three consecutive National League pennants since the 1942–44 St. Louis Cardinals, but those dreams ended when Ryan Howard took a called third strike from Giants closer Brian Wilson to end the series. While the Giants met Lee and the Texas Rangers in the World Series, Amaro met with his advisors to talk about the future.

If they could sign Werth or Lee, which one would they want?

Nobody hesitated. Everybody chose Lee.

"One hundred percent across the board," Amaro said.

The consensus hardly seemed to matter. Werth and Lee were long shots. Werth had established himself as one of the best right-handed-hitting out-fielders in baseball since he joined the Phillies in 2007, and he was in line for a major payday as a first-time free agent. Werth knew it, too. He fired long-time agent Jeff Borris during the season and hired Scott Boras in September to replace him. Players hire Boras because he finds monster deals nobody else can, and with Werth and Carl Crawford the two biggest bats on the market it was a near certainty Boras would find somebody somewhere to pony up big money for his new client.

The Phillies strongly believed Werth would not re-sign with them, but never said it publicly. But even with that knowledge it wasn't like Lee would be any easier to sign. They remembered their brief negotiations with Darek Braunecker the previous off-season, although they had the knowledge this time that Lee loved Philadelphia.

"You fantasize, but there's nothing realistic about it," Amaro said. "Oh, how amazing would it be to add this guy? We look through budgets all the time and our projected payroll and stuff like that. There was nothing that indicated we would be able to add the salary. And there also was no indica-tion we're going to go more than three or four years on a pitcher anyway. A lot of obstacles. I absolutely didn't even think it would fly."

Lee was the top starting pitcher on the market and the New York Yankees and Texas Rangers were his top suitors. Scott Proefrock laid the groundwork anyway. He sent Braunecker an email on November 2, the Tuesday after the World Series. He complimented Lee on his season and told him that Amaro wanted to meet with Lee in person as early as Thursday to gauge his interest in returning to Philadelphia. Teams could talk to Lee at that time to gauge his interest, but they could not talk money or make an offer. The Rangers held exclusive negotiating rights with Lee until midnight Saturday, although Lee had no intentions to sign before then.

"Thank you," Braunecker replied. "It was a disappointing end. I'll talk to Cliff."

Proefrock later told Braunecker that Amaro wanted Kristen Lee at the meeting, too. Kristen seemed more crushed to leave Philadelphia than her husband.

"I'm not sure you want that!!" Braunecker said in a reply email. "She might let him have it!! Cliff might be in a deer stand. I'll let you know."

"I'll tell Ruben to wear his Kevlar suit," Proefrock replied.

"Good idea."

Amaro and Braunecker spoke over the phone a short time later. Amaro expressed his interest, but made two things clear. First, he didn't think the Phillies could match the Yankees and Rangers in money or years. If Lee truly wanted to return to Philadelphia he would have to bend a little. Second, any talks with the Phillies had to be kept quiet. If word leaked the Phillies were involved, they would pull the plug. The Phillies knew if the Yankees and Rangers discovered they were in the hunt, one or both of them could jack up the price to stratospheric levels. But the Phillies had a more important reason for keeping the talks quiet: public relations.

"We didn't want to gussy the public up to thinking they're in for Lee and then you don't sign Lee," David Montgomery said. "We thought we had a pretty good season coming up and didn't want to tarnish the off-season by saying, 'Not only didn't they keep Jayson, they made an effort at Cliff and weren't successful.' "

To keep things quiet, the Phillies closed their inner circle. Initially, the only three people who knew they were talking to Braunecker and Lee were Amaro, Proefrock, and Montgomery. Pat Gillick, who carries heavy influence in the organization, entered later.

"My wife didn't know," Proefrock said.

Amaro didn't tell his father, Ruben Amaro Sr.

"Hell, no," he said.

Yankees General Manager Brian Cashman flew to Little Rock, Arkansas, to meet the Lees and Braunecker on November 10. Cashman called it a "meet and greet." Rangers President Nolan Ryan, Managing General Partner Chuck Greenberg, and General Manager Jon Daniels flew to Little Rock on November 15, to meet with the Lees and Braunecker. The Rangers touted Texas for its proximity to Lee's home and stressed, while they could not match the Yankees in dollars, Texas has no state income tax, which would make up the difference.

Lee mentioned to Cashman and the Rangers how much he enjoyed his time in Philadelphia. Cashman said later he did not consider that a bad sign. He just thought the Lees were being honest.

"We were in such a fight with Texas trying to get him," Cashman said. "We figured he's going to make his call and be rich either way."

Amaro never met the Lees in Arkansas because Braunecker said it wasn't necessary. Then things got quiet. Every time the Phillies thought they had a good conversation with Braunecker they read how the Yankees or Rangers increased their offer. The Phillies doubted they could make a serious run at Lee, but Amaro took one thing as a good sign: nobody knew the Phillies had been talking with Braunecker, even if they were only casual observers at this point.

The Phillies offered Werth a three-year, $48 million contract. The deal included a fourth-year option that increased the total value to $60 million. The Phillies knew if Werth accepted they had no shot at Lee, but they did not consider it a risk. They knew Werth would not accept. Besides, they kept hearing more and more about the money the Yankees and Rangers were throwing at Lee. Ryan and Daniels flew to Little Rock one more time before the winter meetings. They offered a five-year, $100 million contract, according to ESPNDallas.com.

Shortly before the winter meetings on December 6 in Lake Buena Vista, Florida, Proefrock called Braunecker about two other clients, right-hander Dustin Moseley and left-hander Ryan Rowland-Smith. Naturally, they also talked about Lee. Around that time the Phillies heard from one of their scouts that Lee told a business associate that if everything was equal he wanted to be in Philadelphia. Amaro and Proefrock got a jolt from the news. They started to dream big again. They needed to keep trying.

———————— K ————————

Scott Boras got Jayson Werth his money. He agreed to a seven-year, $126 million contract with the Washington Nationals on the eve of the winter meetings.

Werth was out of the picture. But was Lee in? Darek Braunecker lined up meetings with teams during the meetings at the Swan and Dolphin Resort at Walt Disney World. Braunecker texted Proefrock, letting him know he was available if the Phillies wanted to meet.

"We'd love to meet, but we're sensing we're out of the market and won't be able to play in that range," Proefrock replied.

Ruben Amaro Jr. wanted to jump in, but the years in the deal were an issue. Amaro spoke with Pat Gillick, who was elected to the National Baseball Hall of Fame that week. David Montgomery trusts Gillick more than anybody, which has been beneficial for Amaro. If he is getting close to something or needs help, Gillick can help push his idea over the top.

In many ways Gillick is Amaro's hammer.

"I think they understand now that I've figured out their strategy," Montgomery said months later. "But anybody in my position would be foolish not to reach out to Pat and see what he's thinking."

The Phillies purposely kept their distance from Braunecker at the winter meetings. Proefrock ran into him in the hotel lobby, said hello, shook his hand and kept moving.

"I didn't even want to be seen anywhere near the guy," he said.

Reporters started to mention the Phillies as the third team in the Lee sweepstakes, which Amaro vehemently denied.

"I lied," he said.

He made no trips to the confessional for his sins.

"I don't care," he said. "If we were really going to make a serious run at this we couldn't risk it getting out there because I don't know what the Yankees would have done. It's like asking—and this is a totally different scale and level of importance—but it's like asking the chief military officer, are you going to bomb so-and-so today? Let's just let everybody know. That's not how you do business. Sometimes when you're trying to come to some sort of conclusion on something you can't be all that forthright. This isn't necessarily honest or fair. I'd like to think I'm a fairly honest person, but at the same time. . . ."

If it meant telling the truth about their pursuit of Lee and losing him or lying to reporters and getting him, Amaro would lie every time.

Braunecker wanted to get his offers on the table during the winter meetings, return to Little Rock, and have the Lees make a decision shortly after that. The Phillies had not made an offer at that point because they had no reason to believe Lee would leave tens of millions of dollars on the table.

"I don't believe in engaging just to disappoint," Montgomery said. "If we have a legitimate chance, let's do it. But we did not necessarily feel that we were an eventual destination."

The Phillies heard about the money the Yankees and Rangers were offering and they were not going to outspend them. They also didn't like the idea of making a multiyear commitment to a 32-year-old pitcher. But Gillick, who is a big believer in going no more than three years on a pitcher, knew it was a once-in-a-lifetime opportunity and a great way to position the Phillies to win multiple championships.

"We've got a window here for a period of time," he told Montgomery. "Let's take advantage of it before it closes. At some point it is going to close."

The Phillies left the winter meetings without making an offer. But they left with hope.

——————————— K ———————————

Darek Braunecker returned to Little Rock from the winter meetings on Wednesday, December 8. He met with Cliff and Kristen Lee at a restaurant to discuss the offers from the New York Yankees and Texas Rangers. The Lees said they could be happy with the Yankees or Rangers, who would fly to Little Rock one more time. But the more Cliff and Kristen talked with Braunecker the more they wished Philadelphia would engage.

"I just wish the Phillies would get involved," Lee said a few times over dinner.

Cliff rhetorically asked Braunecker how much money his family needed. He said he wanted to go to the team he thought had the best chance to win multiple championships. He also was intrigued about joining what could be the best rotation in baseball and arguably one of the best of all time. Kristen mentioned how much they had been welcomed into the Phillies family and the relationship they had established with ownership.

Braunecker called Scott Proefrock after the meeting. He said he knew Philadelphia was the right place for the Lees and he was not concerned about getting them the most money. He simply wanted to put them in the right place. He also said he would like to look back and think he played a small role in helping put together one of the greatest rotations in baseball history.

All of that sounded fine, but the Yankees had offered Lee a seven-year, $148 million contract.

"We're not going to be able to go seven years," Proefrock said.

"What about five years?" Braunecker said.

"Would you even entertain five years?" Proefrock asked.

"We'll entertain anything," Braunecker responded. "You know where the market is at. If you were willing to go five with an option there might be something there."

Proefrock had his doubts. The Phillies did not want Braunecker to use them as leverage for the Yankees and Rangers.

"We don't need you guys," Braunecker said.

"You have to give me your word this is genuine interest on your part,"

Proefrock said.

"Scott, I wouldn't be wasting your time or my time. You have to trust me."

"I trust you. I just have to be able to tell that to David with complete sincerity."

Proefrock hung up the phone and recapped the conversation and Lee's desire to return in an email he composed to Montgomery:

"To me this conversation represents an indication and validation of everything we do and stand for as an organization, the way we treat our players and our employees. The impact of bringing him back would be immeasurable, not only for our organization, but for the industry. We are in a Golden Era of Phillies baseball, one that we might not see again for years. We have a chance to win multiple championships and in bringing Cliff back we would be maximizing that opportunity to win and expanding our window to remain in the top echelon in the game for an extended period of time. His addition to Halladay, Hamels, would give us the best chance and the best rotation in baseball for at least the end of Halladay's tenure, which would take us through 2014. For him in his current status as far and away the most coveted free agent on the market to walk away from the highest dollar and possibly the longest term to go where he really wanted to go would validate that thinking for years to come."

The phone call from Braunecker to Proefrock changed everything for Montgomery. They were serious. The Phillies returned to Philadelphia from the winter meetings Thursday, December 9. Ruben Amaro Jr. and Proefrock met in Montgomery's office on Friday. Pat Gillick was on speakerphone. The four talked for a long time about how this might affect the future composition of the ball club. Jimmy Rollins, Ryan Madson, Brad Lidge, and Raul Ibanez were going to be free agents after the 2011 season. Cole Hamels was going to become a free agent after the 2012 season. They would have other holes to fill in the near future. If Lee returned, Montgomery wanted to make sure everybody had thought about the chain of events that would follow. Comfortable with what was said in his office, the four came up with a number to offer Lee.

Montgomery wrote the number on a Post-It note and slid it across his desk. Proefrock picked it up and handed it to Amaro.

They would offer five years for $115 million with a vesting option for a sixth year that would increase the value of the contract to $130 million. (The option vested if Lee finished in the top two in Cy Young voting in 2013 or

2014 or threw 225 innings in 2015; and did not finish the 2015 season on the disabled list.) It was a firm offer, which they could not exceed under any circumstances. Amaro and Proefrock were pumped, while Montgomery kept his cool. He believed Braunecker and Lee would see the offer, realize how far away they truly were from the Yankees and Rangers, and walk away.

Proefrock was driving home to Maryland when he got a call from Amaro.

"Card played," Amaro said. "We'll see what happens."

— K —

Scott Proefrock felt pretty good about the Phillies' chances to sign Cliff Lee that Saturday, so good he asked his nine-year-old son John if he thought the Phillies should sign him.

"Yeah, Dad," John said.

"OK, I'm going to call Mr. Ruben and I'm going to tell him we should sign Cliff Lee just because you told me to."

The inner circle had expanded to Amaro, Proefrock, Montgomery, Gillick, and Proefrock's son John.

About 1,100 miles southwest of Citizens Bank Park, Lee sent Braunecker a text message before he took his family on a one-day duck-hunting trip:

"Kristen really wants to go to Philly."

"What does Cliff want?" Braunecker replied.

"I'd love to be back in Philly."

Braunecker and the Phillies exchanged ideas and details throughout the day and into the night with Braunecker sleeping in his office.

"Hey, buddy, make this happen," Braunecker told Proefrock in a text. "We've worked too hard and it makes too much sense. Everybody wins. I can be creative."

"I'm trying," Proefrock replied.

"I know you are," Braunecker said. "I can't tell you how much I appreciate it. I've done all I can do to pacify all interested parties. Deferred dollars gets it done. Signing bonus. More buyout. You name it. Couldn't be more flexible. We're leaving so much money on the table. Can't leave anymore. I know you understand."

Amaro called Roy Halladay on Saturday night. Halladay had sacrificed free agency to join the Phillies in December 2009. He signed a three-year

$60-million extension with an option for a fourth year. He left tens of millions on the table to come to Philadelphia. Amaro wanted to gauge Halladay's temperature on Lee, who would get a much bigger deal than him.

Halladay responded enthusiastically. He told Amaro he couldn't care less about who is paid more. He just wanted to win.

Amaro hung up the phone with Halladay and called Proefrock.

"I want to get this guy even more after the conversation I just had with Roy," he said.

Amaro was with his two daughters at a Barnes & Noble in Langhorne, Pennsylvania, when Braunecker called him Sunday. He had Cliff and Kristen with him and put them on speakerphone. Kristen had spent the weekend making a list of plusses and minuses for Philadelphia, New York, and Texas. The plusses for Philadelphia included everything from Lee getting a chance to hit to the fans to the atmosphere at Citizens Bank Park to living in Center City.

It was the longest list of the three.

"I've tried everything I can," Amaro told them. "I'm trying everything possible. But the reality is they're only going to let me go so far. I'm sorry."

"You broke my heart once, Ruben," Kristen said. "Don't break it again."

The Yankees had offered Lee a seven-year, $148-million contract. The Rangers had offered Lee two options: a six-year, $120 million deal or a six-year, $108-million deal with $30 million deferred over 15 years once Lee turned 50. Both proposals from Texas could include a seventh-year option. The Phillies were in the ballpark with Texas, but fell far short of New York's offer.

The Yankees had started to hear "drips" the Phillies were involved. Yankees General Manager Brian Cashman got frustrated.

"I wanted to pull our offer off the table but ownership wouldn't let me," he said. "I had just come to a point where we addressed every issue and he still wouldn't say yes."

The Phillies and Braunecker continued to work—Braunecker from his office, Amaro from a Barnes & Noble, and Proefrock at a bowling alley. Proefrock had taken his son to a bowling event that morning. The alley was in a basement, so every few minutes he went upstairs to check his voice mail and text messages.

The Phillies were going well beyond their comfort level of offering pitchers no more than three-year contracts. And they were going to pay Lee more than $100 million on top of that, too. Amaro expressed that to Braunecker.

"Darek, my job is on the line," Amaro told the agent. "You realize this could cost me my job."

"I'm going to tell you this much," Braunecker replied. "The best way to ensure job security is doing this fucking deal. You do this deal and go on to win two, three world championships over the next few years, they're going to build a statue of you next to Rocky."

Amaro sent Proefrock a text just after noon on Sunday that read: "Just talked to Cliff and Kristen and Dennis."

Dennis had become the code name for Braunecker. David Montgomery makes a special point to know people's names inside and outside the organization, no matter how high or low they are on the ladder. It is part of his charm, but one time he slipped and called the agent "Dennis Braunecker" and it stuck. Amaro and Proefrock continued to call the agent "Dennis" because they knew nobody else would know whom they were talking about.

Amaro sent Proefrock another text around 3:15 P.M. that read: "Keep your chin up. We've done all we can do."

The parties had reached a stalemate.

It was over.

Proefrock emailed Braunecker at 3:20 P.M. to apologize. He told Braunecker how much he respected him and Lee for their conduct in the negotiations. He thanked them for sacrificing to "try to make the dream come to fruition."

"I think we both feel this is the right place for Cliff, but we've pushed our limits as far as we can go," he said.

Braunecker responded at 4:29 P.M. He said feelings "will forever linger as to what could/might have been."

Montgomery expressed his appreciation to Amaro and Proefrock.

"You're both doing your jobs by pushing for what you believe in and I should always be available to hear what you think," he said. "Sorry we didn't get to the finish line on this one. Again, thanks for the effort."

Amaro hopped on a plane to meet Gillick in Arizona, where they planned to talk with Ben Francisco and John Mayberry Jr. about replacing Jayson Werth in right field. Proefrock sat dejected in Baltimore. Braunecker felt sick to his stomach in Arkansas.

Braunecker sent Proefrock a text message at 6:42 P.M., just hours after both parties declared the negotiations dead.

"Man, is this eating at you like it is me?"

"I want to cry," Proefrock replied. "I'm withdrawing from my family. I don't want to talk to anybody."

"I know," Braunecker said. "I'm starting to feel sorry for my family as

I've been a total non-factor to them lately. I never thought I would be so anxious to forgo my own personal income for something like this, but when something is so right it makes you forget some of the other things. Man, it's kind of heartbreaking as corny as it sounds."

Proefrock felt another shot of adrenaline and started brainstorming ways to resuscitate the deal. He sent Braunecker an email at 10:54 P.M. that stated, "I don't want to ride this to the end either, but how long do you have before you have to respond to other clubs?"

Braunecker said Lee is close to a decision, but could keep the two teams on hold a little longer.

Amaro's flight landed in Arizona at 11:20 P.M. Proefrock told him that Braunecker reengaged. Amaro called Braunecker.

"You've got to give me something," Amaro told the agent. "I need to take something to David."

It would be fruitless to call Montgomery and say Braunecker reengaged, but was unwilling to make any concessions. Braunecker needed to move in the Phillies' direction. At this point both parties wanted to make this deal happen so badly they worked together to craft Braunecker's counterproposal to show Montgomery, with Proefrock typing it up at his kitchen counter.

"A lot of these things are percolating without my awareness and they're presented to me when they're further down the line," Montgomery said. "It's the nature of the beast."

Braunecker sent the Phillies a long letter and proposal Monday morning speaking of the Lees' willingness to make sacrifices to come to Philadelphia. He proposed a five-year, $122 million contract with a sixth-year option that increased the value to $137 million. The option automatically vested if Lee threw 200 innings in 2015 or 400 innings in 2014–15, which was much more attainable than the option the Phillies originally proposed. It was well received, but Braunecker needed an answer soon. Yankees owner Hal Steinbrenner had called him that morning, pressing for a response. He also had exchanges with the Rangers. He even made a counteroffer to Texas, asking for a seven-year deal. He called Proefrock and told him if the Rangers returned his call and accepted, Lee would honor the deal and sign with them.

The Phillies needed to hurry. But just like Sunday, the deal died again— this time between lunch with Mayberry and dinner with Francisco.

———————— K ————————

I can feel the waves crashing over me.

Those words carried a couple meanings for Montgomery. He no doubt understood the importance of the decision in front of him. He had the power to bring back Lee to Philadelphia to form one of the greatest rotations in baseball history. But he also had nicknamed Proefrock the Wave Maker because he makes things happen.

"I could feel the waves crashing over me because the Wave Maker is pushing for a little more, a little more," Montgomery said with a smile.

Montgomery realized they were close. He stopped looking at the whole commitment and started to look at the difference separating the two. He decided he would close the gap. They would offer Lee a five-year, $120 million contract with a sixth-year club option increasing the value of the deal to $135 million. The option automatically vested if Lee threw 200 innings in 2015 or 400 innings 2014–15, and he did not finish 2015 on the disabled list with a left shoulder or left elbow injury.

Ruben Amaro Jr. called Darek Braunecker to finalize the deal. The phones for Amaro and Proefrock started to buzz as word spread the Phillies were the mystery team. Their phones actually had been ringing anyway because they had been trying to trade Joe Blanton, who would make $17 million over the next two seasons, to clear payroll. Braunecker took that as a good sign and called Cliff and Kristen to tell them about it.

"Hold on because we're going to get this deal done," he told them.

Proefrock knew things were turning in their favor around 9:30 P.M. when Braunecker started to ask about relatively minor details in the contract.

"Scott, was the trade provision and suite on the road intentionally struck from the deal? Or oversight? We have full no-trade provision in other offers and suites. Trying to do a full line-item comparison," Braunecker said.

"We don't do full no-trade and we don't do suites on the road," Proefrock replied.

"OK. That in itself has to be worth $2.5 million, especially against full protection," Braunecker claimed. "No joke. Y'all sell that to Montgomery.

"Any way to add that suite?" Braunecker asked again. "Family travels with him a lot."

"Jesus Christ, Darek. When I'm on the road and I get a suite I'll give it to him," Proefrock replied.

"Can we at least get a verbal when family is travelling with him?" Braunecker replied. "And by the way, you are the man."

In between their discussions, Proefrock was getting texts messages from reporters, other club officials, and even relief pitcher Chad Durbin, who was trying to re-sign with the Phillies.

Amaro called Proefrock a little before 11 P.M.

"Sorry, but we didn't get it done," he said solemnly.

"Fuck!" Proefrock screamed into the phone.

"Gotcha!" Amaro replied.

Amaro called Montgomery to tell him the good news. Montgomery wondered if he needed to call the ownership group to tell them what had happened, but Amaro said he could call them Tuesday morning because they would not announce anything until then. So a little after 11 P.M., Montgomery went to sleep.

Amaro and Proefrock were exhausted. They had been working on one of the biggest and most surprising signings in baseball history and had not been able to tell a single soul about it. That made their efforts even more exhausting. They were the only ones who knew.

"Those couple weeks were about as tough sleep-wise as I've gone through on this job because you don't want to get too excited about the possibility of being able to have him," Amaro said. "And at the same time have to keep it from my family, my kids, my friends, my brother, my dad, and my mom."

Montgomery woke up Tuesday morning to learn the word was out. While the Phillies and Lee's camp would not confirm anything publicly, out of respect, Lee had called the Rangers and Braunecker had called the Yankees to inform them of their decision. The word spread through those teams with T. R. Sullivan, the Rangers beat writer for MLB.com, breaking the story at 10:50 P.M. on his blog: "Cliff Lee is going to the Philadelphia Phillies, industry sources said Monday night. The Rangers were told Monday night that Lee is going to the Phillies. It is a done deal."

Montgomery had to scramble and call the ownership group, apologizing and explaining why they had not heard from him earlier. There have been worse calls to make.

Sorry, I didn't call you last night, but the good news is we got Cliff Lee.

Proefrock drove home to Maryland the weekend after Lee passed his physical and had his re-introductory news conference at Citizens Bank Park.

He handed his son John a baseball, with the inscription:

To John, thanks for helping to bring me back.

Cliff Lee.

THE FIFTH STARTER

Oh, the smell.

Joe Blanton can still smell the manure he shoveled into a wheelbarrow on those hot, humid Kentucky summer days. He grew up on a farm in a small town called Chalybeate, about 30 minutes from Bowling Green; a no-stop-light, no-four-way-stop town with a Dairy Queen and a mini-mart. The Blanton family had beef cows and grew tobacco, and Joe handled a variety of chores whenever his father, Joey, who also worked at the family insurance company, needed help. Blanton stripped tobacco leaves in the winter and fed cows and hauled square bale hay in the summer—picking up the bales in the field and throwing them onto a wagon. Once the wagon was full he tossed the bales into the barn. It was hard work in stifling heat, which choked him while he wore jeans and long sleeve shirts to avoid cutting his arms and legs. But more than he cared to remember, he shoveled that thick layer of fresh manure inside the barn into a wheelbarrow. Once the wheelbarrow was full, he pushed it to the garden, where he dumped it and it became fertilizer.

It smelt god-awful.

"It wasn't every day, and it was only a few hours," Blanton said, "but it felt like forever."

Baseball provided Blanton's escape. He lettered on the varsity team six years—one of the advantages of living in a small town—playing his first four years at tiny Edmonson County High School in Brownsville before transferring to the larger, more competitive Franklin-Simpson High School in Franklin for his final two years.

"Joe was Jekyll and Hyde," former Franklin-Simpson coach Greg Shelton said. "He was just as mild and meek and well-mannered a kid as you'll ever run into. Until you put a ball in his hand. Then he turned into a fierce competitor."

Like the time Franklin-Simpson trailed rival Warren Central by a run in the sixth inning. Shelton told Blanton to head to the bullpen to warm up. If the Wildcats took the lead, he would pitch the seventh. On cue, they hit a two-run home run to take the lead, Blanton entered the game and retired the side in order, striking out the final batter he faced. Blanton was so pumped up he fired his glove against the backstop.

Hell, yeah!

"Just out of his mind," Shelton said. "So out of place for him to show that kind of emotion. But he wanted it so bad. He finally had to let it release, you know?"

Big league scouts followed Blanton in high school, but word spread he would not sign because he planned to attend the University of Kentucky. Former Kentucky coach Keith Madison knew the Blanton family well because he played baseball with Blanton's father at Edmonson. (Young Joe broke Madison's strikeout record at Edmonson.) Scouts figured Blanton had no shot of signing because of that connection, although recruiting Blanton wasn't particularly easy.

Madison called him once a week, per NCAA rules, but those phone calls quickly became a painful exercise. Madison had talked to hundreds of teenagers over the years, but Blanton proved to be one of the toughest. He simply would not talk. Madison tried every conversation starter he could imagine, but each one failed. He started dreading those calls, secretly hoping Blanton's mom or dad would pick up the phone so he would have somebody to talk to.

"He's sort of like John Wayne," Madison said. "He just talks when he has something to say."

Blanton pitched in Kentucky's bullpen his freshman and sophomore seasons, throwing only a fastball and curveball, which convinced most scouts he would be a relief pitcher.

"I was a real raw country kid who tried to throw as hard as he could," Blanton said. "There wasn't a lot of pitching involved when I was out there."

Blanton started for the Wildcats his junior season and impressed Oakland A's area scout Rich Sparks. He was one of a handful of scouts that thought Blanton could be a big-league starter. A's Special Assistant to the General Manager Matt Keough felt the same way, and both kept going back to watch Blanton pitch. Sparks saw Blanton five times his junior season; Keough saw him three times.

"He had some fight a lot of guys didn't have," Sparks said.

The A's had seven of the top 39 picks in the 2002 amateur draft, which is known famously as the *Moneyball* draft, for Michael Lewis' book turned movie about the A's and their player procurement methods. The A's selected Nick Swisher with the 16th overall pick and hoped Blanton would fall to them at 24, which wasn't a lock. Chicago White Sox General Manager Ken Williams had told A's General Manager Billy Beane that he liked Blanton and would take him with the 18th pick.

The Phillies selected Cole Hamels 17th, but the White Sox surprisingly took Royce Ring over Blanton. Beane couldn't believe his good fortune.

"You fucking got to be kidding me!" Beane said in *Moneyball*. "Ring over Blanton? A reliever over a starter? Blanton's going to get to us."

The A's considered Blanton the second-best pitcher in the draft. They got him at 24.

Blanton maneuvered through the minor leagues and spent his first full season with the A's in 2005, posting a 12-12 record with a 3.55 ERA and finishing sixth in American League Rookie of the Year voting. He won a career-high 16 games in 2006 and remained in Oakland's rotation until the A's traded him to the Phillies on July 17, 2008, for Josh Outman, Adrian Cardenas, and Matt Spencer. The Phillies had been looking for a starting pitcher for the stretch run, but finished runner-up for CC Sabathia, whom the Cleveland Indians traded to the Milwaukee Brewers. Blanton was nowhere near as talented as Sabathia, but he fit Phillies General Manager Pat Gillick's philosophy that sometimes marginal acquisitions can push a team over the top.

Gillick divvied teams between himself and Assistant General Managers Ruben Amaro Jr. and Mike Arbuckle. Each man would keep in contact with his assigned teams throughout the year.

"You constantly know your needs and their needs and that could help facilitate a deal," Arbuckle explained.

Arbuckle had the Athletics, and worked with Oakland's Assistant General Manager David Forst on the machinations of the trade. Arbuckle finalized the deal while standing in the parking lot outside of Lake Olmstead Stadium in Augusta, Georgia, where he had travelled to scout a Phillies minor-league team. The A's had been pushing for an additional player in the deal, but the Phillies pushed back. Gillick finally told Arbuckle to tell Oakland, "This is where we are. We have interest in somebody else and we're going to go in another direction if you don't want to make this deal."

Oakland said OK.

"We bluffed them a little bit," Gillick said.

The Phillies viewed Blanton as somebody who not only could help the starting rotation, but the bullpen because he could pitch more than five or six innings, helping keep the bullpen's arms fresh. He went 4-0 with a 4.20 ERA in 13 starts down the stretch, and 2-0 with a 3.18 ERA in three postseason starts, including a win in Game 4 of the World Series against the Tampa Bay Rays.

Game 4 is often called The Joe Blanton Game.

Not too many people remember he allowed just four hits and two runs in six innings. They only remember he hit a two-out solo home run to left field against Rays right-hander Edwin Jackson in a 10-2 victory. The Phillies had a 5-2 lead before Blanton launched his bomb, which was the moment many Phillies fans knew they were going to win the World Series.

Blanton doesn't go long without hearing about the homer.

"I was sitting in Section 143 when you hit it!"

"I was at Chickie's and Pete's!"

"I was on the couch at my parents' house!"

"People remember where they were when I hit it, which I think is unbelievable," he said. "To remember that is pretty awesome."

Blanton had been part of something special in 2008, and figured to be part of something special in 2011. He started the season as part of the Phillies' pitching staff of stars, and though he was the fifth man he hardly minded. He wasn't shoveling manure or hauling hay. He was playing baseball and he loved it.

Ultimately, an elbow strain knocked Blanton from The Rotation in May. The fifth spot was eventually plugged by the unlikely tandem of an embattled veteran and a rookie sensation.

———————— K ————————

Kyle Kendrick is the beloved little brother, the perpetual rookie, in the Phillies' clubhouse.

His teammates swiped his clothes and replaced them with a St. Pauli Girl-style costume at RFK Stadium in September 2007. Of course, he joined Chris Coste (Superman), Michael Bourn (Wonder Woman), Chris Roberson (beauty queen), J. D. Durbin (baby), Fabio Castro (clown), and John Ennis (beer keg) as part of a rookie hazing stunt. Kendrick suffered the indignity of a plunging neckline and sexy skirt for one night of laughs and fun, understanding that next year he would be one of the guys laughing at the rookies.

Except his teammates swiped his clothes again in September 2008. And this time he found black chaps, a cod piece, eye patch, leather cap, leather whip, and chains hanging in his locker. Again? Seriously? Several months earlier, Kendrick became a victim of a famous spring training prank. It started with just a few conspirators, but soon included teammates, coaches, and the front office. After a workout, Phillies assistant General Manager Ruben Amaro Jr. called Kendrick into Charlie Manuel's office at Bright House Field in Clearwater, Florida, where Manuel told him he had been traded to the Yomiuri Giants for Kobayashi Iwamura.

"You were one of the guys in the deal," Manuel said glumly.

"I appreciate what you did last year," said Amaro, referring to Kendrick's unlikely rise from Double-A. "You had a hell of a year for us. You're a classy kid, but I think this is a great opportunity for you to make a hell of a lot of money."

"All right," said an utterly stunned Kendrick while signing some paperwork.

Of course, Iwamura didn't exist. The name was a combination of the hot-dog eating champion Takeru Kobayashi and Tampa Bay Rays second baseman Akinori Iwamura. Amaro handed Kendrick a letter on official Phillies letterhead, while Frank Coppenbarger, the director of team travel and clubhouse services, gave him his itinerary for the flight to Japan, which was leaving at 7:05 the next morning.

Everything looked and sounded official.

"Do you have anything in Philly?" Coppenbarger said, asking about belongings that needed to be shipped.

"Uh, in Philly?" Kendrick stumbled. "No."

Kendrick called his agent, Joe Urbon, who confirmed the news. Amaro then announced the trade to reporters while standing next to the stunned Kendrick at his locker. If Kendrick had not been so shocked, he might have wondered why a Comcast SportsNet cameraman was taping everything from the conversation in Manuel's office, to Kendrick breaking the news to teammates, to Amaro announcing a trade in such an unusually casual manner. But the dazed young pitcher wasn't thinking clearly, so when reporters started to ask him questions, like if he had the necessary shots to travel overseas, he answered them.

Finally, Brett Myers, one of the ringleaders, let everybody's kid brother off the hook.

"You know what I say?" he announced. "You just got punked!"

The clubhouse erupted in cheers and laughter as Kendrick breathed a sigh of relief. He took the joke well, which is why he is one of the most well-liked players in the clubhouse. He is a good spirit, and a good sport. There is an innocence about him, a naïveté. His ego hasn't soared from being in the big leagues. He is still the buddy you call to help you move or pick you up at the airport. He hasn't changed.

The Phillies selected Kendrick in the seventh round of the 2003 draft. He had been recruited as a quarterback at Washington State University, but baseball was his first love and a $130,000 signing bonus, plus college tuition, convinced him to sign with the Phillies to begin his professional career. He replaced one of the Phillies' all-time biggest busts, Freddy Garcia, in the rotation in June 2007, despite not being on the 40-man roster or making an appearance with the team in spring training. He went 10-4 with a 3.87 ERA in 20 starts, earning a start in Game 2 of the National League Division Series against the Colorado Rockies. Not bad for a kid who thought he was coming from Double-A for one fill-in start that June.

Kendrick's career has been in flux since. His ERA ballooned to 5.49 in 2008 and he failed to make the postseason roster. He spent most of the 2009 season in Triple-A Lehigh Valley, where the Phillies ordered him to work on his secondary pitches. He went 11-10 with a 4.73 ERA in 2010, but again did not make the postseason roster. He always seemed to be fighting to stay in the rotation, trying to convince Phillies Pitching Coach Rich Dubee he was worthy, but entering this season he knew he had no shot. Roy Halladay, Cliff Lee, Roy Oswalt, Cole Hamels, and Joe Blanton had the rotation locked up. He would be pitching in the bullpen as a long man, unless somebody got hurt.

If that happened—and somebody always got hurt—he would be ready, and his teammates would be pulling for him. Everybody loves Kid Brother Kyle. They just show it in unusual ways.

———————— K ————————

Vance Worley probably had 40 scouts watching him pitch his final regular-season game at Sacramento's C. K. McClatchy High School in 2005. He knew what it meant. He would be selected in the first few rounds of that June's draft.

But then he felt a pop in his right elbow. He finished the inning, but his velocity had plummeted. The gaggle of scouts had seen enough. They packed up their radar guns and headed home.

"Everybody just booked," he said. "They knew."

Worley's chances of getting drafted in the first few rounds ended the moment he sprained his elbow. He followed the first few rounds of the draft on the Internet, but no calls came. The next day he and his girlfriend decided to hit Six Flags Discovery Kingdom in nearby Vallejo. Right before he headed out the door, he randomly put on his Phillies cap. The phone rang. It was Phillies area scout Joey Davis.

"We just picked you," Davis said.

Worley took off his Phillies cap—he had a collection of several different ones—and looked at it.

That's weird.

"I'll come by your house tomorrow to talk about what you want to do," Davis said. "If you want to sign, I'll try to get a dollar figure for you."

Worley talked with Davis the next day. The Phillies wanted him to try to pitch summer ball. If his elbow improved and his velocity returned, they would offer him second-round money, despite Worley being a 20th-round selection. But Worley, who was just 17, wasn't sure. He had a scholarship to Long Beach State. If he tried to pitch in the summer and blew out his elbow, the Phillies would not pay him and he would jeopardize his college career. Worley decided to try college.

"You guys can try to pick me up again in three years," Worley told Davis.

Worley had a nondescript freshman season and strained his elbow twice as a sophomore, which he blamed on the coaching staff for shuttling him from the rotation to the bullpen. He was upset, ready to leave the school, and prepared to tell off his coaches. But in his end-of-the-year meeting the coaching staff surprised him and spoke glowingly about his future.

He stayed, but knew he needed to make changes.

It was the birth of the Vanimal.

Worley had been a quiet kid, meek. He knew he needed to improve physically and mentally. First, he began to work out like he had never done before. Then he made an attitude adjustment. He decided to get mean and nasty on the mound, treating hitters like they had no business standing in the batter's box against him.

As a reminder, he took a Sharpie and wrote, "Fuck you!" inside his cap.

The changes worked.

"Sit down!" he told hitters after striking them out.

If he walked a hitter, he followed them up the first-base line.

"Why aren't you swinging?" he barked. "I'm giving you fastballs. I'm giving you something to hit."

He pitched well enough for the Phillies to select him in the third round of the 2008 draft. He signed and went 3-2 with a 2.66 ERA in 11 starts for Class A Lakewood, bringing the Vanimal into the South Atlantic League. But he struggled in 2009, going 7-12 with a 5.34 ERA with Double-A Reading, while jumping up two levels. The Phillies almost traded him that July. They had a deal in place to send Worley and right-hander Heitor Correa to the San Diego Padres for Scott Hairston, but the Padres backed out at the last second and sent Hairston to Oakland instead.

Worley reported to Clearwater the next spring, looking to rebound and get his inner Vanimal back. But first Phillies minor-league instructors convinced him to get into better shape. They thought he had gotten too soft and put on too much weight the previous season, and that if he tightened up a bit, it would translate to improved success on the mound. He dropped the weight and went 9-4 with a 3.20 ERA in 19 starts with Reading before making his big-league debut on July 21. He went 1-1 with a 1.38 ERA in five appearances with the Phillies, including two starts.

He had gotten a taste of the big leagues, and he wasn't intimidated. The Vanimal wouldn't let him be.

He would become a fan favorite, in part because of his distinctive look. He is half-white, half-Chinese and Taiwanese. He has a Mohawk. His ears are pierced, something he did after his sophomore year at Long Beach State as a way to rebel after he couldn't bring himself to tell off his college coaches like he had planned. He has a dab of facial hair on his chin, which was against the rules in college, but biologically a challenge in high school as well.

"Obviously, being an Asian kid . . ." he joked.

But Worley's most distinctive feature is his prescription Oakley glasses, which he wears whenever he pitches. Worley has tried to wear contact lenses, but the man that scribbled the f-bomb in his cap and barked at hitters in college can't get the dang things to stay in his eyes. So instead of contacts, he has footed the bill for glasses.

"You pay for those?" Cliff Lee asked him early in the 2011 season. "You've got to call your agent. He'll get you hooked up."

"I've tried," Worley replied.

Worley would need to get some wins under his belt before the Oakley rep started coming by and outfitting him with glasses.

Those wins would come quicker than he expected.

THE SUPPORTING CAST

A couple of months after the Phillies won the 2008 World Series, Carlos Ruiz was relaxing at home in Panama.

His telephone rang.

The man on the other end wanted to know why Ruiz wasn't going to play for his country in the World Baseball Classic in March 2009.

Ruiz' answer was not a surprise to anyone who knows how dedicated he is to his pitching staff. And that's just the way he looks at it—as *his pitching staff*.

"I think I need to stay in camp and work with my pitchers," the Phillies catcher told the man in Spanish.

The man on the other end of the telephone said he understood Ruiz' reasoning, but before saying *adios* asked Ruiz to give it a little more thought.

"This is for your country," Martin Torrijos told Ruiz before hanging up.

Ruiz reconsidered and ended up playing in the WBC.

Why?

"Because I love Panama," he said.

"And how could I say no to our president?"

No starting pitching rotation can stand alone. Even the best of pitchers need to be backed by firm defense, solid run support, and good bullpen work. A slipup in any one of these areas can unravel even the best of starts. It could be argued that above all, a starting pitcher needs a soul mate, someone to team with mentally, physically, and sometimes emotionally, from the late-afternoon game-planning session, to the bullpen warm-up, to the final pitch of the night, and, if all has gone well, to the postgame victory beverage, be it a cold beer or a protein shake.

Ruiz is soul mate to The Rotation.

"Everyone here loves him," Roy Halladay said. "He's your favorite guy to root for."

Underdogs always are.

The Phillies began their rise to the top of the National League East in 2007. Not coincidentally, that was also the year a stocky Panamanian named Carlos Ruiz established himself as the team's No. 1 catcher. By the end of

2008, Ruiz was walking to the mound in the ninth inning of Game 5 of the World Series to discuss strategy as closer Brad Lidge was bearing down on Tampa Bay's Eric Hinske. The Phils were one strike from winning the World Series. The potential tying run was on second. There was little question that Lidge would throw his signature slider, but Ruiz wanted to offer a quick directive. Lidge, you see, threw three different sliders during his storybook 48-saves-in-48-chances season in 2008. He had the get-me-over slider, a nice easy one that he knew he could throw for a strike early in a count. He had the one that he tried to "backdoor" over the outside corner with a lefthanded hitter at the plate. And he had the Torpedo—the Good One, as Ruiz calls it, the one that approached the plate looking like a fastball, and then dove sharply into the dirt. It was a wipeout pitch, a championship pitch, and throwing it meant Lidge had to have confidence that his catcher would block it.

"Give me the Good One," Ruiz instructed Lidge on the night of October 29, 2008, as the packed house in Philadelphia held its breath in anticipation.

Three years later, Ruiz recalled that pitch as being "the best one Lidge has thrown in his life."

As Hinske swung over the pitch for the out that clinched Philadelphia's first major pro sports title in a quarter-century, Lidge famously dropped to his knees, looked heavenward and shouted, "Oh, my God, we just won the World Series!"

He shouted it again as a joyous Ruiz arrived at the mound and started the celebration pile.

"I looked up to the sky, but I also looked forward at the fans and Carlos," Lidge said. "I can't explain the feeling of euphoria I felt seeing the fans celebrate and having the team jump on me. That's what you play the game for."

———————— K ————————

All Carlos Ruiz ever played the game for was a chance.

The World Series was a nice reward.

But it all started with the dream of simply getting a chance.

Ruiz was raised in David, a city in Chiriqui Province, Panama. His father, Jaoquin, a policeman, was killed in a car wreck while on the job when Carlos was just seven. Young Carlos loved the game of baseball and poured himself into it. He was a scrappy little second baseman when he told his mother, Inocencia, that she would watch him play on television, in *las grandes ligas*, someday.

Young Ruiz caught the eye of a local baseball *impresario* named Allan Lewis. Known as the Panamanian Express for his running speed during his playing days with the Oakland A's in the 1970s, Lewis coached a local team and also scouted for the Phillies. He took Ruiz under his wing.

In the fall of 1998, when Ruiz was 19, Lewis phoned Sal Agostinelli, the Phillies director of international scouting, and said, "I got this kid. . . ." Agostinelli went for a look and immediately saw why a lot of the other teams had stayed away. Ruiz, squatty and maybe 5-8, did not have the kind of athletic body that the Phillies favored, but Agostinelli figured he'd give him the full look. Besides, it was nice and hot in David that day and Agostinelli, a former Phillies minor-league catcher, was eager to throw some batting practice and work up a sweat. Ruiz took his hacks. Agostinelli liked the kid's swing. He measured off 60 yards so he could watch Ruiz run. The kid came in at a below average 7.09 seconds. Ruiz took some ground balls at second. Pretty good. But not good enough to get Agostinelli to bite.

"I think he can catch," Lewis told Agostinelli.

Agostinelli's eyes lit up.

Catcher is a premium position. Many can do it, but few do it well. Scouts are always on the lookout for catching talent.

Agostinelli turned to young Carlos Ruiz.

"Can you catch?" he asked.

Though he had never really caught, Ruiz nodded in the affirmative. Of course, he would have done that if Agostinelli had asked if he could recite the Gettysburg Address.

"If he can catch, he becomes a different animal," Agostinelli told Lewis.

On that hot day in David, the scrappy little second baseman eagerly jumped behind the plate. His throws to second base impressed Agostinelli. His pop times—from catcher's mitt to second baseman's glove—were consistently under two seconds, which is very good.

"He immediately showed an above-average arm," Agostinelli said. "He was quick around the plate and his hands were good from playing second base. We figured, if he hits, with that arm, he's got a chance."

And that's all Ruiz wanted.

In the summer of 1998, the Phillies signed their first-round draft pick, outfielder Pat Burrell, to a big-league contract worth $8 million. Three months later they signed Carlos Ruiz for a relative pittance—$8,000. A decade later, both players were in that mob of celebrating bodies the night the Phillies won the World Series.

"I didn't care about the money," Ruiz said of his bargain signing bonus. "I just wanted a chance to play professional baseball."

Unlike Burrell, Ruiz did not rise quickly to the majors. Underdogs seldom do. It took him eight seasons to get there, and there were some frustrating moments along the way. He considered quitting during his first season in the Dominican Summer League. There were times when he struggled at the plate and would spit out a cuss word in Spanish. Over the years, a cleaned-up variation of that unsavory word became his nickname, and there's hardly a night that goes by at Citizens Bank Park when Ruiz doesn't come to the plate accompanied by the familiar chorus: *Chooooooch!*

Chooch showed early in his pro career that he could catch, throw, and hit a little bit, but learning to be a big-league catcher, a legitimate big-league catcher, required more than that. He needed to learn to call a game and work with a pitching staff, lead a pitching staff, become a soul mate to the guys on that little bump in the middle of the field. And he needed to learn enough English to communicate with pitchers. When he first arrived in the United States to play in the Gulf Coast League in 2000, his English was limited. He knew the word *chicken*. He knew how to say, *How you doing?*

The Panama native's English got better and better over the years—so good, in fact, that he could have chosen to speak English when he told his mother he'd made the big leagues in 2006, but did so in Spanish and his mother wept; so good that he does a hilarious imitation of teammate Shane Victorino employing one of his favorite catch phrases. "You know, like I said. . . ." Ruiz will say with an impish grin whenever Victorino uses that line in an interview with reporters. If comic relief is needed, Ruiz is always there with a masterful imitation of a teammate's pitching delivery or batting stance. He does a belly-splitting imitation of former teammate Aaron Rowand adjusting his wristbands and going into his unique batting stance. He's got Kyle Kendrick's delivery down pat. And it didn't take him long to pick up Roy Oswalt's mannerisms on the mound. Oswalt is always moving his feet, grooming the dirt on the mound. Chooch nails it.

Ruiz credits many for his transformation from a scrappy second baseman that nobody wanted to a frontline big-league catcher. Pitching Coach Rich Dubee, Bullpen Coach Mick Billmeyer and former Phils' pitcher Jamie Moyer all worked with him on the art of calling a game and setting up a hitter.

"I remember when I first saw him in 2006, he was a timid little guy who'd catch in the 'pen," Moyer said. "He learned a lot in 2007, and kept improving. He's evolved in a nice way. He has a certain confidence, almost an aggressiveness to him now that says, 'I'm in charge.' Pitchers like that. He's definitely become a thinking catcher."

Ruiz is a thinker.

When he's behind the plate, he tries to think like a hitter and a pitcher. *What is the hitter looking for here? How can I fool him here?* Dubee and Billmeyer say they have seen Ruiz learn to read a hitter's swing and make adjustments in a game plan from pitch to pitch.

"He sees a hitter two or three times in a game, understands what they're trying to do, and figures out a way for a pitcher to attack the hitter," Dubee said.

"He's very good at thinking right along with the pitcher," Billmeyer said.

Ruiz prides himself in becoming at one with his pitcher and when the two minds synchronize, well, it's a beautiful thing: The pitcher envisions the pitch he wants to throw, and in a split second, Ruiz has called for that very pitch. Halladay did not shake off Ruiz at all—not once—in his debut start with the Phillies on April 5, 2010. It was the beginning of a wonderful friendship. Six months later, Halladay shook off Ruiz just once while throwing 104 pitches in a playoff no-hitter against Cincinnati.

Though he often hits eighth in the Phillies' lineup, Ruiz likes to swing the bat and wants to be a productive hitter. It bothers him when he doesn't contribute at the plate. One day during the 2011 season, when Ruiz was struggling at the plate, a reporter asked for a minute of his time.

"Not if you want to talk about my hitting," he said glumly.

"It's about the pitching staff," the reporter said.

Ruiz brightened.

He's always willing to talk about the pitchers because he understands his connection to them and understands they come first. No matter how well or how poorly he is swinging the bat, his focus is always the pitching staff. It has to be. A hitting slump can get Ruiz down, but he can't let it affect his performance behind the plate. Handling a staff is his priority, and the pitchers appreciate that.

"He does so much for our team behind the plate and often doesn't get a lot of credit for it," said Halladay, who calls Ruiz the best catcher he's ever worked with.

Cliff Lee echoed those remarks after his sixth shutout of the season on September 5, 2011.

"Chooch did an unbelievable job calling the game, and I felt like he had [Atlanta] off balance from the start," Lee said. "He gets a lot of credit for [the shutout]. I might have shook him off once or twice the whole game. He's really impressive."

In the winter after the 2010 season, Halladay decided Ruiz deserved to be honored for all he does behind the plate. Halladay had just won the National League Cy Young Award. He wanted to do something for his batterymate, his baseball soul mate. He ordered an exact replica of the Cy Young Award he'd won and—in his typical, no fanfare, understated way—left it in front of Ruiz's locker one day in spring training of 2011.

Ruiz was deeply touched by the gesture, and all he could think of was returning the favor.

"Gotta get Doc a ring," he said in the summer of 2011.

———————————— K ————————————

Ruiz isn't the only underdog in the Phillies team picture.

Truth be told, the manager might be the biggest underdog of them all.

Charlie Manuel was born in a car in Northfork, West Virginia, on the way to his grandmother's house, in January 1944, the eldest boy of Charles and June Manuel's 10 children. The kids all had nicknames. Charlie's was Fook, short for Fuqua, his middle name. By the time the family got to the last child, a boy, it had run out of nicknames, so he went by BB, Baby Boy. Manuel's father, a Pentecostal preacher, took his own life when Charlie was a teenager. Charlie and his brothers helped the family make ends meet working in a sawmill in his hometown of Buena Vista, Virginia.

Baseball was Manuel's ticket out of the sawmill. He signed out of high school with the Minnesota Twins, and then kicked around the majors for awhile before landing a big-money deal in Japan. Manuel hit 189 home runs in six seasons in Japan and was league MVP in 1979. Hardly a week has gone by during Manuel's time with the Phillies when a Japanese reporter doesn't approach Manuel and ask the *Aka Oni*— The Red Devil—about his playing days in Japan. How big was Manuel in Japan? Well, he says he did the first-ever commercial for a Sony Walkman. Who knew?

Back in the States after his playing days, Manuel was hardly a household name. He worked as a manager and hitting coach in the Minnesota and

Cleveland systems.

Manuel skippered the Twins' Double-A team in Orlando in 1984 and 1985 when he developed a friendship/rivalry with John Hart, then-manager of Baltimore's Double-A Charlotte club. In those Southern League battles, Hart became impressed with Manuel's will to win—even if it sometimes infuriated him.

In 1984, Hart's club made a 10-hour bus ride to Orlando for a one-game playoff to determine which team would play in the postseason. Hart's club jumped out to an early 7-0 lead. The skies darkened in the fourth inning and it started to rain. Eventually it started to pour. The game was not official. Hart wondered why the grounds crew was not covering the field. He later found out why.

"Charlie paid the guy $100 to take off," Hart said with a laugh years later.

"Our groundskeeper was this guy named Big John," Manuel recalled. "Big John was 6-6 and weighed 350. I knew he liked to drink red wine. We were losing and I saw the rain. I told him to go have some fun. It was pretty funny. Hart was over there yelling for the tarp. I said, 'You want the tarp, put it on yourself!' But he has the story wrong. I only gave Big John fifty bucks."

Big John got his buzz and Manuel got his wish. The game was rained out. Hart's Charlotte team won the makeup and went on to win the league title.

Hart loved Manuel's passion for the game and the way he led a team. When he joined Cleveland's front office a few years later, he hired Manuel. Manuel rose from minor-league instructor to minor-league manager to big-league hitting coach to big-league manager during his time in Cleveland. Hart moved on to the Texas Rangers in 2001. Manuel was fired in Cleveland in 2002 and hired by Phillies General Manger Ed Wade as a scout later that year. After a stormy season in 2004, Wade fired Manager Larry Bowa and hired Manuel as manager. Wade had grown to like Manuel's folksy, easygoing manner. He was impressed with Manuel's gift for building a player's confidence, and figured it would be a good salve for a clubhouse that had trouble with Bowa's barbed-wire ways.

The hiring was ripped in every corner of the city.

Charlie Manuel?

That country bumpkin?

Who's he?

What's he done?

Have you heard the way he talks?

"Wade whiffs at skipper search" read a *Philadelphia Inquirer* headline over a column that proclaimed Manuel as the sixth-best candidate in an eight-man field.

Jim Leyland was the people's choice. He had a World Series ring. And he was tough and hard-nosed, the kind of guy Philadelphians liked. Phillies officials liked Leyland, but he probably had a little too much sandpaper in his personality at a time when club officials were looking for someone the polar opposite of Bowa.

The Phillies finished in second place during Manuel's first two seasons, but that hardly brought him acceptance in the community. He was ripped and ridiculed, but always managed to stay upbeat. When you've survived your father's suicide, a heart attack, a bout with kidney cancer, and diverticulitis so bad that you had to manage with a colostomy bag under your jacket, how much can a rip job on the radio from Howard Eskin really hurt?

Pat Gillick took over as GM before the 2006 season, Manuel's third. Gillick considered letting Manuel go after that season. Gillick stuck with Manuel for 2007 and on the last day of that season, Manuel began to gain a foothold with Phillies fans. The team won the National League East and players nearly tripped over their tongues praising their unpretentious leader. And, oh, by the way, just because he was easygoing, didn't mean he was a wimp. Manuel stood up to players when he had to. He just did it privately without putting on a big show.

If Manuel caught a break in the community in 2007, he gained full acceptance when he hoisted the World Series trophy in 2008 and shouted, "Hey, this is for Philadelphia! This is for our fans!"

Suddenly, his Southern accent and fractured syntax were charming. (How can you not warm up to a guy who described the difficultly of picking an All-Star roster as "a Catch 42 . . . or 29 . . . or whatever it is?") Suddenly, he wasn't the Mayor of Simpleton anymore. He could have been the Mayor of Philadelphia if he had wanted to.

"My favorite memory from the World Series parade was being on a float with Charlie and hearing all the fans yell, 'Chuck for mayor,' or 'Char-lie . . . Char-lie . . . Char-lie,'" said Bill Giles, the Phillies chairman and part owner. "He went from a bum to a monster hero. He was the most popular guy out there."

But even as Manuel gained popularity and earned contract extensions, he never forgot who helped him gain that popularity.

"Anything I've ever gotten as a manager in this game is because of my players," he said.

Players talk. They talk about equipment. *Hey, let me try that bat.* They talk about reporters. *Watch out for that guy.* They talk about restaurants. *Why did they take the bone-in filet off the menu?* They talk about managers. Let's not kid anybody here. Winning and money are the two main reasons that Philadelphia became a destination for star talents such as those in The Rotation. But Charlie Manuel didn't hurt. Guys love playing for him.

"He's the same every single day," said Jimmy Rollins, who has felt Manuel's seldom-seen wrath and been benched a time or two. "As a player, especially when times get a little rough, you want your manager to be the same guy. It's easy to be nice and joke around with everybody when you're winning, but what happens when things aren't going the right way or the team just can't seem to figure it out? All of a sudden is he going to change and completely become a different person? Charlie doesn't do that. If you're struggling, you know he's going to run you out there. He believes in his players."

It's all very reassuring to a team.

The affection that players have for Manuel was evident moments after Carlos Ruiz and Brad Lidge teamed for the last out of the 2008 World Series. Drenched in champagne, Ruiz and Lidge found Manuel in the clubhouse and presented him with the ball. They didn't have to do that. One of them could have tucked it away and taken it home. But they wanted Manuel to have it.

"That was a great honor," Manuel said of the gesture. "It's the best thing I've gotten in my career."

Three years later, in September 2011, Manuel became the Phillies' all-time leader in managerial wins. As always, he credited his players, particularly the starting pitchers that he sent to the mound.

"I don't know where we'd be without them," he said.

————————— K —————————

One of Manuel's favorite expressions is "know thyself." He's a hitting guy, not necessarily a pitching guy, and he knows it. That's why, when he interviewed for the job in the fall of 2004, he told Wade he would need a good pitching coach.

Rich Dubee, a baseball lifer who pitched in the Kansas City Royals system and began coaching in 1982, was promoted from Triple-A and has been at Manuel's side ever since.

"Dubee is my man," Manuel said. "I lean on him. He totally handles our pitching."

Manuel loves to talk hitting. He'll talk about his lineup, why this guy is hitting here and that guy is hitting there. But ask him about his pitching rotation, who'll get the ball on the first day back from the All-Star break, who needs some extra rest, and he'll always defer to his pitching coach.

"I've got to get with Dubee and talk about it," Manuel will say.

Ask him why he stuck with a pitcher in the eighth inning and he'll say, "Dubee and I thought he had plenty left."

The two men are so close that Dubee can finish Manuel's sentences and often does when he sits on daily media sessions during spring training.

While Dubee, Manuel, and Ruiz are prominent members of the cast that supports the Phillies' all-aces pitching staff, there are more, many more, from the playing field, to the front office. In 2011, Phillies pitchers had eight players who had made at least one All-Star team playing behind them, and the bullpen, led by Ryan Madson and Antonio Bastardo, was strong.

Late in the 2011 season, Manuel was asked to name his choice for team MVP.

He thought about the starting pitching and the bullpen, he acknowledged Shane Victorino's strong play and Ryan Howard's sixth-straight 30-homer, 100-RBI season. He mentioned ownership's willingness to spend money on top talent. Finally, Manuel tabbed General Manager Ruben Amaro Jr., the chief architect of the club, as his MVP.

"I don't want to stroke Ruben's ego, and I'm damn sure not kissing him, but he's done a hell of a job," Manuel said.

There is, of course, one more piece of the supporting cast, perhaps the most important of all.

They are the folks who buy the tickets that lead to the sellouts that fuel the huge payroll, the folks that watch the nightly drama—reality television at its finest—and push the TV ratings skyward. They are the folks that give the team the revenues it needs to secure the talent that wins the games that makes more players want to come play for the Phillies.

This is the cycle that led to the Philadelphia Phillies putting together one of the greatest pitching staffs ever in 2011, the cycle that led to The Rotation.

On to the Season.

SPRING TRAINING

The schedule says the new season dawned on April 1 when the Phillies rallied for a late win over the Houston Astros in front of the 124th-straight sellout crowd at Citizens Bank Park, but really it started weeks before that. Seeds for the season of great expectations had been sown in December when Cliff Lee spurned the Yankees and Rangers and signed with the Phillies, the very beau that had dumped him for someone more attractive just a year earlier. Within a week of Lee's pulling on that red Phillies cap at his re-introductory news conference, fans gobbled up 100,000 tickets and the club was on its way to another standing-room-only season.

It wasn't until February 14—Valentine's Day, fittingly—that Phillies fans could really fall in love with The Rotation and all its possibilities.

First workout for pitchers and catchers.

Pitchers and catchers, for short.

Every baseball fan knows what those words mean when they pop up on the schedule. Soon it will be time to store the snow shovels. Soon the sun will coax the crocuses from the ground, the grass will turn from brown to green, and it will be time to tune into the daily narrative of the baseball season. Even in the darkest days of Phillies baseball, pitchers and catchers was a special day, a day when the team was tied for first place in the National League East and hope soared as high as Liberty Place, even if everyone knew it would crash down by Memorial Day. But there was something different about the first day of pitchers and catchers in 2011. Before this day, The Rotation was a collection of names and stats on a piece of paper. Yes, those names and numbers might have been written in gold, but now everything felt as real as the scruff on Cliff Lee's face. The winter was over, and now The Rotation was a reality, all dressed up in crisp new, red practice tops, ready to take to the emerald fields of Carpenter Complex for the first time together.

Standing in the middle of the clubhouse, Rich Dubee, pitching coach of the stars, smiled like a lottery winner.

"I was going to bring a recliner to spring training," he joked.

Dubee had gone to bed on December 13 when a late-night text message alerted him that the Phillies had signed Lee. He scrambled to his computer, verified the news and went to sleep with visions of two-hit shutouts dancing in his head.

"I always said your Number One starter is the guy who is pitching that day," Dubee said. "Now we're running out four Number Ones. Our front office has done a tremendous job piecing together four frontline guys, and Joe Blanton is not chopped liver by any means, so we feel very good about what we've got."

Once upon a time, a signing like Lee's would have been revealed over a bowl of Cheerios in the next morning's newspaper. But news waits for no one in this real-time world of 24-hour updates. From Florida to California, Lee's signing set off a series of beeps and buzzes among Phillies players. Thumbs went into overdrive as quick text messages were sent between the players.

Ben Francisco had just beaten Brad Lidge in a fantasy football game when he delivered some consoling news in a text: "It's OK. Don't cry. We just signed Cliff Lee." At home in suburban Denver, Lidge digested Francisco's text message. His mind immediately harkened back to Halloween Day 2008 when the Phillies rode down Broad Street as World Series champs.

"All right," Lidge said to himself. "This is it. We've got to win this thing."

Now, in Clearwater weeks later for the first day of pitchers and catchers, Lidge was still thinking big.

"When you have four guys like we have, your mind automatically thinks World Series," he said. "Cliff coming here changes the dynamic. Everybody realizes we are the team to beat. To a man, every one of us feels we need to win the World Series."

Yes, that was the feeling in the clubhouse on the first day of pitchers and catchers. Lidge was one of the few willing to forcefully articulate it. Others in the room, though confident, practiced the time-honored baseball tradition of circumspection.

"We have to curb our excitement a little bit, too," Dubee said. "We still have to play baseball. I mean, we're absolutely thrilled with our starting rotation. I don't think anyone who has ever seen baseball would downplay that. But the fact of the matter is we have to play 162 games and play up to our potential."

Even Lidge acknowledged that. Another parade around Halloween was the goal. But this was Valentine's Day.

"It's a long way away," he said, "and we have to perform to our capability."

———————————— K ————————————

Just after 10 A.M., Phillies pitchers and catchers exited the back door at Bright House Field and headed for the dew-covered fields of Carpenter Complex. Club officials dabbed their noses with sun block and descended from their third-floor offices to see the army of arms that they had constructed to be the foundation of the team. Club President David Montgomery, who'd presided over the team's methodical rise from the NL basement to the top of the baseball world, resembled a proud father as he greeted team personnel. General Manager Ruben Amaro Jr. patted Manager Charlie Manuel on the back as the first workout of the new season began. Cameras caught all the flavor—the fresh red uniforms, the green grass, the swaying palms, and most of all, the excitement and optimism—and sent the baseball postcard back to chilly Philly.

Early in camp, pitchers take the field and immediately go through stretching and throwing drills before scattering to different practice stations. Veteran reliever J. C. Romero was jogging between fields when he spotted a man who just a few weeks earlier had become a painful reminder that baseball is fun and games, and no matter how shiny the ERAs and championship trophies are, there's still a real world out there and sometimes it's unbearably cruel.

"Mr. Green," Romero said quietly. "I am so sorry."

Dallas Green, still as hulking at 76 as he was the day he hoisted the World Series trophy in 1980, patted Romero gently on the shoulder. Dark sunglasses hid Green's pain. A month earlier, his granddaughter, nine-year-old Christina—the daughter of Green's son, John, and his wife, Roxanna—was killed by a madman's bullet during an attack on Arizona Congresswoman Gabrielle Giffords at a grocery store in Tucson. Devastated over the loss of his granddaughter and heartbroken for his son and daughter-in-law, Green was back in Clearwater for his 55th year in baseball and 38th as a Phillie. "Baseball helps me," an emotional Green said a few days later. "You sink yourself into your work and you don't see a little girl with a hole in her chest as much."

Seeing Green for the first time since the tragedy was heart-wrenching for many of the people—cold, heartless baseball writers included—who had grown close to him in his years as a pitcher, manager, and adviser with the club. With one small gesture in the middle of the most anticipated workout in Phillies history, J. C. Romero spoke for a lot of people.

For Roy Halladay, there was no easing into the first workout of spring. The guy is an animal when it comes to conditioning his body and preparing it to throw 250 innings. The first workout of spring is as important to him as a postseason start. While his teammates had begun to trickle into the clubhouse in the days before the first workout, Halladay's locker had been occupied since December. The pitcher lives in nearby Odessa and works out religiously at the Phillies spring facility, starting in December. He arrives at the ballpark around 5 A.M. when no one is around and not even the crickets can distract him from that day's plan. By the time Halladay takes the field, he's already pushed his body in the weight room and on the stationary bike, but you'd never know it by the way he goes through his first official team workout. Three and a half months after winning his second Cy Young Award, he is the picture of intensity as he leads the way through every drill, executing them perfectly, giving even the most mundane exercise his full attention as a crowd of fans gather five deep around the chain-link fences.

"They're parking them across the street," a longtime security guard said. "I've never seen that for the first workout."

Even the players turned into fans during the first workout.

"I was stretching between Roy Oswalt and Cliff Lee," said Michael Schwimer, a reliever in his first big-league camp. "I'm not going to lie. I was like, 'Where's the camera?' I was trying to hide the fan in me as much as possible."

Mike Stutes, another first-timer in camp, was also caught up in the excitement of working aside the game's most decorated starting staff. He found himself mesmerized by how hard the starters worked away from the pitcher's mound.

"Even on days when they're tired, when they've thrown fifty pitches and run, they still do all their work and they work harder than anyone," he said. "Halladay is a machine. I watch him all the time. It's impressive. He's always in a rush going somewhere for his next drill or workout. I just try to stay out of his way."

Smart, kid.

Disrupting Halladay's workday can be like thrusting a butter knife into an electrical socket.

Zap.

——————————— K ———————————

If you have ever wondered why spring training lasts six weeks, look no further than the pitching staff. Hitters can hone their swings in less than a month, but pitchers need those six weeks to build the arm strength and endurance that will carry them through a six-month season. And for The Rotation, six months was a minimal expectation. Anything less than a seven-month season, with a trip deep into October culminating with confetti flying in Citizens Bank Park, would be a huge disappointment.

"We all feel like we're on the same page," Halladay said in spring training, two months before his 34th birthday. "We all feel like we're at the similar points in our careers. Cole probably has a lot longer left than the rest of us, but we all feel like we've accomplished personal things, we've set ourselves up, and now it's the ultimate goal—trying to win. The reason I'm playing now is to try to win and win a championship as a team. That's the driving factor for all of us."

Lee confirmed as much, saying he chose the Phillies because he believed they gave him the best chance to win a World Series, a better chance than he'd get with the Yankees, he said, who were getting old.

After a morning of conditioning, throwing and fielding drills on the first day of pitchers and catchers, it was time to start building arm strength at 60 feet, six inches—the distance from the rubber to home plate. Pitchers were split into two groups that would throw every other day in the bullpen or in batting practice until exhibition games began. On Day 1, Halladay and Cole Hamels took the mound, each throwing for about eight minutes. Hamels had finished the 2010 season on a roll and was a big reason the team had won its fourth-straight NL East title. In 15 starts after the All-Star break, he had a 2.23 ERA, the fifth best in the majors over that span, and 104 strikeouts, the second-most in baseball in that time. Twenty-seven years old, he arrived in camp serious and confident, and it showed in his first bullpen session.

"Cole could pitch in a game today," Dubee marveled.

In national media circles, Hamels quickly became the hot pick to win the Cy Young. Reporters love to make predictions in February, even if they are meaningless by Memorial Day, never mind by October. On a staff that included Cy Young winners and ERA champs, Hamels would be allowed to blend in and perform in the less-pressurized No. 4 spot in the rotation. Many thought he couldn't help but shine in the role.

But while Hamels was a fashionable preseason pick for Cy Young, he was only part of the reason that Clearwater had become the No. 1 destination for America's baseball media in the spring of 2010. Albert Pujols' contract drama across the state in Jupiter was a hot story for a day or two, but it didn't have the lasting draw of The Rotation and all its promise. Lee's signing had taken a golden rotation and turned it platinum. On paper, this was one of the greatest starting staffs ever. In the history-obsessed world of baseball, and among the people who cover the sport, that's a big story. Everyone wanted a piece of it and that had kept Greg Casterioto awake at night ever since Lee came on board in December.

As director of baseball communications for the Phillies, Casterioto fields all media requests, and once the winter holidays cleared and spring training came into focus, he was deluged. Casterioto, Bonnie Clark, Kevin Gregg, John Brazer, and Scott Palmer—all members of the team's public and media relations staff—tried to come up with a plan to satisfy the media's demand for access to The Rotation without cutting into the pitchers' preparation for what mattered most—the season. The Phillies PR staff couldn't have individual reporters from around the land parachuting into camp seeking a few minutes with each pitcher on a daily basis. That's a lot of potential butter knives around Halladay's locker.

Phillies officials came up with a plan. They would hold a news conference and make the Big Four starting pitchers available after the first workout of the spring. It would last no more than an hour and the pitchers would be free from questions about their potential place in history for the rest of the spring. The news conference would be transcribed and any reporter who wandered in on March 10 would have access to pages worth of quotes. It would be televised live on MLB Network and on Comcast SportsNet Philadelphia. The pitchers would be required to appear wearing their red Phillies tops—a branding opportunity for a ball club that needs to sell a lot of jerseys to support a $175-million payroll.

The player-media liaison in Casterioto thought a group news conference would work. The fan inside him liked it, too. Halladay, Lee, Oswalt, and Hamels all sitting together with bright eyes and big dreams. Wouldn't it have been cool if the Orioles had done something like that in 1971?

The idea was the easy part. Selling it to the pitchers, particularly the introverted, routine-obsessed Halladay, would be a different story. The job began and ended with Casterioto's ability to convince the ace of aces to carve out an hour at the end of a workday that had begun at 5 A.M. to do something he wasn't particularly fond of.

"Sure, I'll do it," Halladay told Casterioto over the telephone one January day.

Inside, Casterioto was elated to hear Halladay's response.

"As long as Joe is there, too," Halladay said.

The numbers on the back of bubblegum cards made it easy to overlook Blanton, and fans, media, and even people who worked for the team were guilty of it. On a staff of stars, Blanton was Average Joe. He had never made an All-Star team. He'd helped the Phillies win the World Series in 2008, but that didn't stop the team from attempting to trade him in the weeks that followed Lee's signing. The Phillies found no takers for Blanton and the $17 million that remained on his contract, and as spring training 2011 approached, he lined up to be the club's fifth starter. Less than a year earlier, Halladay had purchased 65 Baume & Mercier wristwatches—listed at nearly $4,000 a piece—for teammates and club personnel as a gesture of thanks after his perfect game against Florida. "We did it together," the inscription said. Halladay had defined himself as a team player, and in his mind Blanton was as big a part of The Rotation—the team within the team—as anybody. He had to be at that news conference.

"It was the first thing Roy said," Casterioto said. "And he was right. I was mad at myself for not thinking that way at first, but again, I'm a fan and I was caught up in the foursome."

More than 70 media members, local and national, and club officials packed the news conference at Bright House Field. Lee sat in the middle flanked by Halladay and Blanton on his right, and Oswalt and Hamels on his left. This was the media's first shot to hear from Blanton after a winter of trade rumors and hype that completely ignored him. He was the skunk who'd crashed the lawn party, the fifth Beatle, and everyone wondered what that felt like. The question came quickly from David Murphy of the *Daily News*. Oswalt wasn't happy that a lightning bolt was thrust into what—for the pitchers—was supposed to be a ceremonial unveiling, a happy time at the beginning of a long journey. The veteran pitcher rolled his eyes in disgust at the question, but Blanton, who'd been traded before, handled it well. He even had his touché moment when Ryan Lawrence of the *Delaware County Daily Times* asked Hamels about being the only one with a World Series ring.

Blanton perked right up.

"Uh, I've got a ring," said the man who earned the win in Game 4 of the 2008 World Series.

The Rotation's historic potential was the central theme of the news conference. Halladay, who spent a decade in Toronto wondering what it would be like to pitch in the postseason, looked to his left and said he had to pinch himself being surrounded by such quality talent. Lee summed up everything by acknowledging the staff's historic potential, but added a warning. "We haven't thrown a single pitch as a group yet," he said. "It's kind of early to say we're one of the best rotations in the history of the game. Obviously, we're a very talented group, and there is potential for all of that. But it's just that—potential."

The news conference ended and the pitchers headed off to tape an hourlong television special with Michael Barkann of Comcast SportsNet. All in all, it was a seamless day. The pitchers got their work in and killed a slew of media demands with one stone. No butter knives were thrust into any electrical sockets and Casterioto was happy about that.

When it was all over, long after the luxury cars and SUVs had pulled out of the players' parking lot, a spent Casterioto sat at a picnic table behind the clubhouse and reflected on the day he and his colleagues had been planning for—and dreading a little—since January.

His iPhone buzzed.

His eyes bulged in mock horror as another media request rolled in.

"Greta Van Susteren," he said incredulously. "What's next, *Oprah*?' "

———————— K ————————

Media interest actually continued for a couple more weeks with several national types joining the locals who'd been there all along. *Sports Illustrated's* Gary Smith spent more than a week in Clearwater. Widely hailed as America's best long-form sportswriter, Smith was raised near Wilmington, Delaware, and educated at LaSalle University. He had grown up a Phillies fan. Now, with his unique eye for detail and obsession with finding out what makes people tick, Smith was here to chronicle what was *the story* heading into the 2011 baseball season—The Rotation.

Smith was one of the first to arrive in the clubhouse every morning, right there with the beat writers, observing the pitchers as they ate breakfast at the cool kids' table in the clubhouse. (There are two long tables in the Phillies' spring clubhouse. The veterans congregate at one, the rookies and non-roster players at the other). Computer bag slung over his shoulder and yellow legal pad in his hand, Smith constantly scanned the room for interesting details. Patient and polite, he waited for days to get his shot to interview the pitchers one-on-one. He also conducted lengthy interviews with teammates and club officials for a 5,000-word piece that ran in *SI*'s baseball preview issue.

Not everyone was as patient as Smith. Pat Jordan spent 11 days in Clearwater working on a story for the *New York Times* Sunday magazine. Jordan had been a highly touted pitching prospect in the Braves' system in the early 1960s—he chronicled the death of his baseball dream in his 1975 memoir, *False Spring*—and big hitter at *Sports Illustrated* in the 1970s. He recalled doing interviews with Tom Seaver while the two drove to Shea Stadium. Those were the days when a player would show up in the clubhouse and chat leisurely with a writer while putting on his uniform, the days when a player would grab a brew and rehash the day with a scribe in front of his locker after a game. Those days, of course, are over.

Clubhouses used to be locker rooms. Now they are glorified coat rooms, places to hang your clothes and change before hustling off to get treatment in the trainer's room, lift weights, work with a strength and conditioning coach—a new addition to the baseball world in the last decade—or watch video, all in areas off-limits to media. Players simply don't have the time—and in many cases, the interest—for media interaction as they once did. Oh, the young ones like to be written about and will give you all the time you need to promote their prospecthood. But things often change once they've made it. All this is compounded by the increase in media. There are more people asking for a minute of a player's time than ever before. Walls have gone up, leaving old-school grads like Jordan frustrated.

"I've never done a story where the people I've needed to speak with are so difficult to get," he said.

Jordan spent days wandering in and around the clubhouse, tiptoeing around Halladay's and Lee's work schedules. He always looked ready for a Jimmy Buffet concert as he wore shorts and untucked Hawaiian shirts and never took off his Ray-Ban sunglasses. Outside the back of the clubhouse, the gray-bearded writer puffed on a cigar as the sound of clinking metal could be heard through the open doors of the weight room.

"You can't smoke around here," a team official told Jordan. "The smoke is blowing in the weight room."

Imagine that story? HALLADAY MISSES START DUE TO SMOKE INHALATION.

Jordan rolled his eyes. He had no patience for the new breed of player, media relations officials, or modern, regimented spring camps, and it showed in the story he produced for the *Times* magazine. He wrote learnedly about the art of pitching and how it pertained to The Rotation, but he left no doubt that things were better in his day. Maybe if they had let him smoke, the tone would have been different.

Everyone was looking for an angle to best capture The Rotation. Legendary *Sports Illustrated* photographer Walter Iooss had the most unique. When it came to access, the pitchers had no qualms giving it to Iooss. He was safe. In his own way, he was as talented as the pitchers and they knew it. And he would only make them look good. So good they could hang it on the wall.

On the morning of March 5, Hamels was scheduled to throw a between-starts bullpen session. Usually these are solemn workouts, a trip into the pitching laboratory where pitcher and pitching coach smooth out deliveries and adjust release points by a tenth of an inch. On this day, Hamels' "bullpen," as they call it, was a show. Iooss and his staff had spent two hours setting up strobe lights and reflectors, all powered by a humming portable generator. The lights lured curious minor leaguers out of their clubhouse. Everyone was in the mood for a show. Hamels, in full uniform, delivered.

The lanky left-hander began by throwing fastballs. Iooss, kneeling on a towel a few feet away, started snapping pictures—10 frames per second so he wouldn't miss the sweat rolling down Hamels' cheek or the veins bulging in his neck. In time, Iooss was laying on the ground, shooting up at the pitcher with the blue Florida sky as a background.

Hamels was remarkably focused with such a production buzzing around him.

"Nooo," he spat after throwing a pitch that he didn't like. He conferred with Dubee about the importance of releasing the ball on a downward angle.

Hamels didn't need much persuading when *SI* asked to shoot him at work. (They don't call him "Hollywood" for nothing.) He had been the subject of Iooss features in the past and liked the photographer's work. Iooss had promised to give Hamels some of the pictures.

"Cole likes to be photographed," Iooss said. "He feels he looks good and that helps, too. He's self-confident about how he comes across in pictures."

Iooss began shooting sports, everything from Super Bowls to Olympiads, in the 1960s. He's been around the block.

"Cole's a great-looking guy with personality," Iooss said. "He's lucky he's married. Road life can kill a man."

Before leaving camp, Iooss got The Rotation together for a shot that

ON THE ROAD *UGH*-AIN

One of the perks of being a major-league veteran is getting to occasionally skip a long spring training bus trip.

You don't get a day off, per se, but working out in Clearwater and taking a short day sure beats a two-and-a-half-hour drive over the Sunshine Skyway Bridge to Fort Myers at 7:30 in the morning. And don't even get us started about the ride back.

The schedule makers had the Phillies taking that trip on March 3 for a game against the Red Sox. At midday the day before, Bench Coach Pete Mackanin pinned the travel roster to the clubhouse bulletin board.

Cole Hamels was on it because it was his day to pitch. The only other veteran regular on the list was Shane Victorino, a fact that didn't elude third baseman Placido Polanco, who was staying back in Clearwater.

"Hey, Vic," Polanco called over as Victorino packed his bag for the early ride down I-75 the next morning. "Bring me back something from Fort Myers."

Victorino is the biggest needler on the club, so teammates relish the opportunity to give it back to him. He took Polanco's ribbing in stride and laughed as he placed his spikes in his red travel bag.

"They have oranges down there?" Polanco asked Victorino. "Bring me back some oranges."

Victorino is a live wire, the chattiest of all Phillies. That doesn't always go over well on a long, morning bus ride.

"I have my iPod all charged up so I don't have to listen to him," Manager Charlie Manuel deadpanned.

Victorino only played four innings in that game. He was replaced in center field by utility man Wilson Valdez. Funny thing was Valdez wasn't even supposed to make the trip. He was one of the lucky ones scheduled to stay in Clearwater, take a few swings, and go home. But when the bus rolled out of Bright House Field, Valdez was on it. He'd assumed he'd be making the trip and never looked at the travel list.

"That's OK," Valdez said with a laugh. "I like to play. But I will look at the list from now on."

appeared on the cover of *SI*. It was Lee surrounded by the other starters, a shot modeled after a 2007 *Rolling Stone* magazine cover depicting the rock band Maroon Five. *SI* editors debated which pitcher to put in the middle—Halladay or Lee? They went with Lee "because he came back and created all this drama," Iooss said.

Cognizant of the media pull on the pitchers, Iooss recalled something Michael Jordan used to tell him.

"I like you, Walter, because you're good and you're fast," Jordan would say.

"At this point they're all pretty fed up with pictures," Iooss said after the group shot of the Phillies pitchers. "I was trying to get it over as fast as humanly possible. I got them out of there fifteen minutes early."

Maybe Pat Jordan could pick up that extra time.

Nah.

———————— K ————————

In the days that followed the first workout for pitchers and catchers, the clubhouse filled as position players trickled in before the February 19 first full-squad workout. Pitchers no longer owned the room. Big personalities such as Shane Victorino and Jimmy Rollins arrived. Ryan Howard's hulking presence seemed to fill one side of the clubhouse.

It wasn't long before that the Phillies were a team known for its thundering lineup, but Hamels' development and the acquisitions of Halladay, Oswalt, and Lee had turned the Phils into a pitching-based team.

The hitters were fine with that.

"It's good having the attention directed at them," Rollins said. "We had it for a long time and now we have the right guys to get that attention and deserve it themselves."

Placido Polanco checked in and wondered what it would be like to be an opposing hitter and have to face the Phillies pitching staff. His solution? Sick day!

"Oh, my neck hurts," he said. "I've got the flu. That cheesesteak I just ate doesn't feel too good on my stomach."

Once the full squad arrived, Manager Charlie Manuel gave his annual team address. Veteran Manuel observers know the skipper tends to ramble a bit when he gets loosened up. "All my speeches are different," he once said, "because I say different stuff." Shy and reserved by nature, Halladay simply listened to Manuel's speech in 2010. More comfortable in his second year with the club, the always-organized, always-methodical pitcher gave his manager some advice.

"Bring notes," Halladay said.

Manuel took Halladay's advice and stayed on point, telling the club that its success had not only made fans eager for more but it had left a target on the team's back and other clubs would be taking aim. Be ready, be prepared, and believe, Manuel told his team. Assume nothing. Make it happen.

Rollins always holds a news conference early in camp, the State of the Jimmy, as the scribes call it. It's usually held under palm trees at the picnic table behind the clubhouse and it's a highly anticipated event because the outspoken shortstop usually says something spicy, be it bold prediction or a jab at the Mets. On February 19, 2011, a little more than four years after his "we're the team to beat" comment, Rollins went big again, predicting 100-plus wins.

"But that requires being lucky enough to stay healthy and having everybody do their job on the mound, in the field, and in the batter's box," the 32-year-old shortstop said.

Rollins alluded to the great fear of all professional sports teams—injury. Nothing can scuttle a team's hopes faster than too many trips to the MRI tube. Just three days after Rollins' prediction of 100-plus victories, news flashed across the clubhouse television that St. Louis Cardinals' right-hander Adam Wainwright had suffered a season-ending elbow injury. The news on Wainwright resonated with particular strength in the Phillies' clubhouse because he ranks among the game's elite arms, having finished second and third, respectively, in NL Cy Young voting the previous two seasons.

Wainwright's injury was a reminder to all of the fragility of pitching, not that the Phillies really needed one. Just weeks earlier, Lee had tweaked a muscle under his left armpit during off-season workouts in Arkansas. The Phillies immediately told him to stop working out and he traveled to Philadelphia for an examination. It proved to be nothing major, but the team took it slow with its $120 million investment at the start of camp. A month later, Oswalt took a line drive behind the right ear in a game against Tampa Bay in Port Charlotte. Oswalt went down in a heap, clutching the back of his head as a sunburned crowd held its breath. Thank goodness Manny Ramirez didn't get good wood on the ball. Oswalt might not have been laughing as he did the next day.

"I told Charlie I'm not supposed to be making road trips," Oswalt said. "This is what happens when you make road trips."

Other than Lee's early ache and Oswalt's late scare, the pitching staff accomplished its top goal in spring training. It stayed healthy. Everything else fell into place after that: the conditioning, the pitching, and the all-important bonding that turned five pitchers into The Rotation.

———————————— K ————————————

Every morning, the pitchers, sometimes a couple of them, sometimes all five, ate breakfast at the cool kids' table at the north end of the clubhouse. Over yogurt and fruit, they laughed and joked, talked fishing and pitching, and occasionally peeked up to see the latest highlight on the flat-screen television on the wall. One day, they all turned into autograph-seeking fans when country music ace Kenny Chesney visited the clubhouse. Another day, with camera crew in tow, they played a round of golf with MLB Network analyst John Smoltz, whose own credentials on the mound helped him score access to the spring's hottest story.

For six weeks, the pitchers worked out together in the weight room and sat in the dugout together during games. It was a perfect time to compare changeup grips, or simply get to know each other. Nearly every day, they walked off the field together, as a group, to the applause of picture-snapping fans dreaming about where this staff could lead this baseball team.

"A starting staff is a team inside a team, and when you've got five guys who like being around each other it makes it even easier," Oswalt said. "We've got great guys on this staff. We mess around with each other all the time. If one guy's got to pitch, he feels like he's missing out what's happening on the bench. It's fun."

Oswalt, 33, and Lee, 32, hit it off immediately, "a couple of rednecks," from Mississippi and Arkansas, respectively, as Lee said. Before long, they were sneaking off after practice to a nearby fishing hole. Oswalt reeled in 40 largemouth bass one day.

"No way he's going to beat me," Oswalt said of Lee.

Oswalt and Lee actually began bonding years earlier, in Philadelphia of all places. On the same day in October 2003, both pitchers had injuries repaired by Philadelphia-based surgeon William Meyers. Oswalt, then with

Houston, had a groin injury. Lee, then with Cleveland, had a hernia. The two pitchers didn't know each other at the time.

"I remember a guy being in there with me, but we were pretty drugged up coming out of anesthesia," Oswalt said. "I remember telling the doctor I felt good and walking out of the hospital. The other guy was going to walk out but he stood up and said, 'Noooo, I'll think I'll stay here.' "

Eventually the anesthesia wore off and Lee left the hospital, in and out of Philadelphia so quickly that he didn't get to take in any tourist attractions. That's OK. When he rejoined the Phillies in spring training 2011, a red shirt emblazoned with the image of the Liberty Bell and the word BOOM hung in his locker. He wore it daily during spring training and it soon became the hottest-selling item back home.

Finally, after two weeks of bullpen workouts and friendly fire—pitchers throwing to teammates in batting practice—the first Grapefruit League game arrived on February 26 against the Yankees in Tampa. It would have been great theater had it been Lee's day to pitch. After all, he was the guy who did what few ever do: he turned down the Yankees, and bitterness over his decision stretched all the way to the press box.

"What day does Mrs. Lee pitch?" asked one New York wag, a clear reference to Kristen Lee's desire to have her husband work in Philadelphia and not New York.

Hamels got the ball in that first game and impressed with two strong innings in a 5-4 win. Seven years earlier, as a 20-year-old in big-league camp for the first time, he dazzled the Yankees with his vaunted changeup. Back then he was a string bean. Now, he had muscles and sturdy shoulders under that uniform and he featured a fastball that popped at 94 mph.

"I finally hit two-hundred pounds this winter," Hamels said. "I've been chasing it since I was eighteen. I really think the extra strength will prevent me from wearing down this season."

———————————— K ————————————

Larry Shenk started working for the Phillies in 1963, rising from publicity director to vice president of public relations. Shenk tells stories of driving over to Clearwater Beach in the early 1970s, back when spring training was still a mom-and-pop operation at Jack Russell Stadium, and giving away tickets to games to spring-breakers. Now, there's no need to give away tickets to get fans to come to games. Spring training is big business, especially in Clearwater, where the top ticket is $30 and Bright House Field is packed for just about every game. In recent years, spring training has become a destination for winter-weary Philadelphians eager for a little sun on their noses and a peek at their baseball team. In March, flights from Philadelphia to Tampa are packed with fans wearing red Phillies gear. A quick stop at the rental car counter and they're off to Bright House Field, where they sit around the festive tiki bar and pound $6 Yuenglings while arguing which member of The Rotation will be the first to 20 wins.

In the spring of 2011, no Phillie was more embraced than Lee. Fans fell in love with his scruffy, blue collar, no-nonsense approach to pitching in 2009—he went 4-0 with a 1.56 ERA in five postseason starts that October—and their love for him grew deeper when he turned down the Yankees to be a Phillie again.

After more than two weeks of side sessions, Lee finally pitched in a Grapefruit League game on March 1 against the Tigers. The cheers were huge as he took the mound and the usually unflappable pitcher seemed a little unnerved by the excitement. Lee pitched 212⅓ innings in 2010, hit just one batter, and walked just 18. But in his 2011 spring debut, he hit the first batter he faced. In two innings, he allowed a walk and two runs while striking out three.

"He's still getting his spikes broken in," said Dubee, explaining Lee's shaky debut. "Guys get a little juiced up in their first start and their deliveries are off."

Of course, Halladay never gets too juiced up. His spring debuts in 2010 and 2011 were as eagerly awaited and wildly received as Lee's and he sailed through both without giving up a run.

Lee couldn't help but notice the electricity in the crowd as he warmed up in the bullpen before his spring debut.

"It's nice to know the fans are excited about me being back," he said. "They have reason to be excited. We have a good squad."

The crowds kept coming to Bright House Field and The Rotation continued to inch toward being ready for Opening Day. For the second-straight year, Halladay would get that start. With each passing day, his focus on the April 1 season opener against Houston grew sharper. He started watching video of Astros hitters and formulating a game plan 10 days before Opening Day. From his first start of the spring, Halladay looked ready to win and four weeks of Grapefruit League games had brought his competitive juices to a boil. By the time he made his final spring start, a three-inning test drive on March 27, he was ready to burn someone. That someone turned out to be Art Thigpen.

Thigpen was the home plate umpire for Halladay's final spring start against the Braves at Disney's Wide World of Sports. With two outs in the third inning, Halladay thought he'd thrown a cutter for a strike to Nate McLouth. Thigpen called it a ball. Halladay's blue eyes turned to daggers as he stared in at Thigpen. Halladay then threw a sinker that he liked. Thigpen called it a ball. The daggers turned icy hot. Halladay composed himself and got McLouth to ground out to shortstop on the next pitch. Deep down inside, Halladay wanted to shoot one more look at Thigpen, but that isn't his style. He kept his focus, trained his eyes forward and walked off the field, ready for the regular season after a spring that saw him go 4-0 with a 0.42 ERA in five starts. In 24⅔ innings of Grapefruit League action, he allowed just 16 hits and one run while striking out 19 and walking six. With Halladay, there's no "I'm just getting my work in." He's always there to dominate and he did it, with arm and attitude, in the spring of 2011, right down to his last pitch.

After the game, Halladay ran sprints under the searing Florida sun. His face was red and he was drenched with sweat as he met with reporters 50 minutes after staring down the umpire in a game that didn't even count.

"Jeez, you want to compete," Halladay said. "As a pitcher, we want all the pitches we throw to be strikes."

The countdown to Opening Day had begun in Halladay's mind.

"You put in a lot of work over the winter and in spring training," he said. "To be able to actually put it to use is kind of a relief."

———————————— K ————————————

The final week of spring training means different things for different people. Veteran players comfortably pack their bags for the trip north. Fringe players walk an emotional fault line, not knowing if they are headed to Philadelphia or the minor leagues. Management frets over the final roster decisions.

Spring training 2011 was not the smoothest the Phillies have ever had. Everyone got a vocabulary lesson when Chase Utley was diagnosed with chondromalacia and tendinitis in his right knee. The team's quiet leader didn't play an inning in Florida. Closer Brad Lidge checked into camp feeling healthy and checked out with a tear in his shoulder. Hotshot prospect Domonic Brown slumped badly and then broke his hand. Veteran Luis Castillo came in for a late look at second base but failed to make the club because, well, it already had enough brittle thirtysomethings.

But through it all, The Rotation stayed healthy and the possibilities excited even the hardest of baseball men.

"When I look at the Phillies rotation from a distance I am in awe of what they could possibly accomplish," said Hall of Fame pitcher Don Sutton, a Braves broadcaster. "I know the book isn't written yet, all we have is an outline, and I don't think we'll be able to evaluate until we look back on it. But looking forward to it, I think it should be the envy of every major-league ball club. If you don't want those four guys running out there for you, there's something wrong with you.

"It has the potential to be the best rotation in all of baseball and one of the best in history."

APRIL

Roy Halladay sat in front of his locker and spoke to a small and attentive audience in a corner of the Phillies' clubhouse.

He wore a red hooded Phillies sweatshirt, blue Phillies gym shorts, and red sneakers. Several sheets of paper, each one showing different hitters and how he planned to attack them, rested on his lap. Pitching Coach Rich Dubee sat to his right, reading glasses perched on the end of his nose. Catcher Carlos Ruiz sat across from him, hunched over, hanging on every word as if his life depended on it. It was 10 A.M. on April 1, nearly three hours before Halladay would throw his first pitch on Opening Day of the most highly anticipated season in franchise history, and he was running the show.

Pitchers, catchers, and pitching coaches talk strategy before every game. They discuss the strengths and weaknesses of the opposing hitters and the pitch sequences and locations they plan to use. It's an exchange of ideas. The pitcher offers his opinions. The pitching coach and catcher offer theirs. But when Halladay pitches, he does the talking. He keeps detailed notes on every hitter he has faced and has studied video of every hitter he has a chance to face in that day's game.

Halladay started studying film of the Houston Astros, the Phillies' opponent that Friday afternoon in front of a sellout crowd at Citizens Bank Park, more than a week earlier.

He knew exactly what he wanted to do.

The meeting lasted about 15 minutes. Dubee and Ruiz, who barely uttered a word, stood up and quietly walked away. Halladay turned toward his locker, picked up his iPod, put an ear bud into each ear, and switched on the device. Teammates leave Halladay alone the days he pitches. He gets 33 or so chances a season to help his team win and he treats each opportunity like it's his last. Teammates know better than to puncture the ace's meditative balloon.

A buzz filled the clubhouse on this snowy, Opening Day morning. (Yes, players drove through a snow flurry on their way to the park.) In the corner opposite Halladay, Michael Martinez, a career minor-league infielder who finally made the big leagues at age 28, beamed in front of his locker. The

Phillies selected him in the Rule 5 Draft in December and, thanks in part to an injury to Chase Utley, he earned a spot on the roster. Martinez put on his uniform and smiled. The lowest-paid player on the roster—which boasts seven players making more than $10 million per season—Martinez would make the league minimum $414,000, but the money was life-changing and would help his family in the Dominican Republic.

"Back in the Dominican, we are from the 'hood," said fellow countryman and Third-Base Coach Juan Samuel as the clubhouse buzzed with activity before the season opener.

J. C. Romero strutted through the clubhouse, whistling the tune playing on his iPod. Brad Lidge reached into his locker and checked his cell phone before retreating to a back room. Lidge would open the season on the disabled list with a tear in his rotator cuff. Ordinarily, the smart and affable veteran reliever might be giving a rundown on the season's goals to reporters before the season opener. But on this day, Lidge goes about his business unbothered. Players are seemingly invisible when they are on the disabled list, even former World Series heroes.

Relief pitchers Danys Baez, Jose Contreras, and Antonio Bastardo sat in chairs, conversing in Spanish a few feet away from Martinez. Baez and Contreras are best friends who share a bond as Cuban defectors. An impressive young talent—but one who had trouble staying healthy, pitching consistently, and showing maturity in previous seasons—Bastardo served as the heir apparent to Romero, the team's top left-handed relief pitcher. But Dubee and Manager Charlie Manuel made a point in spring training to say he had proven nothing yet. The coaching staff knows players read media reports about themselves, no matter how much they insist publicly they do not. Even if they don't read the stories, a family member or friend does. And if something negative is written about him, the player will hear about it within minutes.

Dude, they're killing you in the paper!

In the case of Bastardo, the Phillies didn't want him to just think he is good. They wanted him to prove it.

Jimmy Rollins ambled through the clubhouse, wearing a full-length white robe with red pinstripes and his last name and No. 11 on the back. The robe drew a few chuckles from onlookers and Rollins responded by flashing his toothy grin. Nobody else had a robe like this, but nobody else *would* have a robe like this. The most confident and stylish player in the Phillies' clubhouse, Rollins pulled it off.

A few feet from him, clubhouse attendant Sean Bowers handed Roy Oswalt different-sized caps to try on until he finally found one he liked.

Cliff Lee was across the room from Halladay's locker, which used to house Pat Burrell, and then Matt Stairs. Lee reclined in his chair, playing on his iPad, a popular way to kill time in the clubhouse. In 2003, hunting magazines filled the clubhouse at Veterans Stadium with outdoorsmen Jim Thome, Turk Wendell, Rheal Cormier, and Brandon Duckworth on the roster. In 2005, players filled down times with Sudoku puzzles. In 2007, they had PlayStation Portables, and linked up to play first-person shooters on cross-country flights.

For the 2011 season, it was *Words with Friends* or *Angry Birds*.

Lee glanced at Halladay, whose head remained buried in his locker. He was excited to watch the ace of the aces pitch.

"He knows what he's doin'," he said.

Instructions for the pregame festivities hung on a wall in the middle of the clubhouse. Above the instructions, two clubhouse TVs showed video of Astros pitcher Brett Myers, who would pitch against Halladay in the season opener. One TV showed video of Myers facing right-handed hitters; the other showed him facing left-handed hitters.

Bruce Springsteen's "Glory Days"—with its sentimental reference to baseball—played over the clubhouse speakers, and the Boss' words sounded particularly meaningful on the first day of the new season.

It felt like a personal message to the Phillies, who would try to win their fifth-consecutive National League East championship and—if all went well— a second World Series in four years. The Phillies know they must take advantage while they can because the team is getting older and the window of opportunity won't stay open forever. They don't want to look back on this season with regrets.

---------------- K ----------------

Springsteen stepped aside for Led Zeppelin as Halladay took the mound in front of a huge crowd and threw his warm-up pitches before the top of the first inning.

Of course, Halladay did not hear the music. He never does. Hours before his first start at Citizens Bank Park in 2010, Phillies Manager of Video

RESPECT AMONG RIVALS

The Atlanta Braves' rotations of the 1990s are regarded as the best in history, with three Hall of Fame-caliber pitchers in their prime in Greg Maddux, Tom Glavine, and John Smoltz, and quality fourth starters like Steve Avery, Denny Neagle, and Kevin Millwood. The 2011 Phillies had the talent to compete with those rotations, a fact that wasn't lost on Braves President John Schuerholz and former Braves Pitching Coach Leo Mazzone, both of whom were on the field before games against the Phillies at Turner Field in April.

"They have the opportunity to be as good as any rotation in the history of the game for a short period of time," Mazzone said. "When you're talking about the guys in Atlanta, you're talking about three Hall of Famers. Now what I'm saying, for a year or two—or the window that they have—they have the opportunity to be as good as anybody. But nobody will ever be able to be as good as the Braves' rotations because of the longevity of it."

Schuerholz, who was Atlanta's general manager in the 1990s, saw plenty of similarities between the Braves and the Phillies, but it stood out how the Braves quietly stole Maddux from the Yankees like the Phillies quietly stole Lee from the Yankees.

"We were always stealth," Schuerholz said. "No one ever heard or knew by rumor or innuendo or by leak what we were thinking. My view about that as a general manager is, the more people who know what we are thinking of doing— or even thinking—it disadvantages us as an organization from getting the best job done. We keep this information to ourselves. It's very proprietary and very confidential. If it leaks out, we are hurt. You may make yourself a hero telling somebody an inside story, but you're hurting us. And don't let me find that out."

Schuerholz closed his inner circle; Ruben Amaro Jr. closed his. Amaro shared Schuerholz's insistence for secrecy to the point he said he would lie if he believes it will protect the deal he is working on. And why would Schuerholz need more opinions on Maddux anyway?

"Hell, we knew Greg was one of the greatest pitchers to ever take the mound," Schuerholz said.

The Braves won 14 consecutive division championships from 1991 to 2005. The Phillies hoped to extend their run to five in 2011.

"I've compared the Phillies of today to the Braves of the nineties," Schuerholz said. "We worked it. We worked it for fifteen years. They've got a nice run going."

Services Kevin Camiscioli asked Halladay what warm-up music he wanted. This is an important decision to many pitchers and hitters, but Halladay told Camiscioli that he could not care less because he wouldn't hear it anyway. Nothing comes between him and his focus on the game. With the decision in his hands, Camiscioli told Phillies Music Director Mark Wyatt to play some Led Zeppelin. Wyatt, who sits in the Phanavision booth in the second deck along the first-base line, chose the combination of "Moby Dick" and "Good Times Bad Times." Those two songs have played every time Halladay has pitched in Philadelphia.

Halladay pitched well against the Astros, although he certainly had pitched better. He allowed five hits and one run, and struck out six in six innings as the Astros ran up his pitch count to force him from the game earlier than expected. But off-season concerns about an aging and impotent offense showed through the first eight innings. Myers allowed just three hits and one earned run in seven innings as the Astros carried a 4-2 lead into the bottom of the ninth. The Phillies' willingness to swing early in the count had Myers shaking his head the next day. He could not throw his curveball for a strike, but the Phillies never figured that out because they kept swinging early.

Anxiety filled Citizens Bank Park. The Phillies were without Chase Utley, who was injured, and Jayson Werth, who was in Washington after signing a seven-year, $126-million contract with the Washington Nationals. The Phils had invested more than $175 million in payroll, but the thought occurred to the thousands of fans in the stands that a bad offense could torpedo the season, no matter how well The Rotation pitched.

One fan mocked the Phillies as they jogged off the field before their final at-bat in the ninth.

"You can't hit American Legion pitching!"

Rollins chuckled.

"Maybe it inspired us," he said.

The Phillies strung together six singles—the final one coming from John Mayberry Jr.—to score three runs against Astros closer Brandon Lyon to win the game, 5-4.

Whew.

Opening Day is just one game in a six-month, 162-game season, but disaster had been avoided in Philadelphia. A 0-1 start in Philly might as well be a 0-20 start. Nobody knew that better than Rollins, Philadelphia's longest-tenured professional athlete.

"It wouldn't have been received well, especially with Roy on the mound and not being able to come up with a victory," he said. "That was just desire to win. Nobody wanted to make that last out."

The Phillies kept their fans happy one more day.

"Games like today's go to show you we're going to have to win as a team all year," Halladay said. "As much as they talk about our pitching, we're going to have to play as a team if we want to achieve our goals. This was a good example of that."

———————————— K ————————————

If anybody questioned why *Sports Illustrated* positioned Cliff Lee in the middle of its Phillies rotation cover shot, they got the answer when Lee left the bullpen following his warm-up pitches before his first start of the season the next night.

Fans stood and cheered his entire walk from the bullpen to the dugout. No Phillies player had received an ovation like that since Jim Thome, when he played his first game at Veterans Stadium in 2003. Thome symbolized a rebirth of baseball in Philadelphia; Lee symbolized the Phillies' place among baseball's elite. Fans showed their love and appreciation. They cheered his jog to the mound in the top of the first inning. They cheered his first at-bat, even though he struck out. They cheered him after every inning, after each of his 11 strikeouts, and after he executed a sacrifice bunt to set up a two-run rally in the fourth inning of a 9-4 victory over Houston. He allowed four hits, three runs, and no walks in seven innings.

Lee left the ballpark that night feeling he made the right choice returning to Philadelphia.

"I could definitely hear the volume when I was walking in," he said. "It's louder just because of the circumstances, obviously, getting a chance to come back. These fans have a knack for getting a little louder than everyone else. I don't know what it is. I don't know if it's alcohol-induced or what."

Two starts into the season, The Rotation was 2-0.

Carlos Ruiz walked into the trainer's room following Lee's performance and a teammate asked him how much fun he had catching Halladay and Lee in consecutive games.

"Oh, my God," he said. "I can't believe it. And tomorrow we've got Roy."

Roy Oswalt allowed two runs in six innings in a 7-3 victory over the

Astros as the Phillies started 3-0.

"Chooch, how much fun was that?" Danys Baez asked Ruiz.

"Oh, man," he said. "And then we've got Cole Hamels."

But Hamels' season debut wasn't in line with those of the first three aces. He allowed six runs in just 2⅔ innings against the rival New York Mets, and fans showered him with boos as he walked off the mound in the third inning of a 7-1 loss. The Rotation would not be perfect. That wasn't surprising. Perfection is hard to come by in pro sports. What was surprising was the lack of patience fans had for Hamels, a 2008 World Series hero who had a strong season in 2010.

Toughened by five seasons in Philadelphia, Hamels kept the boos in perspective. He shrugged them off and threw seven scoreless innings in his next start against the Atlanta Braves at Turner Field on April 10.

"I've been booed many a time," said Hamels, who acknowledged he once booed Adam Eaton while watching him pitch for his hometown Padres. "If you kind of get that response, it's the understanding that people know that you're good. They expect you to do well and when you don't, they're disappointed, just like anybody. It's human nature."

—————————— K ——————————

The Phillies won the early-season series against the Braves, the team that figured to be their top challenger in the National League East. Music thumped over the clubhouse speakers as the team packed its bags and moved on for a three-game series in Washington at Nationals Park, where they would see former teammate Jayson Werth in a Nationals uniform for the first time.

Music blasts following every Phillies victory, which makes the silence following a loss a startling contrast.

Jimmy Rollins is the music man in the Phillies' clubhouse. He appeared in MC Hammer videos while growing up in Alameda, California. He started the Jimmy Rollins Entertainment Group, through which he got involved in the music business. He owns a share of the publishing rights to songs like Snoop Dogg's "Sexual Eruption" and Sean Kingston and Justin Bieber's "Eenie Meenie." Rollins takes music seriously, but in previous seasons he passed the postgame music responsibilities to Werth.

LMFAO's "I'm In Miami Bitch" became a theme song of sorts for the

2008 Phillies, playing following every victory, although not everybody caught on. Late in the season in Atlanta, former Phillies left fielder Pat Burrell's ears perked up as he finally listened to the lyrics.

"Is this song saying what I think it's saying?" Burrell asked.

Yes, it is.

"Who is this?" he asked.

LMFAO.

"LMFAO? What does that mean?" Burrell asked, furrowing his brow as he tried to come up with an answer.

"Leave me the fuck alone?" he guessed, with a perplexed look on his face.

His answer drew a couple chuckles, partly because he got it wrong—it's Laughing My Fucking Ass Off—and partly because the answer fit his personality. Burrell was a good teammate and treated people directly involved with the team—players, coaches, the manager, and clubhouse attendants—well. But he had little use for anybody else, especially the media.

The Lonely Island's "I'm On a Boat" was the 2009 theme song, which Rollins couldn't stand. But Werth was the DJ, so it stayed.

"We had some anthems over the course of four years," Werth said. "It was more just to give a vibe and get everybody on the same page. Keep it fresh. Keep it new. If you're in a little lull and you're not playing good, the music's got to go. It's never our fault. It's always the music's fault."

Players get tired during the season. They get down. They get angry. Werth sandwiched absurd songs like "I'm In Miami Bitch" between legitimate rap and hip-hop for a reason.

They kept things loose.

———————————— K ————————————

Baseball lifers like to say pennants cannot be won in April, but they can be lost. A bad start can be a killer. Every bloated ERA and subterranean batting average is magnified. Players start to press, fans start to boo, and the next thing a team knows it is July, it's buried in the standings, and its general manager is trading its star pitcher in a fire sale.

Phillies General Manager Ruben Amaro Jr. said in spring training the Boston Red Sox were the best team in baseball, but the Red Sox started the season 0-6. The Tampa Bay Rays won the American League East in 2010, but also started 0-6. Red Sox fans jammed the panic button. (The small handful of Rays fans didn't even notice, and continued eating their grouper sandwiches at Frenchy's.)

The Phillies started the season 15-6 for the best record in baseball. They were winning as everybody expected, but it often didn't feel that way. It seemed like they were catching too many breaks and the pendulum eventually would swing the other way. They swept the San Diego Padres in a four-game series starting on April 21 at PETCO Park, but the team had scored four or fewer runs in 13 consecutive games. Manager Charlie Manuel got more and more frustrated with every runner left on base and every ball popped up in the infield with a runner on third.

Manuel's in-game hunches backfired, too, putting him in a sour mood. He chose right-handed John Mayberry Jr. to pinch-hit against Nationals right-hander Livan Hernandez with the bases loaded and one out in the seventh inning on April 12 at Nationals Park. Manuel typically would have had left-handed Ross Gload hit in that spot, but Manuel chose Mayberry because he thought he could hit a grand slam based on the way the wind was blowing out to left.

Sabermetricians' collective heads exploded with that reasoning.

Mayberry struck out swinging and the Phillies lost the game, 7-4.

"I knew when he went up there somebody was going to say something about it," Manuel said after the game. "That's fine, you know?"

Manuel sounded annoyed. He was.

He got more agitated when questioned about a pitching decision on April 15 in a 4-3 loss to the Florida Marlins. The Marlins had the bases loaded and one out in the seventh inning when they sent lefty-swinging Greg Dobbs to pinch-hit against Phillies right-hander Danys Baez, who had just issued a walk and a single. The Phillies had left-hander Antonio Bastardo warmed up and ready in the bullpen, but Manuel stuck with Baez. Dobbs singled to score two runs to give the Marlins a one-run lead. Manuel said after the game he let Baez pitch because if he had brought in Bastardo, the Marlins would have countered with right-handed hitter Wes Helms.

Most would have chosen Bastardo vs. Helms over Baez vs. Dobbs.

Managers make thousands of calls and moves in a season. Some work. Some don't. Sometimes the player executes. Sometimes he doesn't. It's all part of a game played by humans, not robots, and sometimes it calls for a sense of humor.

"When we go real good, I'm the pitching coach," Manuel joked later in the month. "When we go bad, [Rich] Dubee is. Same with hitting. When we get twenty hits, I'm the hitting coach."

Manuel never joked about being a doctor or trainer. Injuries torture him because he cannot manage them. If a pitcher struggled, he could pull him. If a hitter struggled, he could sit him on the bench for a few games. But injuries? He just had to wait for his players to get healthy. With Chase Utley and Brad Lidge already on the disabled list, the Phils got another scare on April 15, when Roy Oswalt left the game with a strained back. It was an alarming sight, watching one of the four aces leave the mound after throwing a few warm-up pitches in the top of the seventh inning. Oswalt downplayed it after the game, but he had a history of back problems, spending time on the disabled list in 2006 and 2009 because of them.

"This is totally different," Oswalt insisted. "This is nothing like that. This is middle back. It's not really lower back. This is middle. I felt like I could have gotten through the seventh, but I didn't want to go out there, get in trouble, and then have to bring somebody in to clean up the mess."

Oswalt said he expected to make his next start, but after finishing interviews with reporters, he gingerly walked away, favoring his back.

It certainly looked more serious than he made it seem, which was a reason to be concerned. Injuries seemed to be the only thing that could derail The Rotation.

Other players started dropping. J. C Romero strained a calf muscle. Jose Contreras went on the disabled list with an injured elbow. He had appeared in five games in seven days in late April, which had reporters asking Manuel if he had overused the 39-year-old Cuban. Manuel angrily defended himself before a game in Arizona.

A sore back wasn't the only thing that plagued Oswalt early in the season. He left the team following a poor start in Arizona on April 26, when he learned that a series of tornadoes had torn through his home area in Mississippi. Some speculated that Oswalt's head might not have been in the game, considering a tornado had destroyed his parents' home the previous year. But Oswalt's fastball had lacked its normal zip in his two starts since he'd strained his back against the Marlins, indicating that it was indeed an issue.

"I'm a little concerned," Manuel said of Oswalt's health. "But we'll see what happens."

Nobody knew when Oswalt would be back.

The injuries and absences weighed on Manuel, but the team's offensive struggles ate at him most. From April 10 to April 27, the Phillies hit .216, with a .613 on-base-plus-slugging percentage. Their 3.25 runs per game in that 16-game stretch ranked second-to-last in the National League.

"I know people will say, 'Well, you've got the starting pitching. You've got the pitchers,'" Manuel said. "Yeah, that's part of it, too. But at the same time, usually when you talk about a World Series team or something like that you're talking about a top-notch team. I'm not saying we don't have that. We could have it, but it's going to take some work."

The Phillies beat Arizona, 8-4, on April 27 at Chase Field to prevent a Diamondbacks' sweep. A victory on getaway day—the last game of a series when the team packs its bags and heads elsewhere, in this case, back home to Philadelphia—is a victory worth enjoying. But the clubhouse that afternoon felt different. All month long the Phillies seemed to have trouble hitting their stride. Maybe it was the injuries. Maybe it was the inconsistent offense. Maybe it was the expectations. And now, more health concerns emerged in The Rotation and elsewhere. Joe Blanton cut short a bullpen session before the game because of a problem with his right elbow, an injury he had privately dealt with since spring training. And catcher Carlos Ruiz had strained his back on a swing and left the game early.

There was no music after this victory. There was no laughing. There was no chatter.

It was strangely quiet.

The players seemed tight, the mood heavy.

The expectations of a new season seemed to be weighing on them. They seemed to be running in place.

"Hey, we're in first place. Anybody notice?" Bullpen Coach Mick Billmeyer told a reporter as the Phillies packed their bags in Arizona.

"I've never seen a first-place team have less fun," the reporter replied.

"Don't worry," Billmeyer said, throwing a bag over his shoulder. "It'll turn around. We'll start having fun. You watch."

MAY

May began with a stirring show of patriotism at Citizens Bank Park, but between injuries, poor run support and the occasional gopher ball, the weeks that followed caused several bouts of indigestion for The Rotation. It all culminated with Cliff Lee's belching in front of his locker after having his lunch handed to him by the Washington Nationals on the final day of the month.

That May 31 start ended up being Lee's worst of a stellar season. He gave up a pair of home runs, including a three-run blast to Washington second baseman Danny Espinosa, as the Nationals did something they had rarely done against the Phillies: win a series.

After games, it is customary for the starting pitcher to stand in the middle of the clubhouse or in front of his locker and take questions from reporters. Lee was clearly perturbed after this game. Not only had he given up the two damaging long balls, but he had walked three, raising his season total in 80 innings to 19, a number that stood out like a belch in church because he is traditionally one of the game's best control pitchers. In fact, he'd walked just 18 batters in 212⅓ innings the year before. Lee wasn't happy with his performance, nor was he particularly enthused about having to rehash it with reporters. As he arrived at his locker, he let out an audible belch. Must have been the meatballs he served up to Espinosa.

Lee was spectacular—everything the Phillies thought they were buying— in June and August, but May was a month of highs and lows for the left-hander. There were games in which he pitched brilliantly, such as his 16-strikeout effort against the Braves in a 5-0 loss on May 6. Lee's mates let him down offensively and defensively in that one. Later in the month, he pitched eight shutout innings against his former club, Texas. There were games in which he was knocked around, such as the one in Washington, and games in which he thrilled the fans with his work as a hitter, such as his win over Cincinnati on May 26, when he drove in three runs in a 10-4 win.

That was a rare offensive explosion for the Phillies, a team that on many nights in May didn't score enough runs to fill one of Betsy Ross' thimbles. On April 30, Roy Halladay went the distance to squeak by the Mets, 2-1.

That April finale pushed the Phils to 10 games over .500, but it was a foreshadowing, as the team scored three or fewer runs in 15 of its next 22 games, wasting some pretty good pitching along the way. Pitchers get frustrated when their teammates don't score runs, but they are loath to admit it. They know things even out over the course of 162 games, that there will be nights when they allow six early runs and the offense will bail them out. They know negative emotion can unravel a pitcher on the mound and lead to a beating. So it's best not to whine, best just to focus, as the tired cliché goes, on what you can control, even when runs are scarce.

"You just go out and pitch, one pitch after another," Halladay said after taking a 2-1 complete-game loss in Miami on May 10. "Jack Morris told me that. When you bring emotions into it, it makes it difficult."

At one point during the month, the Phillies went 27 innings between runs while Lee was on the mound. He followed the Jack Morris ideal and kept emotion out of it, shrugging as he always does while employing his favorite expression.

Whatever.

"There's nothing we can do about that," Lee said of the lack of run support after a 3-1 loss in St. Louis on May 16. "We hit once every nine hitters. We've got to do our job with the bats and so do the position players and everyone else. It's a complete game. You've got to hit, play defense, and pitch. If one of those things are lacking, you're going to lose. So whatever. It's not my job to worry about runs scored. It's my job to focus on preventing other teams from scoring and I'm going to keep focused on that."

Runs remained scarce throughout the month, but there was no stopping Halladay and Lee on May 20 and May 21. They got just enough support to beat Texas by scores of 3-2 and 2-0. Roy Oswalt wasn't as fortunate in the series finale, which he lost, 2-0, despite allowing just a run over seven innings. After that game, Oswalt, who pitched with a sore back, described what it's like working with the slim margin for error that a lack of run support creates.

"You've kind of got to dance between raindrops out there and not give up too many hits in one inning," he said. "One or two here and there, but you have to make big pitches at big times."

———————— K ————————

Halladay knows all about making big pitches at big times. He and Lee are both strike throwers who don't let hits bother them. They dare hitters to hit their pitches, and rely on their defense and ability to manage an inning when they do. Nobody manages an inning better than Halladay. You can almost see him bear down, raise his intensity, and put a little extra on a pitch in a threatening situation. He did plenty of that on May 29, 2010, when he survived seven three-ball counts on his way to pitching a perfect game against the Marlins in Miami.

Halladay's opponent that night was Josh Johnson, the Marlins' ace. Johnson was really good that night, allowing just an unearned run in seven innings, but Halladay was better. At 27, Johnson is one of the most talented young pitchers in the game, a big, strong right-hander like Halladay.

In the pitching fraternity, Halladay is considered the best in the game, a total package superstar from his preparation—both mental and physical—to his unshakable mind-set, to his prowess on the mound. It's not uncommon for Halladay's pitching teammates to confer with him, trying to integrate some of what makes him special into their games. Kyle Kendrick seemed attached to Halladay's hip when Halladay arrived in Clearwater in the spring of 2010. It's no coincidence that Cole Hamels' development of an assassin's mentality blossomed when Halladay became a teammate and frequent dinner partner.

Even opposing pitchers want to know what makes Halladay tick.

Several weeks after Halladay outpitched Johnson in that 2010 perfect game, the Marlins were in Philadelphia. One day Johnson and Halladay were both scheduled to throw between-starts bullpen sessions at Citizens Bank Park. The bullpens in Philadelphia are two-tiered structures beyond the center-field wall. The visitors' bullpen sits above the home team's bullpen, and they are separated by a staircase. Johnson had finished his session as Halladay was arriving on the mound to begin his. Halladay's bullpen sessions are serious exercises. He's not out there goofing around. He works on polishing his mechanics, refining his grips on the baseball, and trying to locate every pitch with a sniper's precision. Pity the poor sucker who gets in Halladay's way during one of these work sessions.

"The concentration and the effort he applies out there, the focus and the attention, it's amazing," said Pitching Coach Rich Dubee, who, along with a catcher, is usually the only one to get an up-close look at Halladay in his bullpen operating room. "He's out there trying to make pitches. He doesn't just flip it up there. There's a purpose to everything he does. He wants to do his work and he doesn't want to be bothered."

Johnson finished his workout that day in 2010 and slowly descended the bullpen stairs at Citizens Bank Park, stealing a glimpse of Halladay as he began to limber up. Johnson lingered.

"I was waiting for the blowup," Dubee recalled a year later. "I've seen camera guys wander up there and . . . oh, boy."

Zap.

Johnson asked if he could watch Halladay at work. Halladay motioned that it was fine. Johnson was no camera guy. He was a member of the pitching fraternity, a gifted All-Star and Halladay was OK with him taking mental notes, even if Johnson could use the knowledge gained to someday beat him.

"I would be interested, too," Dubee said. "Johnson's no dummy. Doc's a special guy. Johnson's special, too, but Doc has done it for a long time. You have an opportunity like that, you take advantage of it."

Johnson watched with laser-like intensity as Halladay branded the catcher's mitt, time and time again, with darting sinkers, sharp cutters, biting curveballs, and changeups that disappeared as they reached the plate.

Halladay did it all with the seriousness of an anesthesiologist.

"I stayed for the whole thing," Johnson said. "Really, really impressive."

What impressed him most?

"You can go up and down the list," Johnson said. "His attitude. The way he goes about it on the field. The work he puts in. He's somebody you want to model yourself after."

The funny thing about Johnson's little study session in 2010 is it probably would have never happened if not for Phillies fans and the team's relievers in 2004. When Citizens Bank Park opened that year, the home bullpen was on the top tier and the visitors' bullpen was below. After a preseason exhibition series, Phillies relievers complained to management that they were being heckled by fans hanging over the bullpen from above. Phillies relievers complained that it was difficult to concentrate.

Management moved the Phillies to the lower bullpen and threw the visitors to the fans. Raw meat, meet the Philadelphia lions.

Fans above the visitors' bullpen are so close to the visiting relievers that in April 2004, Cincinnati reliever Danny Graves asked one of them if he waxed his eyebrows.

"I could tell that he did, but I asked anyway," Graves said. "It's pretty wild out there. They're ruthless."

A few weeks later during that inaugural season at Citizens Bank Park,

Montreal Expos relievers timed a fan as he booed for 13 minutes straight.

Six years later, Johnson was glad the visitors had been moved upstairs. If they had stayed on the bottom tier, he would have finished his session that June day in 2010 and walked out of the bullpen possibly without knowing Halladay was above him. He can thank the lions and those whining Phillies relievers of 2004 for his up-close look at Halladay's workday.

Fans' interacting with relievers in the bullpen has long been part of the game. Former Boston Red Sox reliever Bob Stanley used to hose down sun-baked fans in the Fenway Park bleachers on hot days. More than a few phone numbers have been exchanged between pretty girls and relievers—bachelors, of course—and an occasional hot dog from the concession stand has made it into a bullpen. One classic bullpen moment in recent Phillies history came when sharp-tongued closer Billy Wagner was warming up in the bullpen in San Francisco. The bullpens in San Francisco are practically in the box seats and a fan was going to town on Wagner, who stands just 5-9.

"Hey, midget," the fan shouted at Wagner.

Wagner, the hardest-throwing lefty on the planet at that time, kept firing pitches.

"Hey, Frodo," the fan shouted.

Wagner kept firing.

"How tall are you anyway?" the fan shouted.

Wagner seized his opportunity.

"Five-nine," he drawled between pitches. "Six-six when I'm standing on my wallet."

---- K ----

Since the day the Phillies signed Cliff Lee, there was a tendency to think of the club as the Big Four starters and a bunch of complementary players. While the impact of the team's star-studded rotation couldn't be disputed, there was more to the club than four guys named Halladay, Lee, Hamels, and Oswalt.

As everyone from the front office to the clubhouse had mentioned since this campaign began on Valentine's Day in Clearwater, it takes a full team to win a championship. All the pieces matter, as Lester Freamon said in *The Wire*. Whatever the case, the first home stand of May was a good reminder of all this. The Phillies went 6-3 on that home stand, even though Joe Blanton and Roy Oswalt were hurting. Two of those wins came from Vance Worley, who went from being farmed out in March to a double-digit winner by Labor Day. The other came from Kyle Kendrick. The right-hander replaced the sore-backed Oswalt on May 7 and, in his first start of the season, pitched five shutout innings in a 3-0 win over Atlanta. Worley and Kendrick pitched 17 innings as starters on the home stand and allowed just one run combined.

Not too shabby.

"Those guys are on a different level," said Kendrick, referring to the big-name starters. "But it is nice to help out."

Blanton struggled with elbow issues the entire month. He was scheduled to pitch against Colorado at home on May 19. Rain washed out batting practice and most of the players milled about the clubhouse before the game. Even the elusive Halladay, often tucked away watching video or riding a stationary bike to Europe, was there, his attention to his workout regimen interrupted by another passion—aviation. Kendrick was playing with a remote-control helicopter. A number of teammates looked on in amusement as the popular Kendrick, joystick in hand, struggled to get the delicate toy airborne. When he finally did, it stayed up for just a couple of seconds and crashed to the floor amidst the chuckles of onlookers.

Halladay, who says he would have become a pilot if he didn't become a ballplayer, picked up the helicopter and made some adjustments to the blades, as if he were tinkering with the grip on his changeup. He grabbed the joystick from Kendrick and flew the helicopter smoothly for 20 seconds before landing it softly and handing the joystick back to Kendrick. All that was missing was Halladay channeling fiddler Charlie Daniels and saying, "That's how you do it, son," but anyone who knows Halladay knows he's way too humble to do something like that.

"He's good at everything," one reporter said to another after watching Halladay pilot the toy helicopter, which was about the size of a middle infielder's glove.

Clearly inspired by Halladay's flawless flight, Kendrick took the joystick and promptly crashed the helicopter into the back of a chair occupied by Blanton, that night's pitcher. It was rather symbolic. Blanton experienced more pain in his elbow as he tried to loosen up and was scratched. He would not make another start until the final week of the season. Kendrick made the emergency start that night and was torched for a pair of home runs by Jason Giambi in a 7-1 loss to the Rockies.

The defeat was the Phils' fifth in six games and they scored more than two runs in just one of them. Their only win in that span was a 2-1 victory over Colorado behind Hamels.

Where were the runs?

It was a question Phillies pitchers asked all month, and, regrettably, would ask again.

————————— K —————————

Back on May 8, Hamels could have asked, "Where are the runs?" He pitched seven innings and allowed just three runs, but the Phils suffered a 5-2 loss to Atlanta on that Sunday night.

The Phillies began an eight-game road trip in Miami the next day. They didn't reach their hotel until after 3 A.M. Players and coaches arrived in the clubhouse the next day, bleary-eyed but upbeat. The hangover that comes with a difficult loss can't last long when you play nearly every day for six months. Several members of the team's traveling party had been relaxing at the hotel pool a couple hours earlier. One staff member spoke of seeing a 250-pound woman sunbathing.

"Some people just shouldn't wear bikinis," he said.

A few feet away, Bullpen Coach Mike Billmeyer, the team's ambassador of laughs, perked up when he heard of the 250-pound bathing beauty.

"Did you give her my number?" he asked.

The Phils beat the Marlins that night, with Blanton getting his only win of the year despite pitching through the elbow injury that would eventually scuttle his season.

The second game of the series was another matchup between Halladay and Johnson, and you couldn't help but wonder if Halladay had given Johnson a little too good of a peek in the bullpen at Citizens Bank Park a year earlier. Johnson pitched seven innings and allowed just one run, lowering his ERA to a microscopic 1.63. Halladay and the Phillies lost the game, 2-1. Not only were runs scarce, the defense betrayed Halladay as normally sure-handed shortstop Jimmy Rollins made a costly error to put the go-ahead run on base in the eighth inning. Halladay followed with a rare wild pitch before Chris Coughlin broke the tie with a bloop hit to center. As Coughlin's feathery blooper found the outfield grass, Halladay shouted a profanity. It was

"WILSON IS PITCHING!"

Danys Baez went 5-8 with a 5.81 ERA in 80 games over two rather forgettable seasons in Philadelphia.

But he'll always have May 25, 2011.

So will Wilson Valdez.

Baez, the last man in the bullpen, and Valdez, who played the first 18 innings at second base, were two of the biggest reasons the Phillies beat the Cincinnati Reds, 5-4, in a 19-inning marathon on that night.

In one of the most entertaining games of the year, Baez, who seemed to be on the verge of being released all season—he actually was let go in July—came out of the bullpen in the 14th inning and pitched five innings of one-hit, shutout ball before Valdez took over and earned the win with a scoreless 19th inning.

Baez threw 73 the pitches, the most since he was a starter with Cleveland in 2002. He had no choice. The Phils were out of pitchers.

"Great job by Baez," starter Roy Halladay said. "The guy's a great teammate. He sucked it up for us."

Valdez hadn't pitched since his sandlot days in the Dominican Republic. The super-sub infielder had always impressed scouts with his whip-like arm.

"Now, we get to see how hard he throws," one team official said to another in the club's executive suite.

Valdez hit 89 mph on the team's radar gun. That's about an average major-league fastball.

Pitching Coach Rich Dubee had told Valdez in the 16th inning that he might have to pitch, so he wasn't surprised to get the call. His family, however, was. His wife was sleeping at home in New Mexico when her mother phoned her and said, "Wilson is pitching!" Kamie Valdez sprung from bed and turned on the TV just in time to see her husband strut off the mound like he'd been there before. A game-winning sacrifice fly from Raul Ibanez in the bottom of the 19th made Valdez the first player since Babe Ruth in 1921 to get the pitching victory after starting the game as a position player.

"It was one of my most fun games ever," said Valdez, who oozes appreciation for being a major-leaguer after bouncing through 10 different organizations over 15 years.

Valdez wasn't the only one who had a lot of fun. The game started with a sellout crowd in the seats, but ended with just a smattering of fans in the house at 1:20 A.M. The fans loved every minute of the late-night/early-morning drama, though one of them was guilty of not paying complete attention. In the 17th inning, as Baez—the Phillies' seventh and final reliever—was starting to tire, a fan leaned over the railing and offered Bullpen Coach Mick Billmeyer some advice.

"The guy said, 'Hey, get somebody up!' " Billmeyer recounted. "So I stood up."

an uncharacteristic show of emotion for the stoic pitcher, but it was that kind of night—frustrating all the way.

"That was a tough way to lose a game," Manager Charlie Manuel said afterward.

Halladay spoke softly, blandly after that game in Miami. It was difficult to tell whether he was more frustrated with himself, the defense, or the lack of offense. But deep down inside, it had to be comforting for the pitcher to know that, across the state in Clearwater, second baseman Chase Utley was about to play in his first minor-league rehabilitation game after missing the start of the season with the most famous case of right knee tendinitis in Philadelphia history. Halladay had once called Utley "the driving force" of the Phillies and compared him to Derek Jeter, the heart of the most recent New York Yankees dynasty. With Utley now playing in minor-league games, it wouldn't be long before his bat and intensity would be back in the lineup.

"One person can mean a lot, especially the caliber of player that Chase is," Manuel said. "We're going to get better when Chase gets back."

With the offense struggling, Phillies officials were also keeping an eye on top prospect Domonic Brown, who had recovered from a broken hand and was now heating up at Triple-A. Manuel was eager to insert Brown's bat into the lineup, but he was willing to be patient. He didn't want a player who wasn't ready to contribute, and neither did the pitchers who were starving for consistent run support.

"Go ask Halladay and Lee and them," Manuel said. "We're here to win. I'm not here to babysit. When Domonic's ready to tear the cover off the ball, he'll come."

That was the idea, at least.

But in baseball, everything is subject to change.

Especially when the offense stinks.

---- K ----

After Miami, scoring runs continued to be a problem in Atlanta and St. Louis. The two games in St. Louis, both losses, were brutal. The Phils scored a total of two runs in starts by Lee and Oswalt, who had returned from the disabled list and held one of the best-hitting clubs in the league to a run over five innings.

After the second loss, players dressed quietly in the clubhouse and boarded buses to Lambert-St. Louis International Airport for the flight home. Players usually ride the second bus while coaches, staffers, and other members of the traveling party ride the first bus. As radio broadcaster Scott Franzke was about to get off the first bus and walk to the plane, he heard a pounding and shouting at the back of the empty coach. He walked down the aisle and opened the lavatory door. Veteran broadcaster Chris Wheeler, red-faced and frazzled, emerged holding a broken doorknob.

Wheeler's pleas to be liberated from the locked lavatory seemed to be a fitting metaphor for a shackled Phillies' offense. But freeing the bats wouldn't be as easy as springing a locked bathroom door. That's why management decided to do something bold. After weeks of stressing patience with Brown, the organization brought him up on May 20. The decision to promote the 23-year-old outfielder was made an hour after that helicopter-crash loss to Colorado on May 19. Moments after that game, Amaro announced that Shane Victorino was headed to the DL with a hamstring strain. At the time, Amaro essentially ruled out bringing up Brown to replace Victorino.

"We don't think he's ready," Amaro said during a news conference.

Almost as soon as he spoke those words, Amaro began to reconsider. While it was true that he believed Brown needed more minor-league seasoning, he wondered if Brown might be able to contribute while continuing his development in Philadelphia. After emerging from the news conference, Amaro huddled with his assistant, Scott Proefrock, the man whose tireless behind-the-scenes work made the Cliff Lee dream a reality. Together, Amaro and Proefrock decided that maybe this was a good time to bring up Brown. The young outfielder would be coming to replace an injured player, not to be a savior for a sputtering offense. That would reduce pressure on the kid, they believed. Amaro and Proefrock floated their reasoning by Club President David Montgomery, who got on board with it. Four floors below, Manuel was still in his office unwinding after the loss. Amaro popped in and ran the plan by Manuel, who, just a week or so after saying he didn't want to see Brown until he was ready to tear the cover off the ball, was all for adding a bat to his lineup, even one that wasn't quite big-league ready.

A few days later, on May 23, the Phils added another bat when Utley returned to the lineup after missing 47 games. Utley was everybody's favorite Phillie long before Lee came to town and took a piece of that mantle. Another sellout crowd greeted Utley with a thunderous ovation.

"I tried to tune it out, but it was a little too loud," the second baseman said.

Utley did not get a hit that night, but his presence seemed to inspire the Phillies. Every other starter did get a hit and the team beat Cincinnati, 10-3.

"There was a new energy with him in there," Hamels said of Utley.

Hamels was the team's best and most consistent pitcher in May. He began the month with a complete-game five-hitter against Washington and ended it with 10 strikeouts over seven innings of two-run, walk-free ball against the Mets. For the month, he went 4-1 with a 2.93 ERA in six starts and the club went 5-1 in those games. He was well on the way to the All-Star Game and Cy Young candidacy. He picked up his sixth win of the season the night that Utley returned for that 10-run explosion against Cincinnati and he was glad to have the run support, though he admitted that the lack of it in previous weeks had helped to harden The Rotation.

Showing a healthy arrogance, Hamels said, "We have the confidence that we know we can go out and pitch seven to nine innings and give up zero runs to maybe one or two. I think we just have the confidence we can shut an opposing team down no matter what we do as an offense."

With Utley back, the Phils took three of four from Cincinnati and moved on to New York, where Brown came off the bench and had two big hits to rally the team to a 6-4 win over the Mets on May 27. Three days later, the Phils were in Washington for a holiday matinee with the Nationals. The month had started with a profound sense of patriotism when President Obama announced the killing of terrorist Osama bin Laden late at night on May 1. The Phillies were playing the Mets at Citizens Bank Park when the news broke. In the stands, fans read reports on their cell phones. The game began to feel secondary in importance and before long, chants of "USA! USA! USA!" filled the air. It felt a little like Lake Placid in 1980.

"I don't like to give Philly fans too much credit," Mets third baseman David Wright said with a wry smile after the game, "but they got this one right."

Four weeks later, the Phils were playing against a patriotic backdrop once again with Halladay on the mound in the nation's capital on Memorial Day. It was a searing 92 degrees for the 1 P.M. start. By the middle innings, it was 95 and the heat index was 99. Sweat poured off Halladay as he worked under the broiling sun. Desperately trying to stay hydrated, he drank water and Pedialyte between innings. In the top of the fifth inning, he raced up the stairs behind the dugout and into the clubhouse where he changed his entire sweat-drenched uniform, right down to the socks, and made it back to the mound in a fresh uniform in time for the bottom of the inning. Halladay said the game was one of the most arduous he'd ever pitched. He trailed 4-3 after giving up a solo homer in the bottom of the sixth, but his teammates rallied for two in the top of the seventh—after a month of little run support, the boys with the bats owed their ace one—to take the lead. Halladay allowed a double and a single to open the bottom of the seventh inning, but survived the turbulence, and, on his 111th pitch, blew a high fastball by former teammate Jayson Werth to end the inning. Antonio Bastardo, Jose Contreras, and Ryan Madson closed out the win.

"I was fortunate that the offense picked me up," Halladay, his face beet-red after pitching under the hot sun, said after the game. "It was a grind out there. The strikeout [on Werth] was a nice way to end it, for sure."

Things took a downward turn 24 hours later when the Nationals, led by Espinosa's two home runs, laid a 10-2 whooping on Lee on the final day of the month.

And so May ended on a sour note.

But, hey, the Phils were still 13 games over .500 and two games up in the division.

That was nothing to belch at.

JUNE

The numbers lied to Roy Oswalt, so he lied to himself.

He had a 1.50 ERA in three starts since rejoining the roster on May 17, following a trip home to help his family recover from tornadoes in Mississippi and a trip to the disabled list to treat his ailing back. The pain in his back bit him every time he threw a pitch, but as long as he had that stellar ERA, he figured he could fight through it.

Oswalt looked like a new man when he joined the Phillies in July 2010. He had escaped the Houston Astros, then freefalling to the bottom of Major League Baseball's standings, for a chance to win his first World Series. The change rejuvenated him. He went 7-1 with a 1.74 ERA in 13 games, out-pitching Roy Halladay and Cole Hamels down the stretch. He had the fourth-best ERA in baseball in that span. He endeared himself to Phillies fans when he played left field in a 16-inning loss to the Astros on August 24 at Citizens Bank Park. (He caught the only ball hit to him, bringing a grin to his face.) He volunteered to pitch in relief in Game 4 of the National League Championship Series against the San Francisco Giants. (He took the loss.)

But just weeks into the 2011 season his back had betrayed him and he looked miserable, like he wanted to be anywhere but at the ballpark. Oswalt had back problems before. An MRI exam from his time in Houston had revealed two degenerative discs, which had required trips to the disabled list and cortisone injections. In the past, the injections worked. But Oswalt received a shot on April 28 in Houston, two days after he surrendered five runs in three innings against the Arizona Diamondbacks in Phoenix, and it did nothing.

Did he really want to pitch in pain the rest of the season?

His fastball averaged 92.3 mph from his first start with the Phillies in July 2010 through April 15, 2011, when he injured his back against the Marlins. It had been 90.8 mph since. Oswalt downplayed the lack of pop of his once-exploding fastball. He told reporters in May, upon returning from the DL, it would take time to get his velocity back. But deep down, he knew better. That late life would never return to his fastball while his back throbbed; and without that late movement and separation in velocity from his other pitches, hitters would have a much easier time against him.

He allowed six hits, two runs, two walks, and one home run while striking out three in five innings in a 2-1 loss to the Nationals on June 1 at Nationals Park. It wasn't a bad performance, but he clearly wasn't the guy that dominated the National League in 2010. He wasn't attacking hitters. His back wouldn't let him. Still, despite opponents hitting .316 against him in his first four starts back and Oswalt striking out 45 percent fewer batters than he had the previous season, he was giving the Phillies a chance to win.

So he kept quiet.

"I'm fine," he replied coolly anytime somebody asked him about his health.

Oswalt's body language betrayed those words. Folks inside and outside the organization could see he was not OK. He looked miserable, as if something heavy weighed on his mind. He nearly lost his mother in a tornado the previous spring and the most recent storms in Mississippi had rattled his young children. And now he had a bad back. People inside and outside the Phillies organization wondered if the pitcher's concerns for his family's welfare, coupled with his ailing back, had sapped his desire to play baseball.

"Baseball is a gift you've been given to play, but this comes third or fourth on my list," Oswalt said after returning from Mississippi on May 5. "I can walk away from the game and be happy as long as you have your family. They're going to be there a lot longer than this game will be. A lot of people don't look at it that way. A lot of people think this is who you are as the game goes. Baseball doesn't mean more than my family, for sure."

One rival executive became convinced Oswalt would not finish the season. He wasn't the only one. Oswalt had talked openly about retirement before and after he joined the Phillies. He had indicated his current contract, which expired following the season—unless a 2012 mutual option worth $16 million was picked up—could be his last.

"I heard it," Oswalt said. "People were asking me if I wanted to finish."

He could have quit. He had been playing baseball since he was four years old. He was 33. He had a wife and kids and enough money to take care of his great-great-grandchildren. He could walk away and people would remember him as one of the best pitchers of his era. Nobody would question that. But Oswalt still felt a pull toward the mound.

He felt he owed the game a better finish.

———————— K ————————

Oswalt's setback in Washington gave the Phillies back-to-back losses for just the fourth time in 2011, but they opened a three-game series in Pittsburgh feeling fine because they had their projected Opening Day lineup on the field for the first time since Game 6 of the 2010 NLCS.

Chase Utley had returned from his knee injury on May 23 and Shane Victorino had been activated from the disabled list on June 3 after missing three weeks because of a strained hamstring. The Phillies had the gang back together—Carlos Ruiz, Ryan Howard, Utley, Placido Polanco, Jimmy Rollins, Raul Ibanez, Victorino, and Domonic Brown—and they hoped it translated into runs. They needed some. The Phillies were averaging a measly 4.07 runs per game, which ranked 10th in the National League. The front office had been telling Charlie Manuel to relax, reminding him scoring was down everywhere in baseball. And they were right. Scoring was down everywhere in baseball. But Manuel didn't give a crap about what the rest of the league was hitting. He cared how the Phillies were hitting, and they were wasting too many great performances from their rotation.

A full lineup hardly helped as the Pirates beat the Phillies, 2-1, in 12 innings in the series opener. After the game, Manuel vacillated between frustration and resignation as he talked about the offense, which squandered another fine effort from Cole Hamels, who allowed just one hit and one run in eight innings.

"We can get started anytime they want to, that's how I look at it," Manuel huffed after the game.

Rollins fouled a ball off his right knee the next night and left the game after a few innings in a 6-3 loss to the Pirates. He would not be in the starting lineup for another five games, giving the everyday lineup less than two full games together. It was the second time this season the Phillies had lost four consecutive games.

Roy Halladay snapped the losing streak with a 7-3 victory over the Pirates on June 5. Cliff Lee made his first start of the month the next night against the Los Angeles Dodgers at Citizens Bank Park, opening a season-high 11-game home stand. Lee entered June just 4-5 with a 3.94 ERA, which had not been the beginning everybody imagined when he slipped on his Phillies jersey during his re-introductory news conference in December. Some fans wondered if something was wrong with him, when in reality he had two awful starts that skewed his numbers. Erase a poor start in Atlanta on April 8 (six earned runs in 3⅓ innings) and a poor start in Washington on May 31 (six earned runs in 5⅓ innings) and Lee was 4-3 with a 2.90 ERA.

Not so bad.

Lee struck out 10 in seven scoreless innings in a 3-1 victory over the Dodgers. He entered the season with nine double-digit strikeout games in his career, but already had picked up his sixth in 2011. Lee, who was leading baseball with 100 strikeouts, couldn't explain why he was striking out so many more hitters than in the past. He didn't care to know. He just wanted to get on and off the mound as quickly as possible.

That wouldn't be a problem the rest of the month. Nobody knew it at the time, but it was the beginning of the best month of Lee's career and one of the best months for any pitcher in baseball history. The $120-million man was giving the Phillies their money's worth.

———————————— K ————————————

Oswalt followed Lee in the rotation throughout the month, providing a contrast of results. Oswalt allowed eight hits and four runs in six innings in a 6-2 loss to the Dodgers on June 7. His velocity showed no improvement, and this time he couldn't fake it. The Dodgers got him, giving the Phillies their sixth loss in nine games. The Phillies might have Halladay, Lee, Oswalt, and Cole Hamels in The Rotation, but they had just lost to pitchers Jonathon Niese, Jason Marquis, John Lannan, Charlie Morton, and Rubby De La Rosa.

Damn.

Manuel spoke after the game about Oswalt's struggles, which were becoming more of a concern.

"How do I explain it?" he said. "Basically, he's not as sharp as he was. When we got him last year . . . he was very aggressive. He pounded the strike zone."

Oswalt's back screamed with every pitch. And now the pain had started to shoot down his leg. Reporters asked him why he was allowing so many more base runners and why he wasn't striking anybody out. After allowing just 8.58 base runners per nine innings from his first start with the Phillies in July 2010 through April 15, 2011, he was averaging a whopping 14.90 base runners per nine innings. After averaging 7.8 strikeouts per nine innings from his arrival in Philadelphia through April 15, he was averaging a pedestrian 3.7.

"I look for wins," Oswalt said. "I don't really look for nothing else. Strike-outs are nice if you get 'em, but if you get wins, that's what you shoot for."

The grilling of Oswalt had begun and the pitcher began to bristle at questions. A reporter followed by asking if a lack of sharpness was contributing to the increase in base runners.

"The reason for what?" Oswalt responded.

For all the extra base runners, the reporter repeated. Oswalt is as mild-mannered as they come, but after a couple weeks of being asked about his vanishing fastball and all those base runners, he had started to lose patience. He said he got caught up trying to throw too hard, "listening to you guys, trying to strike guys out and trying to throw a little harder than I needed to."

Oswalt got another follow-up question mentioning Manuel's comments about how aggressive he was last season and if he felt he was close to being that pitcher again.

"Um," Oswalt said.

He paused.

"I mean, I'm just trying to win."

He chuckled dismissively. He was being asked why he sucked and when he thought he would stop sucking, and he knew it.

"What the other guys do, I don't try to pitch like them," he said. "I try to pitch like myself. I've done it for thee hundred or four hundred starts. There's a big difference between pitching and throwing, and sometimes you get caught up in throwing, trying to get strikeouts and trying to do something you don't need to do. If I can get through six, seven, eight innings, and only strike out one or two and we win, that's all I'm looking for. I ain't looking to pad my numbers. That has nothing to do with it. I'm just looking to win ball games."

Oswalt got another follow-up, trying to clarify the previous question.

Roy, this isn't about you pitching like your peers. It's about dominating like last season.

"It ain't as easy as it looks," he said, clearly annoyed. "I think I've thrown four games since I've been back. The other three games, there wasn't much said about it, but I've felt like I've put the team in position to win a lot of those games. We just didn't win them."

Oswalt was frustrated. He wanted to scream, *"My back is killing me! You guys don't understand! I thought I wiggled through the game pretty well for not being healthy."* But he didn't want anybody to know, so he kept quiet and kept his cool with reporters.

That's not always easy.

———————— K ————————

Veteran baseball writers love to tell stories about how they used to grab a beer in the hotel bar with players, coaches, managers, and general managers. There was plenty of trust between the two sides. Stories were swapped as tongues got to wagging.

Times have changed. The world has changed. The 24-hour news cycle has made players and club officials a little more guarded around reporters. A player really has to trust a reporter before he opens up to him or her. That guardedness extends to his life in the community, where a player steps out for a night out on the town with the realization that he could be on YouTube in an hour. Some players have talked about entering an empty restaurant, bar, or club, and the place suddenly filling up because somebody tweeted their location. OMG, CHASE UTLEY IS AT MORIMOTO'S!!

In the Internet age, everything has become a big deal. On-field mistakes are analyzed and criticized *ad nauseum*, and innocent off-field events are blown out of proportion. Ryan Howard sprained his ankle in 2010 and took his son to Dorney Park in Allentown, Pennsylvania, on an off day. A fan snapped a photo, emailed it to the Philadelphia sports blog Crossing Broad, and suddenly Howard was being ripped for the sin of . . . taking his son to an amusement park! It didn't matter that the ankle was immobilized and in no danger of being aggravated.

In some cases, reporter-player relationships have suffered because of this changing world. Don't misunderstand—solid working relationships can be forged between reporters and the people they cover. It's just tougher than it used to be.

Regardless of the era, there are always times when the best of relationships can get a little offtrack, as first-year *Philadelphia Inquirer* beat writer Todd Zolecki learned in June 2003. The Phillies had won 10 of 12 games that month when Zolecki wrote about a possible reason for why they were playing so well: citing an anonymous source, Zolecki reported the front office had sought the opinions of players following a tough road trip and one player told the front office it would help if Manager Larry Bowa was more positive in the dugout. The story was accurate, but the timing did not sit well with Phillies Third-Base Coach John Vukovich, who grew up with Bowa near Sacramento, California. The two were like brothers, and Vuke was fiercely protective of Bowa—not only because they were close friends, but also because Vuke, who was widely admired and respected in the organization, was old-school, and old-school coaches always protected their managers.

The next afternoon at Veterans Stadium, Vukovich confronted Zolecki in the middle of the clubhouse before batting practice.

"Oh, big man with your anonymous source," Vukovich bellowed. "Big fucking man. If you're a real man, you'd name your source. Name your goddamn source!"

"You know I can't do that," Zolecki said.

Vukovich started screaming, inching closer and closer to Zolecki's face. Players, reporters, and coaches stopped to watch. Bowa listened intently from his office.

"Name your goddamn source," Vukovich demanded.

Zolecki had been on the beat for only a couple months and had never been reamed out like this, not even as a kid.

"Uh, I . . ." he stammered.

"You know why you won't name your source?" Vukovich said, moving even closer.

Vukovich lifted up his right hand and curled his index finger and thumb into the tiniest circle he could make. He put the circle in front of Zolecki's face.

"Because your nuts are this fucking big," he shouted. "Your nuts . . . are this . . . fucking . . . big."

Vukovich walked away.

Ho-ly crap.

The next day Vukovich and Zolecki passed each other in the tunnel leading to the Phillies' dugout.

"How are ya, Todd?" Vukovich said with a friendly smile on his face.

"Uh, good, Vuke. How are you?"

"Great, thanks."

It was over. Vukovich made his point. He defended his manager—strategically in front of the players—and let off some steam and was ready to move on. Vukovich was hard-nosed, which rubbed some players the wrong way, but he was a golden-hearted man that cared about people. He especially cared about the Phillies. Vukovich died in 2007 from brain cancer, but he and Zolecki often joked about that afternoon at Veterans Stadium. It always brought a smile to Vukovich's face, and a hearty laugh. And for good reason. It was one of the all-time chew outs with one of the all-time kicker lines.

Years later, Roy Oswalt was clearly getting tired of answering questions about his health and his desire to keep playing. He wanted to scream as he spoke with reporters that night in Philadelphia, but chose to suppress his inner Vuke, and the reporters were happy for that.

——————————————— K ———————————————

Davey Lopes, who had some old-school in him like Vuke, chuckled as he thought about Cole Hamels' true spot in the Phillies rotation.

"I don't think I need to answer that," he said.

He tried anyway.

"Let me put it this way," he said. "I don't think you'd rank him fourth."

Lopes had been the Phillies' first-base coach for four seasons before leaving to join the Los Angeles Dodgers in 2011, so he had seen Halladay, Lee, Oswalt, and Hamels up close. He had watched Hamels progress over the years, and what he saw on June 8 was a mostly finished product. Hamels struck out nine in eight scoreless innings in a 2-0 victory over the Dodgers. Hamels was quietly developing into one of the best pitchers in baseball, not just one of the best left-handers in the game. From June 9, 2010, through June 8, 2011, he had a 2.58 ERA, the third-best ERA in the big leagues over those 12 months. Only Florida's Josh Johnson (2.16 ERA) and Seattle's Felix Hernandez (2.16 ERA) had been better. Falling immediately behind Hamels were the Los Angeles Angels' Jered Weaver (2.63 ERA), Roy Halladay (2.64 ERA), and Roy Oswalt (2.66 ERA).

"He's definitely different," Dodgers catcher Rod Barajas said of Hamels. "The best I've seen him."

Barajas knew Hamels well. He caught him during his one forgettable season with the Phillies in 2007.

"He was primarily fastball-changeup and the curveball could be out of the strike zone and you didn't have to swing at it," Barajas said. "Now he mixes in the cutter and throws the curveball for strikes. You can't lay off it anymore or assume it's a ball."

"He's grown up a lot," Charlie Manuel said. "He's way more mature. He's been around guys like Jamie Moyer and Halladay and Lee and Roy Oswalt and guys like that. He has a better work ethic now. He's getting stronger. He's bigger than he used to be. If you see him with his shirt and stuff off, he's developing into a man."

Manuel caught himself before he finished that last sentence and started to laugh.

What the hell was he saying about admiring Hamels with his shirt off?

But the Phillies were living dangerously. They beat the Dodgers because Hamels was fantastic, not because the offense did anything. The Phillies had

GONE FISHIN' (DON'T FORGET YOUR PANTS)

The Phillies flew from Seattle to St. Louis on June 19, a Sunday evening. They had no game scheduled for Monday before opening a three-game series on Tuesday against the Cardinals at Busch Stadium. Looking for a little fun on their day off, Roy Oswalt took Cliff Lee, Cole Hamels, Carlos Ruiz, and Ross Gload to his reserve in Missouri to fish.

"Every two minutes we caught something," Hamels said.

Hamels also caught poison oak, which began the most miserable month of his career. The poison oak spread over the back of his legs, which swelled up so much his ankles disappeared. The sores split every time he pitched, creating the sensation of somebody cutting him with razor blades. Mix in the sweat and 100-degree heat in late June and early July and he could barely think straight.

"I was so miserable," Hamels said. "You're itching so bad you don't sleep."

Gload and Ruiz, who were wearing shorts like Hamels, also caught some poison oak, but not as bad a case of it. Oswalt and Lee, who were wearing jeans, were fine. Lee had his arm wrapped around a tree with some poison oak on it, but still never got it.

"Cliff probably grew up around it like me," Oswalt said. "I probably had it on me so much when I was a kid I'm probably immune to it. I haven't had poison oak since I don't know when. I was deep in it. I walked everywhere Cole walked. Southern California probably doesn't have a lot of poison oak."

A couple months later, Hamels, who said he had poison oak growing up in San Diego, pointed to the scars on the back of his legs. They were everywhere.

Hamels made four starts with the poison oak from June 25 to July 10. He went 2-1 with a 1.61 ERA.

"I think I was so focused because I didn't know how many pitches I could be out there for," he said. "It was like, this might be the last pitch because this hurts."

Hamels might have to think twice before fishing on Oswalt's reserve again. Or at least come better prepared the next time he does. Oswalt was already looking forward to taking Lee hunting in the off-season. The Mississippi boy thought he could teach him a few things.

"I'm going to show him how to hunt," Oswalt quipped. "He's an Arkansas boy. Hillbilly."

scored three or fewer runs in 35 of their first 62 games, which was no way to live. Clearly, they had to do something. But even if they could make the finances work, they essentially could only upgrade in right field because they were not going to make upgrades anywhere else. If they did upgrade in right, they would be looking for a right-handed bat to replace Jayson Werth.

"You will not see a major move this year," Ruben Amaro Jr. said. "I don't think we need it."

Right, Ruben, right.

Of course, it made no sense for Amaro to tip his hand or show panic less than two months from the July 31 trade deadline. A lot could change in that time. And he wasn't even sure what he needed most: a bat or an arm in the bullpen. The offense was struggling, but the bullpen was in a state of flux. The Phillies opened spring training with Brad Lidge, Ryan Madson, Jose Contreras, and J. C. Romero in the back of their bullpen. Lidge opened the season on the disabled list with an injured right shoulder and suffered a setback in early June when he felt soreness in his right elbow. Romero, who won two games in the 2008 World Series, had stopped throwing strikes and was designated for assignment on June 16. Contreras went to the DL for a second time on June 23 with an elbow injury, which would end his season. Madson went on the DL on June 28 with inflammation in his right hand. Left-hander Antonio Bastardo, who had made Romero expendable, and rookie right-hander Mike Stutes made more relief appearances than anybody else in June. Former Rule 5 Draft pick David Herndon was third.

Amaro could be patient. Halladay and Hamels were throwing splendidly, and after a couple bad starts the first couple months of the season, Lee was finding his groove. On June 11, Lee walked Chicago Cubs shortstop Starlin Castro with two outs in the third inning. Darwin Barney and Luis Montanez followed with back-to-back singles to score Castro to cut the Phillies lead to 2-1.

It would be the only run Lee would allow all month.

"Sometimes, you get locked in where things roll well," Lee said. "I hope I'm getting into that."

———————————— K ————————————

Lee was rising while Oswalt was falling. Oswalt sagged in his chair like he had just finished 12 rounds with Bernard Hopkins on June 17 in Seattle.

He labored through 6⅓ innings. He allowed eight hits, four runs, two walks, one home run, and struck out three. He had been trying to fool hitters, not bury them, for a month now. He had been trying to keep his back pain quiet. But now the numbers had started to betray him. He could no longer point to the sub-2.00 ERA. He was 1-5 with a 4.17 ERA in his last eight starts. He was drowning.

He had his right leg propped up as he stared into the back of the locker in front of him. Minutes had passed when he slowly got up and turned to face the handful of reporters that had gathered a few feet away. He made eye contact with them, his indication he was ready to talk. He said little. After answering the nuts-and-bolts questions about the start, a reporter asked him if he was having as much fun as last year.

"Yeah," he said flatly.

He wasn't. He hated this. He was tired of the pain. He stepped onto the mound every five days just trying to survive. He started to have anxiety just thinking about his next start. He started to fear he would finish his career on the disabled list, just like former Astros teammate Jeff Bagwell, who retired because of a chronically injured right shoulder. Oswalt didn't want to go out like that, but he wasn't sure how bad the back was going to get.

He finally succumbed to the pain on June 23, when he left his start against the St. Louis Cardinals at Busch Stadium after allowing five hits, four runs, and one home run in two innings. This time, Oswalt came clean. He couldn't tell everybody that everything was OK anymore. He was 1-4 with a 5.81 ERA in June.

"I feel it when I sit down, stand up, walk, pitch, sleep," he confessed.

He then acknowledged his worst fear. He might have thrown his last pitch in the big leagues.

"You throw as long as you can and when you can't throw anymore you don't," he said. "Hopefully it's not to the point where I can't throw anymore. If it's at that point, you just have to accept it."

The people who had wondered if Oswalt would finish the season had to be thinking more and more that he would not. He had an MRI scheduled in a few days, and believed it would determine his fate. He seemed prepared for bad news.

And if he got it, what would he think about his career?

"I've had a pretty good one," he said.

————————— K —————————

Pat Gillick had been in professional baseball for 54 years, so he had seen some of the best rotations in history. He also had one of the best eyes for talent in the business. He had been the general manager for the Toronto Blue Jays, leading them to World Series championships in 1992 and 1993; the Baltimore Orioles, taking them to the postseason twice; the Seattle Mariners, leading them to the postseason twice; and the Phillies, helping them win the World Series in 2008. Gillick's acumen earned him a spot in the National Baseball Hall of Fame in July 2011.

He knew what he was talking about. He looked at the rotation in Philadelphia and had every reason to believe it could survive without Oswalt and Joe Blanton.

"I think this one has a little more depth to it," he said.

The Phillies had four aces. The other great rotations had three or two or one. The Phillies could cushion the blow as long as Halladay, Lee, and Hamels kept throwing well. And as a bonus, they were getting good performances from Kyle Kendrick, who went 1-1 with a 3.00 ERA in three starts, before rookie Vance Worley took his place and finished the month 1-0 with a 1.00 ERA in three starts, including a one-run, seven-inning effort on June 29 in a 2-1 victory against the Boston Red Sox. Phillies Pitching Coach Rich Dubee liked what he had seen from Worley, who had shown he wasn't afraid to compete.

Halladay finished the month 3-0 with a 2.00 ERA. Hamels went 2-2 with a 1.31 ERA, while Lee finished 5-0 with a 0.21 ERA. The rotation had a 1.96 ERA in June, the first time a rotation finished a month with an ERA under 2.00 since July 1992, when both the Cubs (a 1.72 ERA with Greg Maddux, Mike Morgan, Mike Harkey, Shawn Boskie, and Frank Castillo) and Braves (a 1.92 ERA with John Smoltz, Tom Glavine, Charlie Liebrandt, Steve Avery, and Mike Bielecki) accomplished the feat.

But Lee's June rightfully received most of the attention. Since earned runs were first recorded, Elias Sports Bureau found only six other starting pitchers who went 5-0 with an ERA that low in a calendar month in base-ball history: Guy Bush in August 1926 (6-0, 0.19 ERA); Fernando Valenzuela in April 1981 (5-0, 0.20 ERA); Nolan Ryan in May 1984 (5-0, 0.20 ERA); Mike Witt in August 1986 (5-0, 0.21 ERA); Orel Hershiser in September 1988 (5-0, 0.00 ERA); and Cory Lidle in August 2002 (5-0, 0.20 ERA).

"I've had better stretches, I think, to be honest with you, but it's good,"

Lee said following his June 16 two-hit shutout against the Florida Marlins at Citizens Bank Park.

Coincidentally, the same night Lee dominated the Marlins, the Yankees and Rangers—who'd fallen short in the Lee sweepstakes—played each other a couple hours north in Yankee Stadium. Minor-league journeyman Brian Gordon pitched that night for the Yankees. He went 5-0 with a 1.14 ERA in 12 appearances for Triple-A Lehigh Valley before the Phillies released him to allow him to pursue a big-league job with the Yankees. It was his first appearance in the major leagues since 2008 and he was waived a week later.

"They got Cliff Lee, I got Brian Gordon," Yankees General Manager Brian Cashman quipped in New York. "I don't think they have anything to worry about."

Lee threw a six-hit shutout against the Cardinals at Busch Stadium on June 22, becoming the first Phillies pitcher to throw consecutive shutouts since Cory Lidle did it in 2004. Phillies fans had seen stretches like this before from Lee, and they loved watching this one. He went 5-0 with a 0.68 ERA in his first five starts with the Phillies in 2009, and 4-0 with a 1.56 ERA in five postseason starts in 2009. In between those special runs, he went 2-4 with a 6.13 ERA, pitching so poorly at times Phillies fans wondered if Lee or Hamels, who had his own struggles that season, should start Game 1 of the 2009 National League Division Series against the Colorado Rockies. But when Lee was on? Forget about it.

"When he's hot, he's smoking hot," Ruben Amaro Jr. said. "He's as good a pitcher as there has been in the history of the game when he's hot."

Lee throws darts at the strike zone, making hitters look foolish with his cutter, often waiting until the later innings before unleashing his curveball, giving hitters just one more thing to think about before stepping into the batter's box. He was fulfilling the Phillies' expectations, and suddenly October couldn't come fast enough. If Lee, Halladay, Hamels, and Oswalt were on, what team was going to beat the Phillies in a five-game or seven-game series?

Lee got fans into a postseason lather on June 28, when he faced the Boston Red Sox's Josh Beckett at Citizens Bank Park. In spring training, Amaro had called the Red Sox the best team in baseball. Boston entered the series with the second-best record in the American League at 45-32, just a half game behind the Yankees, while the Phillies had the best record in baseball at 49-30.

It was a World Series preview.

When it was finished, Lee had fans wishing it was Game 7. He allowed a single to Marco Scutaro in the sixth inning and a double to Darnell McDonald in the eighth inning, but they were the only hits he gave up in a 5-0 victory over the Red Sox, making him the first Phillies pitcher to throw three consecutive shutouts since Hall of Fame right-hander Robin Roberts had in 1950. The victory also maintained the team's 4½-game lead over the Braves.

"Oh man, he was great," Red Sox second baseman Dustin Pedroia said. "He pitched his butt off. That's why he's one of the best in the business. He attacks the zone. He's one of the best, man."

Lee finished the month allowing just one run in 42 innings, riding a 32-inning scoreless streak that tied him with Ken Heintzelman (1949) and Roberts (1950) for the third-longest scoreless streak in Phillies history behind Hall of Famer Grover Cleveland Alexander (41 innings in 1911) and Larry Andersen (32⅔ innings in relief in 1984).

True to his *whatever* personality, the Marlboro Man wasn't about to get too fired up about his work.

"I don't care," Lee said. "I play to win. Later when I'm done with my career I can look back and that's something I can be proud of. At this point, that's good, but it's not time to pat myself on the back. It's the middle of the season, and we've got a lot of work to do and a lot of games to play."

Lee had dominated a potential World Series opponent, but even that was met with a shrug.

"It's June," he said. "We're a long way from the playoffs. I expect us to do something really special. We expect to win the World Series, but we can't do that right now."

But it could not stop everybody else from dreaming about it.

JULY

July provided an illuminating portrait of Roy Halladay.

The ace of the aces positioned himself nicely for a run at a second-straight Cy Young Award by going 3-1 with a 2.57 ERA in five starts, four of them Phillies' wins. But the greatness that Halladay showed on the mound was hardly revealing. Phillies fans had come to expect months like this from him. The pitcher was almost robotic in his ability to turn out quality start after quality start. It was as if they came off an assembly line and he was the stoic, emotionless supervisor standing there, arms folded, overseeing everything, making sure it met his high standard.

But a funny thing happened to the robot in July.

He proved human.

He allowed his heartstrings to be pulled at in Toronto.

In Chicago, his eyes rolled back into his head and he nearly passed out.

And then there was that night two days before the trade deadline when the man who lives by the cliché of never getting too high or two low got so high that he almost seemed giddy.

"This is one of the big reasons I was adamant about coming here," a beaming Halladay said that night, when his World Series dream seemed so close he could touch it.

Halladay joined the Phils in December 2009 after more than a decade of second-division finishes in Toronto. While American League East rivals the Red Sox and the Yankees played meaningful games in late September, he often found himself packing the contents of his locker in boxes. And while the Sox and Yankees punched their tickets for October, Halladay bought a plane ticket home for the winter.

This is not to say he didn't enjoy his time in Toronto. He did. Very much so. He liked the city, his teammates, and the Blue Jays organization. The feelings were mutual. During spring training in 2011, Blue Jays Athletic Trainer George Poulis almost choked up when he talked about how much he missed Halladay—the man. People don't get these feelings when they believe someone is an ingrate. Halladay is definitely not that. Even as he angled for an exit from Toronto and a trade to a winner in 2009, he was careful not to disrespect the organization or the city that had embraced him for a decade. In fact, he took every opportunity he could to show his appreciation to the team and the city. He did not want to look like an ingrate. He did not want to one day return to Toronto and receive the J. D. Drew treatment.

On Friday July 1, Halladay learned he had succeeded in letting Toronto and the Blue Jays know they had a special place in his heart.

The Phillies, rocking a four-game lead in the NL East and the best record in the majors, opened a three-game series against the Blue Jays in Toronto that day. It was Halladay's first trip back to the city where he had won 148 games and the 2003 AL Cy Young Award, and though he had spent the previous few days telling reporters that it was just another trip, that enough time had passed, that he wouldn't feel any significant emotion, no one believed him.

Cincinnati would have been just another trip.

Not Toronto.

The Jays wanted to honor Halladay in some way before Friday's game. It seemed like the perfect time. It was Canada Day—marking the anniversary of that nation's independence—and the atmosphere at the sold-out Rogers Centre was festive. Though their hearts were in the right place, Jays officials knew they had no shot of honoring Halladay before the first game of the series. Halladay was scheduled to pitch the next day and they knew full well that he wraps himself in a steel cage of mental concentration the day before he pitches. There was no way they'd get him to participate in something like that, not 24 hours before a start.

The Jays came up with a plan. They asked the Phillies if Halladay would pinch-hit for Bench Coach Pete Mackanin and take the lineup card to home plate before the first game. A video highlighting the pitcher's time in Toronto would play on the scoreboard and Halladay would not even notice it. Deliver the lineup card. Tip of the hat. Quick. Painless. Get back into the steel cage. No one gets zapped.

Halladay agreed to do it.

The applause started the moment he came out of the visiting dugout and didn't stop until he had tipped his cap not once, but twice.

The Phillies overcame Jose Bautista's 25th homer in the seventh inning— "I was trying to be aggressive and I don't know why," lamented pitcher Kyle Kendrick, who went against the plan to give Bautista nothing good to hit— and pulled out a 7-6 win in the ninth inning on Canada Day.

The next day was a Halladay, too.

——————————— K ———————————

Pitching Coach Rich Dubee and a few others were sitting in the dugout when Chase Utley, often the first to arrive for batting practice, came up the stairs with a hop in his step and a playful look on his face. Even on good days, Utley is grumpy before a game, but on this day, before Halladay's start in Toronto, he was smiling and giving people the business.

"Another day off," he cracked as he walked by Dubee on his way to sign an autograph for a fan at the end of the dugout.

With 12 pitchers to keep track of, there are no days off for Dubee. But Dubee can afford to push the cruise-control button for a couple of hours on days that Halladay pitches. Dubee is an interesting guy. Fifty-four years old. A former Massachusetts schoolboy legend who pitched in the Kansas City Royals system. Son of a cop. Charlie Manuel turns all of the pitching responsibility over to Dubee, and that makes the crusty New Englander the go-to guy for reporters seeking information about the staff. Dubee always provides the information, but reporters occasionally have to jump through hoops to get it. Some days the hoop is coated in sandpaper, some days in barbed wire.

On this Halladay in Toronto, the hoop was coated in honey. Dubee smiled easily as he gave health updates on his staff, and the time was right for him to learn that his favorite fourth estate foil, *Daily News* beat writer Dave Murphy, had lost his passport. With no paper on Sunday or Monday (because of the July 4 holiday), Murphy had decided to drive to and from Toronto. He had hit the road for Philadelphia after Friday's game only to turn up at a Toronto restaurant later that night frantically looking for his passport.

Murphy somehow made it across the border without a passport the next afternoon, but Dubee had his ammo.

"Wait 'til I see that idiot," he said.

The pregame dugout levity continued when Blue Jays broadcaster Buck Martinez, the Jays former catcher and manager, stopped by to visit with Manuel.

"*Que pasa*, motherfucker?" Manuel said to Martinez.

They both laughed hysterically.

Manuel, a no-pretense country boy, is a native of the Shenandoah Valley. Martinez, a silver-haired and silver-tongued intellectual, hails from Northern California.

The two men first met each other in 1971 during winter ball in Puerto Rico. Manuel was playing for Mayaguez; Martinez was catching for Santurce.

Manuel strode to the plate one day and looked at the name on the back of Martinez' uniform.

"*Que pasa*, motherfucker?" he drawled.

Martinez looked up from his crouch.

"Uh, Charlie," he said. "I speak English."

The dugout comedy act was just a warm-up for the featured act that day—and there was no doubt what that was.

Halladay emerged from the dugout about a half hour before game time to begin his warm-up. He walked by a young fan holding a red foam No. 1 finger. It said PHILLIES on one side, but on the other, in handwritten white paint, were the words: Halladay 32 Forever. Halladay wore No. 32 with the Jays. In the outfield, a bedsheet sign read: Welcome Back, Doc, Please Be Gentle.

Becoming the best pitcher in baseball, as he is often called, wasn't an easy journey for Halladay. During spring training in 2001, after more than two seasons in the majors, Halladay was "getting his ass kicked," as Martinez, his former manager said, and was sent to the low minors to rebuild his confidence, delivery, and pitching style. It was a humbling demotion, but the key event that started Halladay's ascension to greatness. He went to Class A ball at the end of spring training in 2001 and didn't return to the majors until ... July 2 of that year.

So here was Halladay, back on the mound in Toronto, on the 10-year anniversary of his return to the majors.

It could not have been scripted better.

In the bottom of the first, Halladay took the mound to a long standing ovation from the crowd of 44,078. For a moment, it felt as if the Blue Jays were visitors in their own park. The ovation was so long and remarkable that one wondered if Halladay would come out of his steel cage and tip his cap, but by this point, he was so mentally locked into the game that he could not bust through the bars and do that.

Halladay pitched his sixth complete game of the season and earned his 11th win in a 5-3 victory that day, and the Jays truly were visitors in their own park. That, at least, was the message delivered by the *Toronto Sun* the next morning. "Atta boy, Doc" read the headline on the cover of the sports section.

It was such an amazing day that no one wanted to miss a single pitch. Witness Manuel in the fifth inning: he was dying to say more than *Que pasa?* to third-base umpire Brian O'Nora after Ryan Howard was rung up on a questionable checked swing with the bases loaded, but decided against it.

"When you go there it's an automatic ejection," Manuel said later. "I didn't want to have to come in here and sit by myself in the clubhouse. Not today, at least. I wanted to watch Halladay pitch."

When it was over, Halladay could finally tell himself the truth.

This was not just another game.

"I was definitely anxious warming up," he admitted. "Walking onto the field was definitely different. It was a cool experience for me. You always want to do as well as you can, and it meant a lot to me to do it here today."

Halladay said he'd never forget the ovations he received while delivering the lineup card Friday and taking the mound Saturday.

He actually thought about tipping his cap during Saturday's first-inning ovation, but had too much respect for his old team to do so.

"I obviously appreciated it," he said, "but I didn't want to go out there on someone else's home field and feel like I was the center of attention. I wanted to be as respectful as I could to their team and the Blue Jays organization. I didn't want to make a huge production."

It was a huge production. The whole day. And it took a toll on Halladay. He was supposed to dine with some old friends that night, but he had to cancel the plans. The often emotionless pitcher was emotionally spent.

———————— K ————————

Six days later, the Phillies returned home for their final series before the All-Star break, and it was as big as a series could be in July.

The Atlanta Braves, just 2½ games behind the Phillies in the standings, were in town for a three-game series. Like the Phillies, the Braves were a team built on pitching. Phillies starters entered the series with a 2.99 ERA, the best in the NL. Atlanta's staff was second with a 3.07 ERA. With a sweep, Atlanta could go into the break leading the NL East. Now, divisions are not won at the All-Star break, but the Phillies knew the importance, even if it was symbolic, of going into the break in first place. The standings freeze for three days and the Phillies wanted to make sure their division lead stood firm as the baseball world took a breather.

Dubee took advantage of an earlier off day and tinkered with his rotation to make sure Cole Hamels would pitch the final game before the break. That meant Atlanta had to face Halladay, Lee, and Hamels in the series. All three ranked in the top seven in league ERA. For Atlanta, it felt a little like

IT'S GOTTA BE THE SHOES!

The Phillies' clubhouse staff found itself in a mad scramble for shoes on July 29.

Not just any shoes. Red Reeboks. The Phillies are one of only two teams to wear red spikes. That makes finding them on short notice incredibly difficult, especially when a trade happens on a Friday night, like the one that brought Hunter Pence to Philadelphia from Houston.

So Frank Coppenbarger, the team's director of team travel and clubhouse services, and Phil Sheridan, the home clubhouse manager, got on the phone and started calling sporting goods stores in the area.

Uh, got any size 12½ red Reebok spikes for Hunter Pence?
Nothing.

In a storage room, the Phillies have plenty of extra Nike and Under Armour spikes because most players wear Nike, and Under Armour is the official footwear supplier of Major League Baseball. But Pence has an equipment deal with Reebok, so his spikes needed to be Reeboks. When the equipment guys struck out, Pence reluctantly wore a pair of red Nikes for his Phillies debut on July 30. The shoes were a half size too small, but Pence felt even more uncomfortable wearing a competing brand, so the next afternoon Phillies Assistant Athletic Trainer Mark Andersen spent 45 minutes spray painting his black Reeboks red.

Pence finally got his size 12½ red Reeboks on August 2 in Colorado.

The Phillies had gotten luckier in past equipment scrambles. In 2006, they acquired Jamie Moyer on August 20 and Jose Hernandez on August 22. Both wore Nike, and both wore the same size shoe. Moyer wore a pair of shoes for his August 22 start against the Cubs at Wrigley Field. The next day those shoes were in Hernandez's locker.

When Jeff Conine arrived on August 27, he became the third player in a week to wear those shoes until his shipment arrived from Nike.

The motto of a big-league equipment man: keep your ear to the ground and be prepared. In July 2009, the Phillies were leaving for a seven-game West Coast road trip. Coppenbarger knew there was a chance they could acquire Roy Halladay, so he had the pitcher's name stitched on a uniform top and hid it at the bottom of an equipment truck.

A year earlier, Coppenbarger and his staff heard rumors the Phils might be in the hunt for Manny Ramirez, whom Boston had put on the trading block. Coppenbarger had Sheridan call Majestic, the league's official uniform supplier, and discreetly order a pair of the baggy pants that Ramirez liked.

"We knew those weren't off-the-rack pants," Coppenbarger said. "Majestic made us a pair with no name in them and we tucked them away just in case."

facing Greg Maddux, Tom Glavine, and John Smoltz.

"Yeah, it does," Braves third baseman Chipper Jones, a holdover from the team's glory days, said with a big, almost wistful grin.

"We were the hunted for a very long time, so I guess it's only right that we, as the Atlanta Braves, spend some of our time being hunters.

"It's tough coming in and getting three of the best pitchers in the National League in one series. We've beaten all of them at one point, but seeing them all in one series is tough. But if you want to be the best, you have to beat the best."

According to Jones, the comparison of the Phillies' Big Three to the Braves' Holy Trinity was legit.

"When those guys walked on the field, we were expected to win," Jones said. "The Phillies have that swagger now."

Does that swagger come from The Rotation?

"Yes," Jones said without hesitation. "People used to ask me who the leader, who the MVP of our club was, and my answer was whoever was on the mound that night. Whoever we sent to the mound that night, we knew we had a good chance to win, and I'm sure the Phillies feel the same way. Their mind-set is they're going to go nine and beat you. As an offensive player that gives you a lot of confidence, knowing it might only take one at-bat or one swing to win a game. That's a big confidence boost for a team."

It took only one swing for the Phillies to win the first game of the series. Raul Ibanez homered in the bottom of the 10th inning off reliever Scott Proctor to give the Phils a dramatic 3-2 victory just as the midnight moon was cresting over Philadelphia. The game, which was delayed nearly two hours at the start by rain, was one of the most entertaining of the season.

Halladay warmed up in the rain, changed into a dry uniform, and proceeded to pitch seven innings of two-run ball as the skies cleared. Young relievers Mike Stutes and Antonio Bastardo each pitched a scoreless inning, and the game went to the 10th inning. Manager Charlie Manuel, his bullpen weak with Jose Contreras and Ryan Madson on the disabled list, gave the ball to 32-year-old minor-league journeyman Juan Perez, who had been called up days earlier from Triple-A. Perez treated the sellout crowd to a rarity: he struck out the side in the 10th inning on nine pitches, becoming the first Phillie to do that in 20 years. Ibanez' homer gave Perez his first big-league win.

That Ibanez' homer came off Proctor, a right-hander, was not insignificant. The Braves entered the series with the best bullpen in the majors, and Phils management—from Manuel to the front office—was very concerned with that unit, particularly the Braves' three lefties, George Sherrill, Eric O'Fla-herty, and Jonny Venters. But all three had appeared in the game by the time Ibanez batted in the 10th. He got a fastball from Proctor and did not miss it.

In the 2009 World Series and again in the 2010 NLCS, the Phillies had been susceptible to left-handed pitching. This is why everyone from front office adviser Pat Gillick—still the most trusted voice in the organization nearly three years after stepping down as general manager—to Manuel had voiced the opinion that the team needed a right-handed bat if it was going to have the season it dreamed of.

"I don't want someone we've already got," said Manuel, putting a little pressure on the front office. "I want a good hitter."

It was right about this time that Houston Astros General Manager Ed Wade sent a memo to every team in the majors. The Astros were in the process of being sold and Wade was under orders to cut payroll. He let it be known that any player on his roster could be had for the right price.

In April, the Phillies had played the Astros and Manuel had kiddingly told Houston Third-Base Coach Dave Clark that he was going to get Hunter Pence from the Astros. Pence was a right-handed hitter capable of hitting in the middle of the order. He also played right field, the only real question-mark area in the Phillies' lineup. Now, on the cusp of the All-Star break, he was available.

Manuel wasn't the only person in the organization that wanted to upgrade the lineup for a big October run. Up on the executive level of Citizens Bank Park, GM Ruben Amaro Jr. was all for it and he initiated dis-cussions with Wade. Down in the clubhouse, Halladay shared his bosses' desire to make the Phillies better and stronger before the July 31 trade dead-line. In Toronto, he'd always found it frustrating when the Red Sox and Yankees made July deals and the Jays sat on the sidelines. He was eager to see the Phillies mix it up, as they had a year earlier when they acquired Roy Oswalt at the deadline.

"We have the players here to win," Halladay said. "But any time you can get better, you take it. Knowing that I'm only here for a certain amount of years, yeah, I'd sell the farm."

As Amaro went to work trying to get the hitter his team needed, the Phillies took two of three from the Braves and headed into the All-Star break with a 3½-game lead in the division. They won the final game, 14-1, with Hamels on the mound.

Who needs another hitter, anyway?

──────────── K ────────────

After Hamels' 11th win, most of the Phillies headed off for three and a half days of R & R, while three-fifths of The Rotation headed to Phoenix for the All-Star Game. Hamels received a $50,000 bonus for being selected to the team and used a chunk of it to charter a private jet so he, Halladay, Lee, and Shane Victorino, and some of their family members, could fly to Phoenix together.

Halladay is seven years older than Hamels and his ship has come in, as they say. When Halladay heard Hamels was footing the bill for the flight he told Hamels to hang on to his wallet, that he'd write the check. Hamels wouldn't hear of it. They were two friends tugging on a dinner check and Hamels was not letting go.

Kid Cole had become a man.

A few days later, as he got set to board a crowded commercial flight back to the East Coast, former Phillie John Kruk, the ESPN baseball analyst, heard about how Hamels had flown his boys to Phoenix in comfort.

Having played for the 1993 NL champion Phillies, a team that thrived on togetherness, Kruk knows a thing or two about team chemistry. He was impressed by Hamels' generosity.

"That's why they win," Kruk said. "They all like each other."

There was some debate about which pitcher NL Manager Bruce Bochy would name as starter. Would he go with Atlanta's Jair Jurrjens, the league's ERA leader at the time, or someone like Halladay, who was ranked fourth in ERA and had put together a tremendous body of work the previous season with a perfect game, a playoff no-hitter, and a Cy Young Award?

Bochy went with Halladay, and in introducing the Phillies ace at a packed news conference the day before the game in Phoenix, committed an interesting Freudian slip that Phillies fans hoped would prove prescient.

"I couldn't have a better guy start the World Se . . ." Bochy began before catching himself, ". . . All-Star Game for us. When you talk about the best, this guy is always on top."

Lee endorsed Bochy's choice.

"Roy's the perfect physical specimen to be a starting pitcher," Lee said. "His work ethic, his mind-set. He equips himself to be the best. He's the best pitcher in baseball. If I were to pick a starting pitcher to win one game, he's the one I'd pick. He's deserving of it. I expect to see him put up a couple of zeroes."

Halladay did just that, throwing two shutout innings before turning the ball over to his teammate. Lee pitched 1⅔ innings and allowed a home run to Adrian Gonzalez, who was putting up an MVP-type season with Boston. The NL overcame that home run and won the game, 5-1, on the strength of Prince Fielder's three-run home run and a defensive gem by a guy named Pence, who—wearing a Houston Astros uniform—cut down a potential run at the plate with a laser throw from left field. The National League had secured homefield advantage in the World Series.

There was some hubbub about Bochy, the San Francisco manager, not using three of his Giants starting pitchers—Tim Lincecum, Matt Cain, and Ryan Vogelsong—in the game while sending Halladay and Lee to the mound for more than an inning apiece. Conspiracy theorists saw Bochy trying to weaken an opponent for the second half. In the end, Bochy's use of the Phillies pitchers wasn't much ado about nothing, but it was much ado about very little. Halladay and Lee did not pitch in the first series after the All-Star break, but Dubee was considering giving both guys extra rest anyway.

Protective of his golden arms, Dubee was mildly perturbed that Halladay and Lee were used for more than an inning, but even he acknowledged that winning the game could have enormous benefit to the Phillies in a few months. The issue surrounding Bochy's use of Halladay and Lee raged for a few days, and briefly when the Giants came to Philadelphia from July 26 to July 28 and Halladay and Lee's turns in the rotation conveniently did not come up. But in the end, this was a non-issue to the men who mattered most. Halladay threw 19 pitches. That's barely a trot for a horse like him. Lee threw 25 and said he wouldn't have minded going out for a third inning.

Case closed.

This was not Halladay's first All-Star start. He got the call for the American League in 2009, but didn't fully enjoy the experience because the Blue Jays, at Halladay's urging, had hung a For Sale sign on him days earlier and rumors of his being on the move flew everywhere.

In Phoenix, Doc had a blast. The man who saves his smiles for special occasions wore one on his face for three days.

"It's fun to be able to come in and talk about good stuff and enjoy it and not talk about uncertain futures," he said. "It's been a great experience coming here with these guys."

He was referring to Hamels and Lee, his brothers on the pitching staff.

Meanwhile, on the rehab trail, Roy Oswalt's bad back was responding well to treatment.

It wouldn't be long before The Rotation was once again fully locked and loaded.

———————— K ————————

Players returned from the All-Star break late Thursday afternoon on July 14 and boarded buses for New York. Though the mathematical midpoint of the season had passed, the first game after the All-Star break is considered in baseball circles to be the start of the second half. The Phils boarded those buses with the best record in the game and optimism for a big stretch drive was high. Not only had the Phils been a great second-half team under Charlie Manuel, but the front office had always made moves to infuse the team with a talent boost for the final months. While the team headed to New York to open a series against the Mets on Friday night, General Manager Ruben Amaro Jr. peeked in on his organization's minor-league talent in Clearwater. Amaro, who was hunting for a bat and bullpen help, spent his time in Florida classifying prospects as touchable or untouchable. His willingness to deal young talent for proven big-league help was popular in the clubhouse and with Phillies fans, who, in addition to racking up sell-outs at Citizens Bank Park, had pushed television ratings for Phillies' games on Comcast SportsNet up 22 percent from the previous All-Star break.

World Series lust was at an all-time high, and the first game back from the break couldn't have gone better. Rotation pledge Vance Worley won his fifth game, John Mayberry Jr. drove in five runs, and Ryan Madson came off the disabled list in a 7-2 win over the Mets.

Hamels couldn't keep the winning going the next day. He left too many pitches over the heart of the plate, was hurt by shoddy defense, and took an 11-2 loss. Every pitcher has a nemesis and the Mets are Hamels'. The loss was his 10th in 16 career starts against the Mets.

"When you play a team so often, that's bound to happen," he said.

The game got so out of hand that the beer-fueled bachelor party in the seats in front of the press box was actually more entertaining. Well, it was until one of the revelers took off his shirt in the late innings and displayed a hideous set of man boobs. One of the partiers waved a dollar bill at the shirt-less man and the whole section cackled in laughter.

Mets fans.

The Phillies bounced back the next day and won the series, their seventh straight, behind underappreciated rotation helper Kyle Kendrick. Now it was on to Chicago.

The Phillies arrived in Chicago as a brutal heat wave gripped the middle of the country. That didn't stop throngs of Phillies fans from traveling to Chicago. In the late 1990s, Phillies fans barely showed up at Broad and Pattison. Now, they go everywhere, and spend big coin to do it. They take over stadiums from Pittsburgh to San Diego. They travel like, well, Eagles fans. There is no better place to swig beer and watch baseball than cozy Wrigley Field. Phillies fans took over Wrigleyville pubs and packed the El as they rode the Red Line back and forth to their downtown Chicago hotels.

Six days after his All-Star appearance, a rested Halladay was set to make his first start of the second half against the Cubs. Phillies fans had come to Wrigley to hail their Doc. Little did they know he'd soon be needing one.

It was 91 degrees for the 7 P.M. game and oppressive humidity pushed the heat index over 100. Halladay took the mound wearing a red-sleeved undershirt, as he usually does. From the beginning, he looked uncomfortable. He did not look like himself. It wasn't so much the first-inning home run he gave up to Aramis Ramirez—that happens, especially in Wrigley—it was more the mannerisms and look on Halladay's face that said something was not right. His face was redder than usual. He frequently stretched his arms high above his head, as if trying to peel the sweat-soaked undershirt from his torso. Halladay got through the first couple of innings, but then began to wilt in the heat while working through an arduous 31-pitch third inning. Twice he hunched over his knees, like Bobby Clarke waiting for a faceoff, and took deep breaths as he strained to fill his lungs with air and cool his overheating body.

Chase Utley is one of Halladay's favorite teammates. They both have serious personalities and an intense, get-in-my-way-and-I'll-kill-you approach to the game. From his post at second base, Utley could tell that his baseball brother was having problems in the heat. Utley tried to buy some time for Halladay. He whistled for the umpire, asked for time out and bent down to tie his shoes, which really didn't need tying at all. Halladay appreciated the gesture and went into a catcher's crouch while Utley methodically untied his shoes and tied them again.

Halladay removed his undershirt after the inning and team athletic trainers tried to cool his body with frozen towels.

Dubee asked Halladay if he wanted to come out.

Halladay was emphatic. He wanted to stay in.

HIT (AHEM) KINGS

Cliff Lee had a lot of reasons for wanting to come back to Philadelphia. He liked the Phillies' chance of winning, he loved the energy in Citizens Bank Park—where "fans don't need a teleprompter to tell them to get up and cheer"—his family liked the city, and $120 million was nothing to sniff at, even if the Yankees had offered more.

Getting to swing the bat again in the National League also didn't hurt.

"I prefer the National League style over the American League style," Lee said. "I like to hit."

All the Phillies starting pitchers like to hit. They work at it in batting practice because they know handling the bat well can help them win a ball game.

Competitive beasts that they are, the Phillies starters staged a season-long competition to see which one of them helped the team the most with his bat. Bench coach Pete Mackanin was the judge and scorekeeper. He devised a points system in which a pitcher was rewarded for a successful bunt, a hit, an RBI, a walk, a line-drive out, a home run, and a quality at-bat of five or more pitches. Mackanin had the authority to award or deduct points at his discretion. You don't think these guys like to compete? Lee once successfully lobbied Mackanin for a half point for advancing a runner.

"It was fun," Lee said. "More reason to take an at-bat seriously."

Joe Blanton and Roy Oswalt fell out of the competition because of injury. In the end, Hamels won with 49 points. Lee had 45, and Halladay 40.

Halladay led the team with 16 sacrifice bunts, which tied him for fourth in the majors. Lee hit .200 (15 for 75) with two home runs and seven RBIs. Hamels hit .159 (11 for 69) with three RBIs, but was deemed to have had better at-bats throughout the season.

"Cliff wasn't happy with the results," Mackanin joked after the season. "We might have to adjust the scoring system."

No one would say what Hamels' prize was, but it's safe to say a group of competitive millionaires weren't playing for a cheesesteak.

He got through the fourth inning and came out for the fifth. He threw one pitch and seemed to have no idea where it was going. Clearly hurting, he backed off the mound and took a deep breath as his eyes briefly seemed to roll into the back of his head. Halladay signaled for catcher Carlos Ruiz to come to the mound and Dubee and athletic trainer Scott Sheridan followed. The bulletproof pitcher could not go on.

"He was lightheaded," Dubee said. "He was having a tough time focusing and seeing the signs."

Halladay was treated by two doctors in the clubhouse. He was diagnosed with heat exhaustion and dehydration. The next day he was back at the ballpark, looking as if nothing ever happened.

"I thought I could get through it, but that last inning I felt like I was about to get wheeled off the mound," he said.

A number of factors played a role in Halladay's overheating that night. Obviously, there was the temperature and humidity. Jimmy Rollins likened it to "one of those old days at the Vet when you'd stick a thermometer in the turf." The venue didn't help. Wrigley Field is 97 years old and lacks the amenities of modern parks. The clubhouse is small and narrow, like a truck trailer, and the cramped dugouts turn into brick pizza ovens on hot days. Halladay couldn't even seek relief in the tunnel behind the dugout because an exhaust vent from a nearby clothes dryer was pumping out hot air.

"Between innings I couldn't get away from the heat," he said. "I couldn't escape it. It got to the point where I kept getting hotter and hotter and I couldn't stop it."

The incident was so scary that the next day Cubs officials opened an air-conditioned room behind the dugout for pitchers to use as a retreat between innings. Vance Worley benefited from it two days after Halladay could have used it. Rollins even sneaked in there as the temperature rose to 97 in the series finale. Halladay, fully recovered, was able to throw a bullpen session before that matinee game. Except for a tour group winding its way through the stands, the old ballpark was empty as Halladay did his work that morning. As Halladay made his way back to the clubhouse after his bullpen session, a young boy sneaked away from the tour group and shouted to the pitcher as he was about to disappear down the dugout steps. Halladay turned, waited for the boy, and signed his baseball. The boy ran back to the tour group with a lifelong memory in his hand.

The visit to Chicago was memorable for other reasons for Halladay and members of the Phillies traveling party. It was downright scary watching him melt on that pitchers mound.

Several days after the incident, it was revealed that Halladay had battled a stomach virus the night before the start. He did not admit that when he spoke about the incident with reporters because, like Utley, he is loath to talk about health issues that can be interpreted as excuses.

Halladay is a man who prides himself on pitching deep into games, finishing what he starts. For years, big, tough major-league managers have felt heat from his glare when they dare to take him out of the game too early. Halladay tried to stare down Mother Nature on that searing night in Chicago, but she got the win. She pulled back the mask and revealed that there was a human being behind that robot. And if you didn't think Halladay was a little humbled by it all, check this out: he actually initiated some small talk with a couple of reporters the next day. It must have been cooler in Hell than it was in Chicago.

———————————— K ————————————

Charlie Manuel walked up the dugout steps and into the Friday afternoon furnace that was Citizens Bank Park on July 22.

"It's hotter than a two-peckered billy goat," said Manuel, who has a one-liner for all meteorological conditions.

The Phils were about to play the San Diego Padres in the first game of a 10-game home stand that featured a couple of huge subplots—the approaching non-waiver trade deadline and a three-game series with the San Francisco Giants, who hadn't visited Philadelphia since they danced on the Citizens Bank Park lawn after beating the Phils in the 2010 National League Championship Series.

July 2011 would prove to be the hottest month ever in Philadelphia. Temperatures were in the high 90s all weekend and the humidity was stifling, but that didn't stop the Phils from taking three of four from the Padres. Cole Hamels bounced back from his worst start of the season the previous weekend in New York and struck out 10 in a 3-1 victory on Friday night.

"Baseball is a game of failure," he said afterward. "It's how you get over it that determines how you succeed."

Six days after his personal Chicago fire, Halladay stared down the Philadelphia heat and struck out eight Padres over eight innings in a 5-3 win, his 12th of the season.

Hamels and Halladay walked a total of two batters in 16 innings in their starts.

San Diego Manager Bud Black was impressed with Hamels.

"I've seen him develop into a pitcher who can do a lot of things," Black said. "His movement on his fastball and on his changeup, and the command of his pitches has really improved. He's showing that being an All-Star is warranted.

"That entire staff throws strikes so you've got to be ready. But the first pitch might not be a fastball the way they all locate."

On Tuesday night, the Giants came to town and became the latest team incapable of solving the rookie Worley, who pitched the first complete game of his career in a 7-2 win.

The 2011 Phillies had never felt better about themselves. Not only had they just beaten the team that shattered their postseason dream the year before, but the offense had finally come alive. The Phils quietly led the NL in runs per game in July, and the pitchers were no longer fretting about run support and trying to hide their frustration when they didn't get any.

None of this stopped the front office from continuing to pursue a hitter. In pro sports, a management team must stare a hole through the good times and continually evaluate a club with cold and clinical eyes. Even as the Phillies' lineup was heating up, Manuel, Amaro, and other team officials could see that the club still needed another bat. And if they needed a reminder of why, it was right in the other dugout, where the Giants had the type of explosive starting pitching staff that could eviscerate a lineup and enough good left-handed relievers to do a job on the Phillies' lefty-heavy batting order.

Amaro investigated the Mets' Carlos Beltran, the White Sox' Carlos Quentin, and Michael Cuddyer and Delmon Young of the Twins, but his top trade target throughout July was Pence. He was in hot pursuit of the lanky Texan even before Giants starters Matt Cain and Tim Lincecum beat the Phillies on July 27 and July 28 in Philadelphia. The losses marked the first time the Phillies had lost back-to-back games since June 3 and June 4. Manuel created a little controversy after the second loss when he said the Giants pitching staff was good but not great. In damage control days later, Manuel said he meant no disrespect to the Giants and Lincecum, the two-time Cy Young Award winner whose slim build and long hair make him look like *The Wizard of Oz* Scarecrow in a baseball uniform. Manuel said his point was it takes years of excellence, not just a few, to be considered great.

Some folks theorized that Manuel was playing head games on the Giants.

There's no doubt that Big Chuck has some fox in him, but his commentary on the Giants' pitchers probably wasn't that calculated. Manuel's analysis probably had more to do with the Phillies hitters than the Giants pitchers. Manuel, you see, is a hitting junkie. He loves to talk about it and study it. He once said he keeps a copy of Ted Williams' book, *The Science of Hitting*, in his bathroom and unashamedly admitted to reading it a thousand times on trips to the john. He made his bones in the majors as a hitting coach for the powerful Cleveland Indians teams of the 1990s. The hitting junkie can't stand it when his team doesn't give him his fix. He takes it personally and doesn't hesitate to vent his frustration. And that's what happened those back-to-back nights against the Giants. The Phillies scored just two runs in those games and both were unearned. Remember Manuel saying, "I want a good hitter," earlier in the month? He was still thinking it—and so was Amaro.

Christmas morning arrived the next day for Phillies fans. It was July 29. On this day in 2009, Amaro landed Cliff Lee in a trade with Cleveland. On the same day in 2010, he traded for Roy Oswalt. Anticipation of another shiny package under the tree reached a feverish high as the Phillies got set to open a three-game series with the Pittsburgh Pirates. As Halladay threw the first pitch that night, there was a strong feeling around the ballpark that the deal was going to come down that night. In the executive offices, Amaro and Assistant GM Scott Proefrock briefed Club President David Montgomery as the deal moved to trigger-pull stage. The Phils' baseball people were ready to send top hitting prospect Jonathan Singleton and top pitching prospect Jarred Cosart, and two other minor-league prospects, to Houston for Pence. It was a steep price. Singleton, just 19, was considered one of the best hitting prospects in the game. "Don't trade Jonathan Singleton," a rival scout said back in March, after a couple of weeks of scouting the Phils' system in spring training. In Cosart, the Phils gave up a 21-year-old with fire in his right arm. "The best arm I've seen in a long time," former Phils pitcher Dickie Noles said in the spring of 2010.

Giving up Singleton and Cosart was enough to make the Phils wince, but they weren't about to let two unproven players from Class A ball hold up a deal that was going to help ensure that this season reached the destination that had been charted back in December, when ownership stretched the pay-roll to sign Lee. The Phils had something special brewing—the best record in the majors, multiple Cy Young candidates, and enough electricity in the stands to light up Center City. They had to make this deal. It was part of their World Series-or-bust mandate.

In the middle innings of that Christmas night game against the Pirates,

Greg Casterioto, the team's director of baseball communications, quietly slipped away from his seat in the press box and did not immediately return. Veteran press-box dwellers knew this was a sign. Casterioto had headed off to his office to write the press release that was about to turn Roy Halladay into a giddy kid on Christmas morning. Hunter Pence was a Phillie.

"We always try to address our needs," Amaro said in a news conference after the game. "We feel this was the missing piece."

Halladay, who racked up his 13th win that night, was elated by the deal. At the All-Star Game two weeks earlier, he and Pence had chatted about Philadelphia.

"He asked me about it and I said for me it's everything I thought it would be," Halladay said. "I told him how much I enjoyed it here. I didn't think at the time it was a sales pitch, but I guess I did a pretty good job if it was."

After years of seeing other teams make late-season improvements while in Toronto, Halladay was ecstatic to be on a team that was willing to sacrifice to win.

"We're a better team," he said. "I'm sure the guys they gave up have a chance to be great major-league players, but that's why guys want to be here, because of the sacrifices the organization is willing to make. I know as a player it's greatly appreciated.

"It's a good feeling to know that even when you're five or six games up, management is still trying to make you a better team. New York and Boston did it. That's one of the big reasons I was adamant about coming here."

Pence hightailed it from the worst team in the majors to the best and was in the lineup in borrowed red spikes the next night. Delirious fans showered him with affection and he loved them back with thumbs-up signs and other gestures of thanks. His 6-5 body could not contain the excitement of being in first place and playing in front of the most electric crowd in baseball. Pence is all arms and legs, and he never stops running. His blue eyes, as big as baseballs, are filled with boyish enthusiasm. He makes Shane Victorino, the hyperactive center fielder, look sleepy.

"Now *he's* high-energy," Victorino said after he heard about the trade. "I'm not the biggest spaz around here anymore."

Pence made an immediate impact. He drove in a run in his first game and started a game-winning rally in the 10th the next day, July 31. It was the final day of the month and the Phils were about to depart on a rugged 10-game West Coast trip. The last thing they wanted was to play extra innings, but that's where the Pirates had taken them.

"Let's get this over with," Victorino shouted in the dugout before the Phils' batted in the bottom of the 10th. "I'm hungry."

Pence, who had begun his day by getting coffee in Center City with teammate/welcoming-committee leader Chase Utley, was hungry, too. Following Victorino's orders, he doubled with one out in the 10th. Raul Ibanez followed with a game-winning double, capping a four-RBI day. As Pence charged across home plate with a huge smile on his face, the Phillies' dugout emptied, the sellout crowd went nuts, and a new team motto was born.

"Good game, let's go eat!" Pence told broadcaster Sarge Matthews in an on-field interview moments after the dramatic win.

It was good to be a Phillie and everyone from Hunter Pence to Roy Halladay knew that. The team headed to the airport 29 games over .500, and the wins kept coming on an eventful West Coast trip.

AUGUST

The month of fun started with a 92-mph fastball into the small of Shane Victorino's back.

Sometimes the good times hurt a little bit.

The Phillies opened August with a 10-game road trip through the National League West against Colorado, San Francisco, and Los Angeles. They swept the Rockies at Coors Field, including a dramatic 4-3 victory on August 1, when John Mayberry Jr. hit a game-tying home run on a 3-2 slider from Rockies closer Huston Street with two outs in the ninth and Victorino hit a game-winning homer in the 10th.

Nothing beats a thrilling late-inning victory.

Well, except maybe a bench-clearing brawl.

The Phillies and Giants had developed a nice little rivalry since the Giants upset them in the 2010 National League Championship Series. The Phillies entered the NLCS as favorites, but the Giants silenced their bats, which had been the concern before Game 1. The Phillies hit just .216 overall and just .178 with runners in scoring position against the likes of Tim Lincecum, Matt Cain, and a strong Giants bullpen. A clutch hit or two and the Phillies possibly win the series. Instead, Giants closer Brian Wilson struck out Ryan Howard looking in the bottom of the ninth inning in Game 6 at Citizens Bank Park, and the Giants celebrated a trip to the World Series in front of 46,000 Phillies fans.

The Giants returned to Philadelphia in July and took two of three from the Phillies to keep the rivalry simmering. Charlie Manuel added a little fuel to the fire when he told reporters afterward that Lincecum and Cain are "good, not great" pitchers. Good, great, mediocre, whatever. They still kept kicking the Phillies' ass. The Phillies simply couldn't beat the Giants, who seemed to be a sure-bet to get back to the postseason to defend their title.

That could mean trouble and the Phillies knew it. But for now, they had a four-game regular-season series against the Giants on their minds.

And what a series it was.

The Phils won the first game of the series, 3-0, at AT&T Park on August

4, when Cliff Lee threw his fifth shutout of the season. They were cruising to a 9-2 victory the next night when Victorino stepped into the batter's box with two on and two out in the top of the sixth. Giants pitcher Ramon Ramirez threw a first-pitch fastball into Victorino's back. Everybody in the ballpark knew he intentionally threw at Victorino, including home plate umpire Mike Muchlinski. He hopped up from his crouch and quickly issued Ramirez a warning. But Victorino couldn't care less about warnings. He was pissed. He flipped his bat and took a couple steps toward the mound. Muchlinski stepped in front of him, trying to block his path to the pitcher. Ramirez dropped his glove and stepped toward Victorino, letting him know he was ready to go if he wanted to take a run at him. Giants catcher Eli Whiteside started hopping up and down in front of home plate. Not since Johnny Lawrence in *The Karate Kid* had somebody looked like a bigger tool before a fight. He was begging for somebody to make a move. He noticed Placido Polanco running in from first base, dropped his mitt, and tackled Polanco at the knees.

Everything went to hell from there.

The dugouts and bullpens cleared. Brian Schneider tried to pull Polanco away from Whiteside, but fell to the bottom of the pile. The players at the bottom started beating the hell out of one another, punching and kicking and doing whatever they could under the cover of their teammates who were pushing and shoving above. Muchlinski tried to keep Victorino away from the action, but he kept moving closer and closer. He finally pushed Muchlinski out of the way only to have Greg Gross pull him back out. Victorino's eyes were the size of saucers. He kept watching the pile, looking for a reason to dive back in.

Whoa, does Pablo Sandoval have Chooch in a choke hold?

Victorino escaped Gross' grasp, sprinted back into the pile, and tackled Giants Hitting Coach Hensley Muelens on his way to save his catcher.

"I felt bad for Carlos," Victorino said.

Eventually, the pushing and shoving stopped, Victorino, Whiteside, and Ramirez were ejected, the game continued and the Phillies won handily.

The Phillies hadn't had a good bench-clearing brawl like that since April 22, 2004, when they battled with the Florida Marlins at Citizens Bank Park. Brett Myers gave up a solo home run to Mike Redmond with one out in the second inning. His next pitch came up and in to Alex Gonzalez, who took exception to it. He pointed and yelled at Myers. Phillies catcher Todd Pratt jumped up to protect his pitcher, benches cleared and fists started flying. Marlins pitcher Carl Pavano had Phillies third baseman David Bell in a chokehold before Mike Lowell threw Bell to the ground.

It was a pretty good fight. But, truth be told, the best punch that afternoon actually happened before the game when Phillies reliever Tim Worrell slugged Pitching Coach Joe Kerrigan in Manager Larry Bowa's office. Phillies pitchers didn't like Kerrigan. He knew pitching, but pitchers didn't like the way he communicated. He condescended. He would overhaul a pitcher's mechanics the first time he saw him. He would print out stat packs and place them in his pitcher's lockers. He wanted his pitchers to pitch to the stats, not how they felt the most comfortable pitching. Any pitcher or pitching coach will talk about the importance of confidence on the mound, the conviction to throw a particular pitch in a particular situation. Kerrigan ignored those feelings—*pitch to the stats*—and many of his pitchers hated him for it.

Kerrigan generally called the game from the dugout with the catcher getting the sign from him before every pitch. Worrell had enough of that. He told catcher Mike Lieberthal not to look into the dugout for Kerrigan's signs under any circumstances. So Lieberthal didn't, and Worrell blew a save in an 8-7 loss in 12 innings to the Marlins on April 21. The next day Bowa and Kerrigan called Worrell and Lieberthal into Bowa's office. The players were sitting as Kerrigan stood over them, berating them, telling them how to do their jobs, telling them he knew best.

Worrell got tired of what he heard, stood up, and did what most pitchers in the clubhouse had wanted to do: he popped Kerrigan. The blow hit Kerrigan's glasses, cutting him. Phillies coaches Gary Varsho and Mick Billmeyer sprinted into the office to help break up the one-sided fight. Kerrigan and Worrell left Bowa's office through a rear exit, so they wouldn't be detected by reporters.

The Phillies enjoyed their fight against the Giants as much as Worrell enjoyed his against Kerrigan. While the Giants barely said a word about the brawl in their clubhouse—other than suggesting that Jimmy Rollins' stolen base in the top of the sixth inning with a six-run lead could have prompted Ramirez to throw at Victorino—the Phillies happily recalled the action, often laughing and joking about it.

"Vic almost has to go, unless he wants his teammates to call him chicken," Charlie Manuel said.

"I had no intentions of charging the mound and escalating the fight for no reason," Victorino said. "It was the heat of the moment, and I just wanted to step forward and be like, 'What was the purpose? Obviously, Eli, I guess from looking at his reaction, thought I was going to and he started jumping around. Obviously, Polanco came in and he tackled Polanco."

Polanco heard Victorino's words behind a circle of reporters.

THE PRYIN' HAWAIIAN

Shane Victorino found himself with nothing to do at Citizens Bank Park on August 18 when he served the first game of his two-game suspension for his role in the brawl in San Francisco. The frenetic Victorino and oodles of free time? That could be trouble.

Before the game, pop singer Ke$ha visited the clubhouse, and Victorino made sure she was aware of his presence.

"Tik, tok, tik, tok, tik, tok!" Victorino screamed in her direction, referring to her hit song, "Tik Tok."

She looked down the corridor to see who was yelling at her.

"My name is Ryan Madson!" he said laughing.

"No, it isn't," Madson said. "That was Shane Victorino making all those noises."

Suspended players cannot watch the game from the dugout, so Victorino watched the Phillies' 4-1 victory over Arizona from a suite. But he got bored during a two-hour, 17-minute rain delay and made his way into the radio broadcast booth, where he hopped on the air with Scott Franzke and Larry Andersen. After getting bored of being on the air, he made his way into the press club, where he sat in the dining room and chatted for awhile. Then he made his way into the press box to slum it with reporters. He started to ask about the official scorer, who on this night was Jay Dunn.

"Are you the official scorer?" he said.

Dunn looked startled. Why in the hell was Victorino standing behind him?

"I've got to be extra nice to you, so you can turn some of those errors into hits when I'm batting," Victorino said cackling.

He turned around, noticed broadcaster Gary Matthews, and started giving him a hard time.

"The game looks real easy from up here, huh?" he said. "You forget what it's like to strike out."

The press box windows were closed because of the rain, but Victorino noticed fans walking in front. So like an orangutan at the zoo, Victorino started pounding on the glass to get their attention. He started to wave and fans started to realize the Flyin' Hawaiian was in the press box, in street clothes, *waving at them.*

A crowd started to gather.

"OK, let's get him out of there," said Anthony Morrison, a ballpark operations employee.

Whoosh, he was off.

"He didn't tackle me!" Polanco said loud enough to draw a smile from Victorino.

Ryan Howard, who sprinted onto the field from the batting cage only after he heard the roar of the crowd, asked if the Phillies beat writers had started fighting the Giants beat writers in the press box. Vance Worley laughed at how he got startled once he realized how big some Giants players were compared to him. Cliff Lee joked that instead of taking a couple shots at some of the Giants pitchers he decided to take a couple shots at Kyle Kendrick, everybody's little brother on the club.

"Nah, I hit *him* in the face," Kendrick countered.

The next day, Cole Hamels threw a complete game against the Giants in a 2-1 victory to give the Phillies a shot at a four-game sweep. Hunter Pence, who joined the team on July 30, going from last place to first place in the process, couldn't have been happier. The Phillies were 8-0 since he arrived and eating everything in sight.

"This is awesome," he said. "This is baseball. I don't know how much of a difference I've made, but I love it."

"Don't kid yourself," Victorino said. "You're a big piece. You've made yourself better. You've made everybody around here better."

The Phillies lost the series finale against the Giants, and then headed down the coast to Los Angeles for a series at Dodger Stadium. SoCal guy Mike Lieberthal stopped by batting practice to visit with his former teammates before the first game. "Hey, bud," said Charlie Manuel, greeting Lieberthal the way the former Phillies catcher greets everyone. Holding his young son in his arms, Lieberthal was all smiles. And, of course, he broke up a few people telling the old story about the Worrell-Kerrigan dustup years earlier.

Roy Halladay and Lee beat the Dodgers in the first two games, with Kendrick getting the win in a wild series finale. The Phillies overcame a 6-0 deficit in the third inning and won, 9-8. They headed to LAX with a 9-1 road-trip record under the arm, completing their best 10-game trip in franchise history to maintain an 8½-game lead over the Atlanta Braves in the National League East.

If 1967 was the Summer of Love in California, then August 2011 was the month of fun for the Phillies in California.

"The Phillies are as good as any team I've seen," said Braves third baseman Chipper Jones, who was following the Phillies' run from the East Coast. "I'd put them up against any of those Yankees clubs of the late 1990s and early 2000s. That club has got it going on and they are flat out playing like it, day in and day out."

———————— K ————————

The Phillies were having a blast, finding different ways to entertain themselves along the way. Victorino worked a walk in the series opener in San Francisco, but instead of dropping his bat at home plate or flipping it toward the on-deck circle, carried it down the first-base line to have the batboy take it from him. The batboy, a Bay Area kid named Cameron Hansen, jogged out to meet Victorino, but slipped on the field and fell as he reached him, drawing laughter from the dugout and crowd. The next afternoon, there was a poster-size picture of Hansen's gaffe, captured from TV, taped to a wall in the visitors' clubhouse.

Victorino signed it: *To Cameron: Slow down . . . wet grass! Shane Victorino 8.*

Before games in San Francisco and Los Angeles, the players shelved Kanye West and Kings of Leon for "Do De Rubber Duck," a reggae song by Ernie from Sesame Street. A couple players had stumbled across the song on Strength and Conditioning Coordinator Dong Lien's iPod. Hip-hop or rock blaring over the clubhouse sound system made way when Roy Oswalt, wearing a mischievous smile, would scroll through the iPod and press play.

The night Cliff Lee beat the Dodgers in Los Angeles he not only threw eight scoreless innings to give him 17 scoreless in August, he hit a solo home run in the seventh inning to give the Phillies a 2-0 lead. The homer proved to be the game winner. But Lee had other things on his mind as he crossed home plate with a huge, giddy smile on his face. As he trotted to the dugout, he looked toward the visitors' bullpen in right field and brushed his right hand with his left hand like he was doling out imaginary hundred dollar bills. He was letting Kendrick know he owed him money.

Lee and Kendrick had made a wager on their offensive performance, and Lee had just scored big with that home run.

Oswalt made sure Kendrick got the message. Shortly after Phillies Pitching Coach Rich Dubee called the bullpen to tell Bullpen Coach Mick Billmeyer to warm up Ryan Madson, Oswalt called down to the pen. Billmeyer assumed it was Dubee telling him to have Madson take a seat, but when he picked up the phone he heard Oswalt's thick Mississippi drawl on the other end.

"Tell *Ken'rick* that Cliff wants his money in hundreds."

Lee and Kendrick enjoy competing with one another. Inside the tiny visitors' clubhouse at Wrigley Field in July, they had a contest a couple kids might have during a lazy summer afternoon. They took one of their red belts and bet who could hit the other the hardest. Kendrick went first. He smiled nervously as Lee stuck out his right forearm.

Slap.

The hit didn't leave a mark.

"That's *dumb*," Lee said with a tinge of disgust in his voice. "Why wouldn't you hit me harder than that?"

Kendrick knew he was screwed right then and there because Lee played to win and if he had a chance to win a belt-hitting contest, he sure as hell was going to win a belt-hitting contest. Kendrick stuck out his left forearm and Lee unleashed a vicious slap.

THA-WHACK!

Lee won. The prize went to the loser: a large red welt on Kendrick's arm.

Rookie reliever Mike Stutes had started carrying a pink Hello Kitty backpack and a long pink feather boa to the bullpen in Los Angeles. It is tradition for rookie relievers to wear an emasculating backpack, which is loaded with snacks and drinks for the game, and Brad Lidge has been the keeper of that tradition for the Phillies since he joined the team in 2008. He picked up the backpack and complimentary boa—you've *got* to accessorize—before the end of the Giants series.

"That's pretty readily available in San Francisco," he joked.

When Lee dozed on a couch in the visitors' clubhouse during the series finale in Los Angeles, teammates used white athletic tape and made an outline of the pitcher's supine body with the No. 33 in the center. It looked like a crime scene.

The Phillies were 77–40 as they flew back to Philadelphia, the first time they had been 37 games over .500 since they finished 101–61 in 1977. The rotation was doing its job, and now the offense was coming around. The Phillies were averaging 5.31 runs per game since the end of June, which was the best mark in the National League in that stretch.

They were winning and they were having a blast.

———————— K ————————

So, naturally, everybody got a scare shortly after they got home. Cole Hamels pitched only five innings on August 12 in a 4–2 loss to the Washington Nationals at Citizens Bank Park. His fastball averaged just 88.6 mph after averaging 91.4 mph for the season. It was 91.4 mph on July 22 against San Diego, 91.2 mph on July 27 against San Francisco, 90.7 mph on August 1 at Colorado, and 90.2 mph on August 6 at San Francisco. It had been dropping for weeks, but this was significant. Something was wrong.

Hamels revealed after the game he felt stiffness in his left shoulder.

Shoulder problems? Oh, boy.

A blown ligament in a pitcher's elbow can be replaced, but shoulders are much trickier. A torn rotator cuff can end a pitcher's career, even after surgery. Hamels, however, didn't seem concerned as he spoke about it, which everybody inside the organization took as a good sign. Hamels suffered so many injuries early in his career, he is extra cautious whenever he feels a twinge or some sort of discomfort. He said that night he felt no pain in his shoulder.

No pain. That was important.

"It's one of those times of the year," he said nonchalantly. "Travelling, pitching a lot of innings—things kind of mount and you just have to battle through it. It just kind of comes up. You don't ever know and you just try to do everything you can to get your body back . . . and I haven't felt that yet. Once I start getting that jump, I think everything will smooth out."

But until Hamels had an MRI, nobody could be certain. There could be a tear in there. Teams announce injuries as stiffness or soreness and often they turn into something much worse. Chase Utley had "general soreness" in spring training only for everybody to learn a few days later he had major knee problems that could cost him his season and possibly his career. But good news for Hamels came following an MRI exam on August 15. He had no structural damage in the shoulder, and while the Phillies placed him on the disabled list to rest, he would return to the mound before the end of the month.

The Phillies would be fine without him. They still had Roy Halladay and Cliff Lee pitching at full strength. Vance Worley was 6-0 with a 2.52 ERA in 10 starts since rejoining the rotation in June, and Roy Oswalt was back.

———————————— K ————————————

The Phillies took two of three from the surging Arizona Diamondbacks the next week in Philly with their only loss coming in the series opener on August 16, when Halladay blew the first ninth-inning lead of his career in a 3-2 loss.

It was Halladay's 65th career complete game and just the 15th he had lost,

IT'S DOC'S GAME

Jimmy Rollins had a big smile on his face when he found Roy Halladay at Citizens Bank Park on August 18.

"You made it, dog," Rollins said.

Huh?

Rollins had been searching for new music for the Phillies clubhouse playlist when he checked out Game's new CD, *The R.E.D. Album*. Rollins was clicking through the songs on iTunes when he started track 17—"All I Know"—which took full artistic license in connecting Halladay's ability to throw a "K" with two of history's biggest villains.

The song is hardly PG material—it's more like NC-17—but Halladay *had* made his way into a rap song by a famous rapper. Yahoo! Sports' David Brown described the lyrics best:

"Hey, wait a second. Associating the Good Doctor with an alleged financial criminal such as Bernie Madoff—that ain't cool. And how can this be a Phillies song *and* a Mets song? However, comparing Halladay ripping off a knuckle-curve or a cutter to firing a 'K'—an AK-47 (Evan Longoria's former gun of choice)—that seems like a reasonable metaphor. And the Hitler thing . . . whatever."

Following batting practice before that night's game against the Arizona Diamondbacks, Rollins played the song through the clubhouse speakers. As the bass thumped and Game rapped, Halladay blushed.

"He turned *so* red," Rollins said.

Rollins announced his discovery later that night on Twitter, eventually striking up a brief conversation with Game.

Game: *dat boy cold JR*

Rollins: *straight up beast*

Halladay previously had made his way into a country Christmas song: "Baseball Glove" by Gord Bamford. That was family friendly, although Halladay isn't the type of guy to be listening to a Christmas song about himself while his children open their Christmas presents.

"I'm not sure what to think about it," Halladay said about "All I Know." "Unfortunately, I can't let my kids listen to it. Yeah, it's cool, I guess. It's definitely interesting, you know?"

but none had happened like this. He had a 2-1 lead entering the top of the ninth. He thought he had struck out Justin Upton on an 0-2 pitch, but home plate umpire Vic Carapazza called the changeup a ball. Upton singled on the next pitch and Miguel Montero followed with a single to left field to put runners on first and second with nobody out.

Phillies Manager Charlie Manuel had Ryan Madson and Antonio Bastardo warming up in the bullpen, but they remained there. This was Doc's game to finish.

"That's my ace," Manuel said.

Halladay rewarded Manuel for his faith under similar circumstances in Washington on April 13, when he carried a 3-0 lead into the bottom of the ninth at Nationals Park. He had allowed two runs to score and had runners on second and third with one out, but struck out the final two batters he faced to win the game. Manuel expected more of the same from Halladay against the Diamondbacks. He struck out Chris Young for the first out, but Lyle Overbay ripped a double off the right-field wall to clear the bases to give Arizona the lead.

"It can be a little tougher to swallow sometimes in the ninth," Halladay said.

Halladay blew a 3-2 lead in the eighth inning in Cincinnati on June 30, 2010. He allowed a run in the ninth in a 1-0 loss in Boston on April 29, 2008. They were the only other times he suffered a similar fate. Fans criticized Manuel for leaving Halladay in the game, which was ridiculous. Had Manuel pulled Halladay for Madson or Bastardo and they had lost the lead, the same fans would have angrily questioned Manuel for pulling his ace. Manuel stuck with his horse. He would do it again if he had the chance.

"There's never been the perfect pitcher or the perfect player," he said.

Cliff Lee kept trying to prove Manuel's theory wrong. He came close in June and he was trying to replicate his success in August. He allowed two runs in seven innings in a 9-2 victory over the Diamondbacks on August 17. At the time, no one thought much about Arizona first baseman Paul Goldschmidt's two-run homer in that game, but it was significant. Those turned out to be the only runs Lee would allow in five starts and 39⅔ innings in the month of August.

———————— K ————————

Roy Oswalt spent July recovering from the pain in his lower back, but a second cortisone injection had him feeling like himself again. He rejoined the rotation on August 7, allowing 12 hits and three runs in six innings in San Francisco. He looked better on August 13 against Washington, allowing six hits and three runs while striking out five in seven innings.

But everybody was waiting for that one start when they could point and say, "Little Roy is back."

Oswalt had been scheduled to pitch against the Nationals in Washington on August 19, but there was a 142-minute rain delay after he threw his warm-up pitches. Phillies Pitching Coach Rich Dubee pushed him back a day—no need to have him warm up again after cooling down, putting unnecessary strain on his back—and started him the next night. It was the right call. Oswalt's fifth fastball of the game clocked 94 mph. He rolled from there, striking out a season-high nine batters in eight scoreless innings in a 5-0 victory.

"He's back," Cole Hamels said. "I think that's pretty much it. He's back. When he has the velocity, you know it's game time."

Oswalt's fastball averaged 92.2 mph. It was 90.9 mph in eight starts from May 17, when he went on the disabled list for the first time, through June 23, when he went on the disabled list a second time. Kanye West blared in the clubhouse after the game. Oswalt's teammates were pumped.

"Vintage Roy," Jimmy Rollins said. "He had that little fastball that he shoots from his chest and by the time the batter swings, it's shoulder-height. I was excited, man. His velocity was super. I was looking up and he was hitting 93 still late in the game. I was like, 'Wow.' You could tell he has confidence in his back and in his arm."

Carlos Ruiz agreed, and Ruiz's opinion carries weight. He is one of the most candid players in the Phillies' clubhouse. He doesn't speak in clichés.

"That was him, you know?" he said. "He hit ninety-three, ninety-four. You can see he was healthy. That's the best part. He likes to compete, but when you're hurt, it's hard. You could see it. He's quiet, but you could see it in his face and body language. Something was wrong. He didn't feel OK. Now I know he's healthy."

If Oswalt was back, Hamels could get healthy, and Halladay and Lee could keep throwing like they had been, the Phillies could enter the postseason at full strength. That would be huge. For years, Charlie Manuel had been asked questions about using pitchers on short rest in the postseason: Cole Hamels in the 2007 NLDS against Colorado; Cliff Lee in the 2009

World Series against New York; and Roy Halladay in the 2010 NLCS against San Francisco. But with four aces, each on top of his game, they could have everybody pitching on normal rest.

— K —

An early afternoon earthquake—5.8 on the Richter Scale—shook Philadelphia on August 23. Citizens Bank Park was ordered evacuated. But it would have taken the Big One to interrupt Roy Halladay's workday. He stayed in the ballpark and finished his afternoon workout. Philly would get another taste of Mother Nature later in the week, when Hurricane Irene barreled toward Philadelphia on August 27. The Phillies postponed their weekend games against the Florida Marlins and flew early to Cincinnati for a four-game series against the Reds beginning two days later at Great American Ball Park.

The Phillies had an unusual amount of time to kill on the road, but they found a way. Halladay, Cliff Lee, Cole Hamels, Kyle Kendrick, Hunter Pence, Brad Lidge, Ben Francisco, Mike Stutes, Ross Gload, David Herndon, Home Clubhouse Manager and league commissioner Phil Sheridan and clubhouse attendants Sean Bowers and Rick Collinson held their fantasy football draft that Saturday in a conference room at the hotel, complete with beers and pizzas. (The only ace not to participate was Roy Oswalt; he had played in 2010, but spent so much time hunting in the off-season he rarely made a roster move or lineup change and decided not to play again.)

The Phillies have had a fantasy football league since Curt Schilling got the ball rolling in 1995. Harry Kalas announced the first few rounds of those drafts, making them easily the coolest fantasy football drafts ever.

With the first pick, Curt Schilling selects, running back, Emmitt Smith, Dallas Cowboys.

This was Halladay's second season in the fantasy football league, and he hoped to fare better than he had in the first. He had no idea how to draft a team in 2010, selecting quarterbacks Tony Romo and Matt Schaub in the first few rounds. Even Halladay couldn't escape the trash talk, and he caught plenty of hell for drafting his backup quarterback so early.

"What?" he said. "I'll just trade one."

Players crushed Kendrick in 2010 because he always pushed the two-and-a-half-minute time limit to select a player. He would catch even more crap in this draft. He picked up a fantasy football magazine that recommended he not draft running backs before the fifth round, advice he followed.

"Strategy, bro," he said after teammates mocked his every pick. "Strategy."

Of course, that strategy—it was so good he should have called it *strategery*—left him without a single starting running back in the NFL.

"That magazine is going to be out of business next year," Lidge said.

"No matter what, though, if I had drafted a good team, they still would have thought my team was brutal," Kendrick said.

But Kendrick quickly realized he screwed up when he texted teammate David Herndon minutes after the draft ended.

"Hey, I was going over our teams and you're pretty strong at running back, but weak at wide receiver," he said. "We should try to work out a deal."

"Dude, it's Day One!" Herndon replied.

Halladay and Lee follow their personas in fantasy football. Halladay came prepared, although he denied it.

"I cheat," he said. "Don't tell anybody."

Lee showed up like he couldn't care less.

"Cliff gets in there and wings it a little bit, just like everything else," Lidge said. "But Cliff finds a way."

"I downloaded an app and I've still got the best team," Lee boasted.

The players with the most time on their hands seem to have the most success in the fantasy league, especially since the Phillies returned to the postseason in 2007. Left-hander Les Walrond won the league in 2008. He pitched in just six games for the Phillies and did not make the postseason roster. Left-hander Jack Taschner won the league in 2009. He pitched in 24 games and went home to Wisconsin after he did not make the postseason roster. Herndon did not make the 2010 postseason roster and won the league.

Trash-talking text messages fly furiously after the players scatter across the country for the off-season. Lee, Francisco, and Gload are the best trash talkers. Lidge isn't bad, either.

"He went to Notre Dame," Herndon said. "He's smarter than everybody."

But Kendrick is learning to talk smack, kind of like a kid learns to swim after being dropped into the deep end of the pool.

"Kyle has taken so much heat he's learning how to talk trash because he's the absolute redheaded stepchild of our league," Lidge said. "But everybody talks trash when it comes down to it. Everybody has good and bad weeks, and everybody is subject to getting slaughtered, which is what makes it so fun."

Like any fantasy football league, it is more about the camaraderie and ball busting than it is about the trophy at the end of the season.

"It's a fun thing to stay on each other throughout the season when we're traveling and all over the place," said Hamels, who won the league in 2006. "We've got like one day a week where we'll still be thinking about each other and still seeing how things are going. It's our bonding time."

———————— K ————————

As the end of the month approached, management tried to add a left-handed bat to the bench, much like it added Matt Stairs in August 2008. They had Ross Gload, but he was playing with an injured hip, hitting .238 (20 for 84), with five doubles, zero home runs, and six RBIs in 72 games before the series against the Reds. He was a decent option, but the Phillies were looking for more pop.

They wanted Jim Thome.

Thome would turn 41 on August 27, and he knew he was running out of time to win a World Series. He also knew the Phillies had positioned themselves better than any other team, and if he could reunite with Charlie Manuel, his old hitting guru, he believed he could give Philadelphia a good couple of months in a pinch-hitting role. But it would be nearly impossible to make the trade happen. Players have to clear waivers before being traded in August and because the Phillies had the best record in the National League, they would have last crack at him. In other words, if the Atlanta Braves knew the Phillies wanted Thome, who was playing with the Minnesota Twins, they could claim him to block him from going to Philly. The Twins would have to trade him to Atlanta or pull him back off waivers if they could not complete a deal. And if the Twins pulled him back, he could not be placed on waivers again.

The Phillies and Twins could circumvent the rules, but it seemed unlikely. Minnesota could unconditionally release Thome, which would make him a free agent. But the Phillies and Twins are known for not rocking the boat when it comes to MLB Commissioner Bud Selig's rules. The Twins were as

NICE TEAM, KYLE

The first round of the Phillies' 2011
fantasy football league draft.

1. Ben Francisco—Texans running back Arian Foster
2. Ross Gload—Vikings running back Adrian Peterson
3. Brad Lidge—Ravens running back Ray Rice
4. Cliff Lee—Chiefs running back Jamaal Charles
5. Roy Halladay—Packers quarterback Aaron Rodgers
6. Hunter Pence—Eagles running back LeSean McCoy
7. Kyle Kendrick—Texans wide receiver Andre Johnson
8. Sean Bowers and Rick Collinson—Jaguars running back Maurice Jones-Drew
9. Cole Hamels—Falcons wide receiver Roddy White
10. Mike Stutes—Lions wide receiver Calvin Johnson
11. Phil Sheridan—Eagles quarterback Michael Vick
12. David Herndon—Rams running back Steven Jackson

unlikely to unconditionally release Thome as the Phillies would be to sign him if it happened.

It never got to that point. The Cleveland Indians claimed Thome, and the Twins and Indians completed a trade for him on August 25. Thome could have blocked it, but it was the only team he had trouble saying no to. The Indians drafted him in 1989, and he spent his first 12 seasons with them before signing a six-year, $85 million contract with the Phillies in December 2002.

It must have been a sinking feeling for Thome. The Indians were grasping at straws when they acquired him. They were 63-64, and 6½ games behind the Detroit Tigers in the American League Central and 14½ games behind the New York Yankees in the AL wild-card race. They had no shot to catch the Tigers, and everybody knew it.

The Phillies talked with the Tampa Bay Rays about Johnny Damon, but they found the price too high. So after falling short on Thome and Damon, they settled for John Bowker, who was playing in the minor leagues for the Pittsburgh Pirates.

They whiffed. Bowker went 0 for 13 with seven strikeouts before the Phillies sent him home following the season. They would have to hope one of their own bench players would have a Matt Stairs moment in the postseason.

———————————————— K ————————————————

The Phillies finished the month with Roy Halladay throwing seven scoreless innings in a 9-0 victory against the Reds on August 30, and Cliff Lee throwing 8⅔ scoreless innings against them in a 3-0 victory on August 31.

The postseason couldn't come quickly enough. Halladay went 3-1 with a 2.62 ERA in August, while Lee went 5-0 with a 0.45 ERA. Lee became just the third pitcher in MLB history to go 5-0 with an ERA under 1.00 in two separate months in the same season. He joined Bob Gibson, who went 6-0 with a 0.50 ERA in both June and July 1968; and Walter Johnson, who went 5-0 with a 0.24 ERA in April and 6-0 with a 0.81 ERA in July 1913. Lee also became the first pitcher to throw at least seven scoreless innings in 10 or more starts in the same season since Dwight Gooden and John Tudor had in 1985.

Pretty good, huh?

Whatever.

Lee needed just one more out on August 31 in Cincinnati to throw his sixth shutout of the season, but got into trouble after retiring the first two batters he faced in the ninth. He allowed a double to Joey Votto, walked Jay Bruce on a full count, and hit Miguel Cairo with a pitch to load the bases. Charlie Manuel reluctantly walked to the mound to retrieve the baseball from Lee's left hand.

"I want Madson," Manuel said.

"You sure?" Lee replied.

"Damn sure."

Ryan Madson got the final out to end the game to maintain the Phillies' 7½-game lead over the Braves.

"It's not very often you go 8⅔ and not give up a run and somehow not feel good about it when it's over," Lee said. "It worked out. Madson came in and got the guy out. It's hard to question the move. Whatever."

Whatever.

Fans and reporters pick up players' little idiosyncrasies over time. Cole Hamels habitually inserts "ya know" in between sentences. Domonic Brown offers an, "Aw, man." Shane Victorino drops "no questions asked" or "you know, like I said" when responding to a question. Pat Burrell always said, "Thanks, guys" to signal to reporters—he despised them—that the interview was over and it was time to go away. Burrell might be gone, but his famous "Thanks, guys" catchphrase lives on with Chase Utley.

But, "Whatever?" That's Lee's.

Lee had a "whatever" moment at the plate in the fourth inning against Cincinnati that night. Reds left-hander Dontrelle Willis jammed him on a pitch and the ball shot straight to Reds second baseman Brandon Phillips. Lee glanced at his bat after he swung through and by the time he looked toward first base he noticed the ball going into Phillips' glove. He took a couple steps toward first base before waving dismissively at the play, like, "Ah, forget it."

Whatever.

"I should have run right there," he said. "There's no way he's throwing that ball away, but that's not good. I should have run right there. But whatever."

"Whatever!" Kristen Lee said a month later. "Oh, my gosh! I finally told him. I've told him for years—just don't say *whatever* about everything. He says that about *everything*. I was like, 'Hey, just so you know, you're known as saying *whatever* just like I've been telling you for years. You're known for that. They're making comments in the media about how you say *whatever* all the time.' Everything is *whatever*."

Kristen started to laugh.

"Just so you know, he does that to me, too," she said. "It'll be, 'Hey, Cliff, Jaxon's teacher said he had trouble at school today or something.' He'll say, 'Whatever. It doesn't really matter.' Yeah, for you. You're 1,000 miles away. Yeah, everything is *whatever*."

SEPTEMBER

S ix and a half months after they had assembled in Clearwater, the Phillies glided into September on the wings of 18 August wins. The season was shaping up just the way they had hoped, just the way it had to, really, considering the blue-ribbon talent management had assembled and the money it had spent to bring it all together. Ownership had gone all-in when it stretched the payroll to sign Cliff Lee, and the baseball ops people had sacrificed a load of blue-chip talent to get Hunter Pence. Since February, the team had operated against a high-pressure, World Series-or-bust backdrop, and now, entering the final month of the regular season, the feeling raged like an inferno.

The Phillies had led the National League East every day but one. They had built their lead to 7½ games and raised their record to 41 games above .500 when they completed a four-game sweep of the Reds in Cincinnati on September 1.

October couldn't come fast enough.

September would be the longest Christmas Eve these guys had ever lived through.

"Win games," Charlie Manuel said after completing that sweep in Cincinnati. "Keep winning."

Despite a clear path to the postseason, there was plenty the cruising Phillies could still accomplish in September:

Never had a Phillies team been 42 games over .500. Getting there would mean something.

No Phillies team had ever won more than 101 games. Eclipsing that mark would mean something.

Individually, September would be an important month for a key member of The Rotation. Roy Oswalt had recovered fully from the back injury that had marred his season and was ready to build the arm strength that would bring the crackle back to his fastball and put him in position to be the October contributor Phillies officials thought he'd be when they dealt for him more than a year earlier.

In addition to all this, Manuel wanted to make sure his club finished with the best record in the majors for the second-straight year. That, coupled with the NL's win in the All-Star Game, would ensure the Phils home-field advantage throughout the postseason. For even as they chugged toward 100 regular-season wins, what mattered most was the 11 postseason wins it would take to win the World Series. Being able to open three separate series in front of home crowds at Citizens Bank Park would be a huge benefit to the team. Or so everyone thought.

Ultimately, what should have been the Phillies' easiest month turned out to be their most difficult. A series of August rainouts eliminated the off days that can refresh a body and a string of lackluster performances, culminating with an embarrassing eight-game losing streak following the division clincher, caused angst in the streets and resulted in more than a few boos in the stands.

Manuel resisted laying into his team during the losing streak. For one thing, he knew a post-clinch hangover was pretty much inevitable for a team riding as high as the Phillies. For another, he wasn't playing his big guns every night. Jimmy Rollins and Chase Utley were working their way back from a groin injury and a concussion, respectively, Hunter Pence had a cranky knee, and Ryan Howard needed time off because of a sore ankle. The Phillies played their regular eight position players in the same lineup just four times in September. What was Manuel supposed to do, air out the Lehigh Valley IronPigs?

Clubhouse eruptions have to be carefully timed and executed. Manuel had chewed out his club a week earlier after a pair of uninspiring efforts in Houston and he knew the surest way to have tirades fall on deaf ears was to have too many of them. This is not to say Manuel is against an old-fashioned airing out. In late August 2010, as the team was being swept at home by Houston, Manuel blasted his players behind closed doors and called them "yesterday's All-Stars." The Phils reacted positively to the spanking and went 27-8 the rest of the way. A season later, the Phillies were a lot closer to the regular-season finish line and were physically bruised and banged-up. Manuel, 67 years old and nearing a half century in the game, knew this was the time for a softer touch. He sent messages through the press that the team needed to pick up its play, but no one got scalded.

"People think you can jump around and scream and kick them in the ass, and they're going to react, but let me tell you something, that ain't going to do anything at all," Manuel said during the losing streak. "I can scream with the best of them, and I can get just as tough as anyone, but believe me, sometimes that ain't the way.

"Players nowadays can tune you out. I can get a response from my players, and I think I have the respect of my players, but at the same time we just got through clinching and we got home-field advantage. We came out the last few days and haven't played good. Now is not the time for me to go in there and start hollering at people."

The Phillies eventually ended the eight-game skid and finished the regular season with four straight wins. In those final days of the regular season, The Rotation served notice it was ready for October. In their final starts of the regular season, the Big Four starters—Roy Halladay, Cliff Lee, Cole Hamels, and Roy Oswalt—combined to pitch 25 innings and allow just three earned runs for a 1.08 ERA.

For the season, the Phillies starting pitchers had an ERA of 2.86, the best in baseball since 1985. Through all the injuries and all the offensive ups and downs, they were the team's one great consistency—just as expected.

One day in late September, someone asked Manuel where the team would be without its starting pitchers.

"I'd say that we might be getting ready to go home," he said.

———————————— K ————————————

After completing their sweep of the Reds to open September, the Phillies flew to Miami for a weekend series against the Marlins. For much of the season, the club had three pitchers in the discussion to be the NL Cy Young winner. A bout of shoulder inflammation knocked Cole Hamels out of the race in August, but Roy Halladay and Cliff Lee remained very much in the hunt, along with Dodgers lefty Clayton Kershaw.

While the NL Cy Young race lined up for a close finish, the competition in the American League was turning into a runaway. Detroit's Justin Verlander won his 20th game on August 27 en route to leading the majors with 24 wins. Verlander also led the majors with 251 innings and 250 strikeouts.

Checking into a Miami hotel before that weekend series against the Marlins, a Philadelphia writer bumped into a scout from an AL club. The scout had just seen one of Verlander's starts.

"He's the best pitcher in baseball," the scout said.

Hold on here.

Best pitcher in baseball?

That title belongs to Doc Halladay, doesn't it?

"Verlander's the best," the scout said emphatically. "Detroit's going to be a bitch if they can get to the World Series and he can pitch three times."

It was difficult to argue with the scout's assessment of Verlander. The right-hander's fastball approaches 100 mph and he commands it like a finesse guy. He walked just 57 in those 251 innings. He changes speeds. He's a horse. Maybe he had indeed usurped Halladay's throne.

"Don't get me wrong," the scout said. "Halladay's great. I mean great. He's done it for a long time, and that means a lot. But right now, Verlander's the best. He's got weapons. He beats you with his stuff. Halladay beats you with his smarts, his pitchability, his mind. He wears you down and never gives in."

"They're both great," the scout said in the lobby of that Miami hotel on that Friday afternoon in early September. "But Verlander's the best."

Charlie Manuel makes his off-season home in Florida. He loves the state. But if he had his druthers, he'd never take a team to Miami on a weekend.

"I don't like those Sunday afternoon games," he said. "Not only is it hot, but you run into that South Beach problem."

Yes, players have always liked "taking their talents" to South Beach on Saturday nights, and sometimes it shows in their play on Sunday afternoons. In former Phillie Lenny Dykstra's case, it was his non-play. On May 9, 1994, a Sunday afternoon, the Phils were set to play the finale of a series in Miami. Dykstra, as they say in baseball parlance, could "run it" with the best of them, and on that Sunday afternoon, he looked like a man who was in no shape to play a ball game and had no interest in doing so. Manager Jim Fregosi knew this but had Dykstra in the lineup anyway, leading off. With no day off, Dykstra orchestrated his own. He led off the game by taking a called third strike, instigated an argument with home plate umpire Angel Hernandez, and was quickly ejected. Mission accomplished. The Dude spent the rest of the day chilling in the air-conditioned clubhouse.

This trip to Florida marked the Phillies' last to the stadium that the Marlins had shared with the NFL's Dolphins since Major League Baseball came to Florida in 1993. Though two World Series championship teams called the stadium home, it had always been a bad fit for baseball, a garish teal and orange behemoth that lacked baseball charm because it had been built for football. Rain delays were frequent at the ballpark, which has had six different names over the years, and fans were few. The Marlins believe things will change on both counts when they move into their new, retractable-roof, baseball-only stadium in 2012.

In addition to Dykstra's day off, the Phillies had some memorable visits to Sun Life Stadium, as it was known in 2011, over 19 seasons. During one trip there, Phillies second baseman Mickey Morandini threatened to knock out the organ player if he didn't stop playing the theme to *The Mickey Mouse Club* when he batted. Bobby Munoz two-hit the Marlins in one hour and 54 minutes on July 27, 1994 (the guys must have been in a hurry to get to South Beach that night). Curt Schilling struck out his 300th batter in his final start of the 1998 season in the ballpark, becoming just the fifth pitcher in big-league history to have back-to-back 300-strikeout seasons. Hurricane Georges forced two postponements that weekend. Phillies players busied themselves by playing paintball throughout the stadium one night—Schilling bought all the supplies—and that didn't make the cleanup crew very happy.

On the final day of the 2002 season, the Phils were bidding to finish with a winning record and the game went into extra innings. Finishing with a winning record meant a lot to Manager Larry Bowa, but not first baseman Travis Lee. The Marlins scored the winning run on a sacrifice fly in the bottom of the 10th. Lee made a catch in foul territory down the right-field line to allow the winning run to score. He could have let the ball drop into foul territory and prolonged the game and the Phillies' chances of winning it, but his forgettable three-season stint with the team was coming to an end. He made the catch and barely broke stride as he hailed a cab to the airport and out of a Phillies uniform. The Phils finished 80-81.

In 2006, Manuel's second as skipper, the Phillies were eliminated from wild-card contention on the final weekend of that season in the Miami ballpark. The Phils' playoff drought grew to 13 years with the elimination. Sitting in the dugout on the final day of the season, the day after the Phils were eliminated, General Manager Pat Gillick tap-danced around questions about Manuel's future. Gillick was clearly thinking of firing Manuel. In the end, he stuck with Manuel and the Phillies have gone on to win the NL East five straight times. They won the World Series in 2008. In December 2010, Gillick was elected to the Hall of Fame. Asked at the time what his best move as Phillies GM was, Gillick said, "Sticking with Charlie."

Of course, the Phillies' finest moment in Sun Life Stadium came on May 29, 2010, when Halladay pitched just the second perfect game in team history. So it was kind of fitting he got the ball for the Phillies' final game ever in the stadium on September 4. It was a Sunday afternoon game, and, to no one's surprise, strange things happened. The Phillies played the game under protest after the umpires took away a potential extra-base hit from Hunter

Pence because of a fan-interference infraction. The umpires made their call after watching video replays. The Phillies squawked because replays aren't supposed to be used to review defensive plays. The umpires said they determined the fan interference while trying to see if Pence's ball was a home run.

"Even if the umpires were wrong in their decision to go in and review it, they got the play right," Florida Manager Jack McKeon said. "Isn't that what we want from the umpires—to get it right? That's like a ballplayer who misses a sign and then hits a home run. He screwed up, yet he got it right and hit it out of the park."

The Phillies lost the protest and the game, 5-4. Halladay was long gone by the time David Herndon walked in the winning run in the bottom of the 14th inning. The game lasted four hours, 47 minutes and finished with only a smattering of fans in the stadium. The Phils ended up going 74-78 in the Marlins' starter house. Even Halladay, who had authored a great personal memory in the stadium, was happy to put the place in his rearview mirror.

"I'll be glad to get out of here," he said as he headed to the team bus for the flight back to Philadelphia and a brief, three-game home stand against the second-place Atlanta Braves.

Lenny Dykstra could not be reached for comment.

———————————— K ————————————

The Phillies looked flat in losing the final two games of the series in Miami. That happens during the course of a long season, especially when a first-place team on cruise control plays a dead-end team in a lifeless ballpark. Charlie Manuel couldn't wait to get out of Miami, not because of South Beach and all its trappings, but because he knew his team was going home where it would be invigorated by the energy of another Citizens Bank Park sellout. What's more, the Phillies were about to embark on a stretch of seven straight games—three at home, four on the road—against Atlanta and Milwaukee, two potential playoff opponents. The intensity figured to be high and Manuel liked that.

With Citizens Bank Park in a full, throaty roar, the Phillies opened a quick, three-game home stand with a 9-0 win over Atlanta. Cliff Lee was masterful in registering his sixth shutout, the most posted by a pitcher in a single season since Tim Belcher had eight for the Dodgers in 1989. Lee held the Braves to just five hits, did not walk a batter, and struck out six as he positioned himself for a backstretch charge in the Cy Young race. Coming out of Miami, Chase Utley had been locked in a 2-for-28 slump and Hunter Pence was 0 for his last 11 at-bats. Both hitters came to life in backing Lee at home. Utley had two hits and Pence three RBIs. Rookie Vance Worley picked up his 11th win the next night.

In a foreshadowing of the damage they would ultimately inflict on the Braves' season, the Phillies swept the series to go 42 games over .500 and run their lead to 10½ games in the NL East, effectively ending the Braves' chances of winning the division. But not everything went well for the Phillies in that series. In the finale game, Utley took a 94-mph Eric O'Flaherty fastball off the back of his batting helmet. When the Phillies' charter flight left for Milwaukee after that game, Utley was not on it. He spent the entire seven-game road trip at home, recuperating from the latest ailment to befall him—a concussion.

The Brewers were rolling toward the NL Central title and figured to be a good late-season test for the Phillies. They had formidable starting pitching with Zack Greinke, Shaun Marcum, Yovani Gallardo, and former Phillies left-hander Randy Wolf, and a power-packed lineup led by the thundering bats of MVP candidates Ryan Braun and Prince Fielder. The Phillies, of course, had some weapons of their own with Cole Hamels, Roy Halladay, Cliff Lee, and Vance Worley set to pitch in the series.

Before the first game, Wolf was running in the outfield when he spotted Rich Dubee.

"Do you have the easiest job in the big leagues, or what?" he playfully shouted to the Phillies pitching coach.

It was a question that Dubee himself had pondered way back in February when he joked about bringing a recliner to spring training.

"To have three starters on one staff with ERAs under three—that's truly remarkable," Wolf said. "And then they have a guy like Worley step in his first year and go 11-2. Facing that team is the equivalent of a pitcher having to face a team full of .330 hitters.

"It's really an awesome staff. Cole throws ninety-four, he cuts it, and has a great changeup. Halladay's ball never stops moving. Cliff has that pinpoint control. . . ."

Wolf, who rejected an offer to stay with the Phillies after the 2006 season, shook his head in amazement.

"Ruben pulled a Houdini," he said of General Manager Ruben Amaro

HAS ANYBODY SEEN DOMONIC?

Domonic Brown had a difficult season in 2011, but he did manage to make some history.

On July 30, he became the first player in major-league history to send himself to the minor leagues.

The Phillies traded for Hunter Pence on July 29. At the time of the trade, the media speculated that the Phillies would make room for Pence on the roster by sending Brown to Triple-A. MLB Network went a step further than speculating. In the crawl at the bottom of the screen, it reported that Brown had been optioned to Triple-A. The network credited reporter Jon Heyman for the news.

Brown read the report when he returned home from Citizens Bank Park after the game on July 29. He rose early the next morning, drove to the stadium, packed his equipment, and headed to Lehigh Valley, arriving in the early afternoon for that night's game. There was just one problem: Brown hadn't been sent down.

Phillies General Manager Ruben Amaro Jr. got a call from a member of the Lehigh Valley staff.

"Domonic's here," the official said. "What should we do with him?"

"What?" said an incredulous Amaro.

Amaro had planned to go briefly with one less pitcher and keep Brown around for a couple of days as a pinch hitter before sending him to the minors.

Amaro phoned Brown from Manager Charlie Manuel's office in Philadelphia.

"Domonic, did anyone indicate to you that you were being sent down?" Amaro asked.

Brown responded that no one had told him anything, that he had read it on his television screen and assumed it to be true. Rather than have Brown drive back to Philadelphia, the Phils went through with the option. They faxed Brown the necessary paperwork, and he played in Triple-A that night.

Brown returned to the big club in September and laughed about the rookie mistake that cost him a couple of days of service time.

"I guess it shows I'm dedicated," he said.

"To his credit, he went right to work," Amaro said.

Jr. "He let Cliff go, then got him back. All you heard was he was headed to the Yankees or Rangers and all of a sudden the Phillies got him. It says a lot about that organization that he would go back."

Wolf added that in addition to being talented, the Phillies staff "probably feeds off each other and pushes each other with a friendly competition."

All season long, members of The Rotation pooh-poohed suggestions of such internal competition. But, on that first night in Milwaukee, Hamels confirmed Wolf's belief. He had just pitched a four-hitter to lead the Phils to a 7-2 win. It was the staff's major-league-best 17th complete game and Hamels' third. He was still four shy of Halladay and three shy of Lee.

"I'm trying to keep up with these guys in complete games," Hamels said. *Aha! One-hundred-forty games into the season, the truth comes out.*

Halladay and Lee followed Hamels with strong starts and the Phillies won the first three games in Milwaukee. The Big Three combined to pitch 24 innings and allow just four earned runs in those starts. The Brewers salvaged a win against Worley in the series finale, but, all in all, it was a successful visit to the land of bratwurst and beer. It was also entertaining. Second baseman Pete Orr, filling in for the concussed Utley, nearly got pancaked by one of Miller Park's famous racing sausages as he made his way to his position in the sixth inning of the second game. Everyone in the dugout had a good laugh as Orr escaped death by encased meat, but it wouldn't have been funny had Halladay been impaled by a Polish sausage. Sacrificing a utility infielder to the baseball gods is one thing, but the best pitcher in baseball? Or the second best? No way.

"I was about to walk right in front of them," Halladay said of those speeding sausages. "I actually saw them coming and stopped. Pete didn't."

It's a good thing Halladay saw the sausages coming. Imagine the *zap* had he been hit by one.

Lee and three relievers combined to beat the Brewers, 3-2, in 10 innings the next night and that brought out some gallows humor from the Milwaukee media contingent as it rode the elevator from the press box to the clubhouse.

"What a grind it must be for Charlie Manuel to manage that team," one reporter said after the game.

"Yeah, tonight he actually had to use the bullpen," another Cheesehead said. "I thought they welded the door shut."

"I hear tomorrow the relievers are going to watch the game at Karl Ratzsch's," added another, referring to the famous German restaurant in downtown Milwaukee.

Yes, the Phillies were flying high. They had won six straight games against potential playoff opponents and, at 94-48, were 12 games up in the division. But even as they steamed toward the regular-season finish line and 100 wins, they knew that six months of greatness would quickly be forgotten with a poor showing in October.

"We're on a great pace," Ryan Howard cautioned. "But at the same time, we know what the main goal is. All of this is fine and dandy, but it's all for naught if you don't go out and achieve the ultimate goal."

The words would resonate all winter long.

—————————— K ——————————

With the magic number for clinching a fifth-straight division title dwindling, the Phillies headed to Houston on September 12 for three games against the Astros. It was a matchup of the team with the best record in the majors against the team with the worst, but you would never have known which was which in the first two games. Houston won the opener, 5-1, as Phillies exile Brett Myers outpitched Roy Oswalt, who made his first start in Houston since being dealt to the Phillies 13 months earlier.

Myers had been the Phillies' top draft pick in 1999. He pitched for the 2008 World Series champions. He badly wanted to stay in Philadelphia, but his pattern of knuckleheaded behavior led the team to cut ties with him after the 2009 season and he was signed by the Astros. Myers entered his start against the Phillies with a dismal 4-13 record. He knew his old team loved fastballs, so he relied mostly on off-speed stuff in holding the Phils to one run over eight innings.

This was Myers' World Series game.

"It feels good to beat them," he said in the Astros' clubhouse after the game. "I don't know if they want to stick it to me more than I want to stick it to them, but—they're going to be in the playoffs in a few weeks and I'm going to be sitting there watching them, so. . . ."

Down the hall in the visiting clubhouse, Oswalt decompressed from a start that also carried much personal significance. He had spent a decade in Houston and was eager to make a good showing against the club for which he twice won 20 games. It didn't happen. He allowed 13 base runners in seven innings and was hurt, as he was quick to point out, by poor defense.

"I thought I made some pretty good pitches that we didn't make the plays on," Oswalt said afterward. "It wasn't a real fundamental game."

Charlie Manuel concurred. In the manager's office, he sat and simmered behind the desk.

"We played a sloppy game," he said. "That bothered me a lot."

The Phils played another ugly game the next night in losing to another former teammate, J. A. Happ. Including a final-day loss in Milwaukee, they had lost three games in a row for the first time since early June and that irked Manuel. All season long, he had been the father of a perfect teenager. The kid did his homework, minded his manners, was always respectful, and never got in trouble. As a result, dad never had to raise his voice and that blood pressure always stayed an even 120/80. But now, the kid was slipping up and dad was getting pissed.

Manuel wasn't so much perturbed by the losses—he had no beef with the way his team played the final day in Milwaukee—as he was with how the Phillies had played the first two nights in Houston. The Phils had been outscored 10-3 in two games against a dog-meat team. They had just 11 hits, and eight of them were singles. They had gone 1 for 12 with runners in scoring position. The defense was poor. The at-bats were lousy. The offense was punchless. And on top of it all, Manuel thought the team's effort sucked. The man who was known as *Aka Oni*—the Red Devil—for his fiery temper during his playing days in Japan had seen enough. He called a private clubhouse meeting after the second loss. He rattled a few cages and let his high-flying team know it hadn't accomplished jack shit yet.

After cooling off, Manuel met with reporters.

"We've talked all year long about where we want to go," he said. "We want to get to the World Series and win it. We're sitting in a hell of a position, but when we come out and play sloppy and don't have a lot of life. . . .

"We need to bear down. If you play right and hustle and don't win, that's OK. But mental mistakes and taking things for granted—we're better than that."

The *Aka Oni* was getting hot again. He took a cooling breath and leaned back in his chair.

"We could put a little more into it," he said. "That's the bottom line."

A manager can look good when one of his tirades is followed by a win the next day. Of course, it helps when the eruption precedes one of Halladay's starts. The ace of the aces stopped the losing skid with a 1-0 shutout in the series finale. Halladay allowed just six singles, a walk, and struck out seven. He needed to be on top of his game because the offense was largely unmoved by Manuel's little motivational speech from the night before.

"What do you mean motivate them?" Manuel said with a laugh. "We came out and got one walloping run."

Halladay's 18th win was significant because it was the Phillies' 95th of the season and it assured them of at least the NL wild-card playoff spot. Once upon a time, an accomplishment such as that would have been reason for celebration for the Phillies. This was, after all, a team that went 14 years without a playoff berth after winning the NL pennant in 1993. But times had changed for the franchise. It had All-Star pedigrees all over the diamond. It had a $175-million payroll. And, of course, it had The Rotation, the best pitching staff in baseball. Only a parade down Broad Street would satisfy this club.

That's why that Wednesday afternoon win in Houston was treated like, well, a Wednesday afternoon win in Houston.

"That's the beauty of being here," Halladay said. "We had some big wins last year, and you came in the clubhouse and the feeling was, *that's what we expected to do*. It's a great mentality to have. There's still business to be taken care of."

That business included winning a fifth-straight NL East title, wrapping up the best record in the game, and maybe setting a new franchise record for wins. The Phillies had all of those milestones at their fingertips as they jetted back to Philadelphia for the season's final home stand, a 10-game run that would bring the jubilation everyone was waiting for—and some frustration that no one expected.

———————————— K ————————————

Three months had passed since the Phillies had last seen the St. Louis Cardinals. The Cards had given the Phillies problems earlier in the season, and now were in Citizens Bank Park with two-and-a-half weeks to go. They were red-hot, and making a late run at the NL wild-card spot. The Cards had been 10½ games behind Atlanta in the wild-card race on August 25, but 14 wins over a 19-game span had pulled them to within four games as they arrived in Philadelphia for a four-game series against the cruising Phillies on September 16. A month earlier, the only drama in St. Louis was whether free-agent-to-be Albert Pujols would re-sign with the Cardinals in the off-season. Now, rabid Redbirds fans had a playoff push—and maybe so much more—to follow.

The Cardinals had given the Phillies trouble back in May, sweeping a two-game series in St. Louis on May 16 and May 17. Cliff Lee and Roy Oswalt pitched well in those games, but runs were difficult to come by that entire month, and the Cards won the games by scores of 3-1 and 2-1. Now, four months later, the Phillies' offense was beginning to scuffle for runs again, but the drought wasn't all that worrisome because the team had built an impressive reservoir of wins and champagne showers were in the forecast.

The Phillies were poised for a celebration when they arrived at the ballpark on Friday afternoon, September 16. Sheets of plastic had been hung above the lockers and were ready to be unfurled. The champagne was on ice, and, surely, someone had a stash of victory cigars tucked away in the clubhouse. The New York Mets beat the Atlanta Braves that night, reducing the Phillies' magic number to one, but the Phillies couldn't fulfill their half of the equation against the increasingly difficult Cardinals, as St. Louis scored a 4-2 win in 11 innings. The Phillies' offense, which had been robust for much of the second half of the season, continued to be a concern as the club was held to three or fewer runs in its eighth-straight game.

The plastic was still rolled above the lockers when the Phillies arrived for work the next day. The 198th-straight sellout crowd made its way through the turnstiles and there was a party atmosphere in the stands.

"Tonight's the night!" a female fan shouted from behind the dugout as the Phillies exited the field after batting practice.

It was the night. In their 150th game of the season, the Phillies sewed up their fifth-straight NL East title with a 9-2 win over the Cardinals. The Phils got big contributions up and down the roster. Hunter Pence knocked in a pair of runs. Shane Victorino homered on his way to a three-RBI night. Raul Ibanez put an exclamation point on the evening with a grand slam in the bottom of the eighth.

The most promising contribution came from Roy Oswalt, who looked like a postseason-ready pitcher in delivering seven shutout innings. He walked none and struck out seven. The ball had excellent life coming out of his hand.

"It was jumping," he said with a smile that was all too rare during the preceding months.

It had been a difficult season for Oswalt. In addition to dealing with a painful bulging disc in his back, he had spent a week at home in Mississippi helping family, friends, and neighbors clean up after a tornado.

"It's pretty special to pitch the game that got us in," Oswalt said as champagne flew around the victorious clubhouse. "Any clincher is special, especially with all the stuff I had to deal with this year."

No sport has a more grueling schedule than baseball. Seven weeks of spring training followed by 162 games. Players often arrive at the ballpark by 2 P.M. and don't leave until close to midnight. Winning a division title is a special accomplishment, and it deserves to be celebrated. But the Phillies' celebration on September 17 was a little different than the club's previous ones. Oh, sure, there were still the hugs and hoots and hollers. The newcomer, Pence, was given the honor of popping the first champagne cork—an honor that had gone to Halladay, Brian Schneider, and Mike Sweeney, all playoff newbies, the year before—and he whooped it up pretty good, dropping to his knees as teammates doused him with bubbly. But on the whole, the celebration was more controlled and less raucous than previous ones. These Phillies had been there and done that. They were saving themselves for a bigger party. Heck, Victorino barely participated in the celebration. He went off to the weight room while his parents wandered around the field looking for him.

"This is a step," Ryan Howard said. "We'll celebrate a little, but we know the true test starts in October."

"This is just one piece," Charlie Manuel said.

After soaking the clubhouse carpet with champagne, Phillies players returned to the field. A smattering of jubilant fans remained in the stands. Players milled around with family members and celebrated with club officials. Behind home plate, Cliff Lee and his wife, Kristen, shared a moment with John Middleton, one of the Phillies owners, and his wife. The couples had met and, as Kristen said, "kind of clicked," two years earlier on the field at Citizens Bank Park as the Phillies celebrated their 2009 division title. Lee, of course, was traded that winter, a move that broke his wife's heart.

At the All-Star Game in 2010, Kristen bumped into the Middletons and told them how much she and her husband loved being with the Phillies and how disappointed they were to be traded away. John Middleton is a powerful, behind-the-scenes force in the Phillies organization, a competitive, physically fit, fiftysomething Main Line billionaire. He shuns the spotlight and media interview requests, but there's no doubt he loves the Phillies—and winning. "He's got a little Steinbrenner in him," one team official said. When the Phillies brought Lee back for $120 million in December 2010, one of Amaro's first calls was to Middleton, who was thrilled by the news.

Now, after stops in Seattle and Texas, the Lees were back in Philadelphia, celebrating another division title with the Middletons.

"Just a little detour," Kristen Lee said. "But it worked out in our favor."

It was a bittersweet home stand for Cliff Lee. Two nights before the clincher, he was one strike away from his seventh shutout when he hung a 0-2 cutter to Florida's Jose Lopez, who swatted it into the left-field seats, tying the game at 1-1. The Phillies won the game, 2-1, in 10 innings, but Lee did not get the win. Poor run support and one bad pitch—how could he have thrown a strike there?—might have cost him the Cy Young Award that night, and deep down inside he knew it. Seven shutouts in one season might have put him over the top.

Oh, well. Lee found solace in the division clincher. He enjoyed it even more than the 2009 clincher.

"This year, I feel more a part of it," he said. "Last time, I jumped in during the middle."

As the celebration died down, Ibanez talked about his eighth-inning party-starting grand slam.

"Every hair on my arm stood up, and if I had any hair on my head, that would have stood up, too," he said.

A moment later, Ibanez, 39 years old and in the final year of his three-year contract, grew reflective. He talked about how lucky he felt to play in front of packed houses every night in Philadelphia, and how lucky he was to play behind The Rotation.

"One day, I'll be telling my grandkids I was part of a team with a pitching staff like this," he said.

From the first pitch of spring training to Oswalt's gem in the division clincher, The Rotation delivered.

"I actually think they've been better than advertised because of the expectations put on them," Pitching Coach Rich Dubee said. "They pitched beyond those expectations. They took it to another level.

"We have a great rotation. Look at the numbers. But right now, we're just getting started."

Yes, with a division title in hand, the Phillies were just getting started.

But how much longer would they last?

That seemed to be a very legitimate question the rest of the month.

———————— K ————————

Maybe the Phillies should have blown it out after clinching the division. Maybe the postgame celebration should have been rowdier and the players should have done the Lambeau Leap into the arms of delirious fans. Maybe Victorino should have skipped his workout, hung a lei around everyone's neck and shouted, "Let's party!" Then there might have been an excuse for the almost unbelievable hangover that dogged this team for the next week.

Twenty-four hours after they clinched, the Phillies got just eight singles in a 5-0 loss to the Cardinals. The Phils had nothing to play for, and it showed. The Cardinals had everything to play for, and it showed. In a performance that would cast a shadow all the way into October, Cardinals' ace Chris Carpenter pitched eight shutout innings to keep his team alive in the wild-card race.

From a Phillies' perspective, the loss was quite understandable. There is an inevitable letdown after clinching a division.

But what made this letdown worrisome was that it lasted eight games. *Eight freaking games.* At one point during the skid, Pence said the team was embarrassed by its play. How many 98-win teams can say they are embarrassed by their play? How many 98-win teams are booed in their final regular-season home games—on Fan Appreciation Night for gosh sakes?

It all happened. The Phillies lost their final six home games, and the skid reached eight games with a pair of losses in New York. Back in February, the Phils had hoped to be a history-making team. They made history, all right. They became the first team in baseball history to lose eight straight after clinching a league or division title. They became the first team to ever lose eight straight after winning its 98th game. The eight-game skid was the team's longest since 2000. High hopes accompanied that season, too. The Phils traded for Andy Ashby, and he was to join Curt Schilling atop a rotation that was going to give the Phillies a chance. Only problem, Schilling needed preseason shoulder surgery and opened the season on the disabled list and Ashby was a flop. Both of them were eventually traded and the team finished the season with a rotation that included Kent Bottenfield, Omar Daal, and Bruce Chen—hardly Halladay, Lee, and Hamels.

As the losses piled up, angst grew in the streets. Even the starting pitchers, frustrated by a lack of run support, were beginning to sound agitated. At first, Charlie Manuel tried to calm frayed nerves by pointing out how banged-up his team was and promising how things would turn around once he was able to get his regular lineup on the field. But after a doubleheader sweep by the Mets on September 24—the Phils squandered a Cole

Hamels gem in losing the opener, 2-1—extended the losing streak to eight games, even Manuel found himself searching for answers. He fielded just two questions from reporters that night in New York. In answering the second question, the old-school Manuel went on a nearly four-minute, stream-of-consciousness rant that seemed to reveal some frustration with the team's health situation and the new-school medical staff's conservative approach to getting players back on the field.

"All of a sudden we want to get our guys who are hurting well," he said. "All of a sudden, we start giving them two and three days off, on one, off one, start deciding when to play them. Look around, and pretty soon you lose your mojo. You lose your timing and you lose your rhythm. I know what I'm talking about. I've been in the damn game for fifty years. I know exactly what I'm talking about. I preach about it every day. People hear it, but they look at me like I'm stupid or crazy. Maybe I am. But that's what's happening. That's what you're seeing. We're out of sync. We're out of focus. We're searching, and nothing's going right.

"We've got 98 wins. We were set to have the biggest year of any Phillie team and we got out of sync. We keep bouncing around, we keep doing things, we keep getting well, and all of that. We've played all year with people hurting. Every day you play the game of baseball, you hurt. Somehow, you hurt. You have aches and pains—ankle, knee, elbow, whatever. Headaches. Believe me. You can ask anybody who ever played this game. I played this game for twenty years, I can tell you. When you lose focus and you get out of sync, you've got to get it back.

"Do we have time [to turn it around]? I don't know," Manuel concluded. "We'll see. But also, too, it'll be a test of how good we are. How about that? This will be a good test. This is the first time this year that we've actually gone bad. And it's not a real good time to go bad. But at the same time, we'll see. This is a good measuring stick for us. You might not like it, but it is. We've created it ourselves, so we'll see. That's all I've got to say."

That was plenty.

Some managers do crossword puzzles to kill time. Manuel doodles lineups. He scribbles them on napkins, dinner receipts, scraps of paper. He might arrive in his office by 11 A.M. for a night game, scribble out three potential lineups, take a walk around the stadium, and scribble out three more when he gets back to his office.

After that eighth-straight loss, Manuel returned to his Manhattan hotel and thought about a lineup he'd been kicking around. The next day he unveiled it. Chase Utley was moved from third to second in the batting order. Hunter Pence was moved from fifth to third. Shane Victorino would have to bat fifth behind Howard, who was back in the lineup after resting his sore ankle. Placido Polanco, playing with two tears in his groin, was dropped to seventh in the lineup.

It worked. The Phils pounded out a cathartic 19 hits and snapped the losing streak with a 9-4 win.

Of course, for a manager, lineup changes are a little like clubhouse tirades: they work best accompanied by a Roy Halladay start. Halladay pitched six shutout innings that day to finish the regular season at 19-6 with a 2.35 ERA. He would be in the mix for a second-straight Cy Young Award, but maybe not good enough to overtake the Dodgers' Clayton Kershaw. One of Halladay's most impressive stats was his 10-3 record after a Phillies' loss. That's the definition of a stopper, and on September 25, in the waning days of the regular season, the 2011 Phillies needed a stopper more than ever before.

And so did the writers who cover the team.

They would have gotten carpal tunnel syndrome if they'd had to transcribe another of Manuel's rants.

———————————— K ————————————

Baseball is a game steeped in tradition. Fans will throw back an opponent's home run in Wrigley Field, everyone will stand for the seventh-inning stretch, and rookies will do what the veterans tell them to do on the last road trip of the season. After eight losses, laughter finally filled the clubhouse when the Phillies won that series finale in New York. Rookie players arrived at their lockers to find their clothes had been replaced by wacky outfits that were to be worn on the flight to Atlanta. The September rookie hazing ritual is one of baseball's most enduring traditions. Sometime during the last trip, veterans sneak out and buy frilly dresses that embarrassed rookies have to wear in public. The tradition used to be funnier back in the days when teams flew commercial and rookies had to parade through airports with all the regular schlubs. Now, baseball teams fly charters and seldom see an airport terminal. The bus takes them onto the tarmac and right to the door of the plane. Only a handful of flight attendants see them.

But even in the era of charter flights, the rookie hazing event is still good for a few laughs, and this one was no exception. The Phillies rookies were good sports as they dressed in costumes cleverly conceived and purchased by Brad Lidge and Ryan Madson. Domonic Brown was resplendent in a pimp's outfit. Erik Kratz, dressed as a beer wench, looked ready to serve up some brews. Michael Schwimer was so perfect as a rabbi that Lidge said, "We forgot to get Schwimer a costume." Justin De Fratus' face was so obscured by his *Pulp Fiction* gimp mask that TSA officials insisted he take it off as they checked his ID before the flight. Hunter Pence took a picture of the group next to the plane and Tweeted it for the world to see. Pence is one of a number of Phillies who communicate directly to fans through Twitter. Jimmy Rollins, Shane Victorino, and Vance Worley are also members of the Twitterverse.

All this Twitter stuff was kind of foreign to the old-school manager. Back in spring training, Charlie Manuel was briefing a group of reporters on some minor developments. One of the reporters said, "I'm going to Tweet that."

Manuel pointed at the guy and in his Southern drawl said, "Yeah, you go ahead, *tweak* that."

It was one of the many simple but hilarious things that Manuel said in the course of the long season. In March, the day after Domonic Brown suffered a broken hamate bone in his right hand, Manuel reported that "Domonic broke his hambone." Later in the year, he talked about how his team couldn't let success spoil its desire and hunger to win. He was trying to say that the club couldn't afford to get too giddy and it came out as, "We can't get too gay." Hey, once upon a time, the words had a similar meaning, right?

Three wins in New York had allowed the tight Phillies team to exhale, to breathe, to smile, and to loosen up as it headed for three days of unexpected intensity in Atlanta. Technically, the Phils had nothing to prove in Atlanta. Yeah, they were still reaching for 100 wins. Yeah, the club record for regular-season wins was still within reach. But both milestones were hood ornaments and wouldn't impact things in October. The trip to Atlanta was three final days to run the engines and make sure everything was set for October. The Braves provided a little intensity and that was a welcome intangible.

The Braves were the second-best team in the National League for much of the season, but had sputtered down the stretch. They had led the NL wild-card race by 8½ games over St. Louis on Labor Day, but their lead over the Cardinals had dwindled to one game entering the final three days of the regular season.

The Phillies' opponent in the division series was directly tied to the outcome of the series in Atlanta. If Atlanta won the wild card, the Phils would play Arizona in the division series; if the Cardinals won the wild card, the Phils would play them. While Phillies fans debated who the better matchup for their team would be—Arizona was considered a more favorable matchup than the rampaging Cardinals—Manuel made it clear that he did not care which club his team played in the first round. In his mind, it was *how* the Phillies played, not *whom* they played, that would determine the team's October success. He was headed to Atlanta to get his regulars some at-bats, his pitching staff some innings, and to go into October with the momentum that comes with winning a few ball games. Former Philadelphia Eagles player and New York Jets coach Herm Edwards once famously said, "You play to win the game," and that was Big Chuck's mind-set heading to Atlanta.

The players shared that view.

Lee allowed just two runs and struck out six—raising his season-total to a career-high 238 strikeouts—as the Phils won the opener, 4-2. It was their 100th win of the season, marking just the third time in franchise history that they had reached that plateau.

Oswalt pitched six shutout innings as the Phils equaled the franchise record for wins in a 7-1 victory the next night.

Manuel liked what he saw in the game. Jimmy Rollins continued to come alive at the plate and reliever Antonio Bastardo, who had shined for five months only to unravel in September, delivered his first clean inning in a month.

"I think we're playing with better focus," Manuel said after his team's third-straight win. "We're more into it. We're playing the Braves and we're getting ready for the postseason."

As Manuel spoke, the Cardinals were finishing off a 13-6 win in Houston to pull into a tie with Atlanta in the wild-card race.

The stage was set for the final day of the regular season and it would prove to be one of the wildest and most entertaining in the history of the game. Not only was the NL wild-card race even heading into the final day of the season, but so was the AL wild-card race. The Boston Red Sox, the team so many had predicted would play the Phillies in the World Series, the team that Ruben Amaro Jr. called the best in baseball back in spring training, had blown a nine-game lead in the AL wild-card race and were now in a tie with surging Tampa Bay.

As tension filled the Braves' dugout in Atlanta, the Cardinals' dugout in

Houston, the Red Sox' dugout in Baltimore, and the Rays' dugout in St. Petersburg, the Phillies remained loose. They rallied in the ninth inning to tie the game, got a game-saving catch from rookie Michael Martinez in the 10th inning, and rallied again in the 13th on their way to beating the Braves, 4-3. In Houston, the Cardinals had already won, 8-0, on the strength of Chris Carpenter (that guy again) and his 11-strikeout gem. In Atlanta, Freddie Freeman crossed first base after making the final out of the game and final out of the Braves' season, and then smashed his helmet to the ground in anger and frustration. The lights had gone out in Georgia. The Braves lost 20 of their final 30 games and were overtaken by the Cardinals, who won 23 of 31 to earn a trip to Philadelphia, where they would be sacrificial lambs— wouldn't they be?—for the Phillies in the first round of the playoffs.

Content to have ended the Braves' season, picked up their record-setting 102nd win, and given Manuel his 646th career win as a Phillies manager— moving him past Gene Mauch for the most wins by any manager in team history—Phillies players retired to the clubhouse at Turner Field and gathered around the big-screen TV for what turned out to be the wildest 3½ minutes of the season. Players watched in amazement as Baltimore rallied to beat Boston, and then turned their attention to the drama in St. Pete, where the Rays had already rallied from a 7-0 deficit against the Yankees to tie the game on Dan Johnson's pinch-hit homer with two outs in the ninth. Boston's loss had assured the Rays of playing at least a one-game tiebreaker against Boston for the AL wild card. Evan Longoria made that game unnecessary when he lined a home run over of the 315-foot marker in left field to give the Rays a surreal 8-7 win in 12 innings and the AL wild card.

You think major-leaguers are jaded? You think they aren't fans of the game? Think again. Phillies players were riveted to the action on the TV.

"Oh, oh, oh," Shane Victorino shouted as Longoria connected. "Did he get it? Did he get it? He did! Oooooh! What did that ball go—three fifteen and a half?"

Victorino's ruckus brought Manuel out of his office. It brought banged-up players out of the trainers' room. Everyone strained to get a look at the TV and the Rays' celebration. The highs and lows of a baseball season, the thrill of victory and the agony of defeat, had been encapsulated in one 3½-minute snippet inside the visiting clubhouse in Atlanta, and everyone, well, nearly everyone, on the team had witnessed it.

"What happened?" asked John Mayberry Jr. as he emerged from the shower and heard all the noise.

What happened?

What happened?

Well, the regular season went just the way the Phillies had hoped it would when they first assembled back on Valentine's Day in Clearwater. Yeah, they had some injuries. Yeah, the offense could be sporadic. Yeah, that eight-game losing streak scared the hell out of a lot of people. But September was over and so was the longest Christmas Eve of their lives. The postseason was finally here. This was why The Rotation had been built.

"This is what you play for," Roy Oswalt said. "This is the fun part."

ONE OF THE BEST

Charlie Manuel extended his right hand to Jim Palmer, who was waiting for him along the third-base line at Bright House Field before a Grapefruit League game in March 2011.

"Big Jim, what's up?" Manuel said.

Palmer smiled, quickly breaking into his Manuel impression.

"Jim sent me to Japan," he said, mimicking Manuel's thick Virginian drawl.

Both men laughed. For years, every time Manuel saw Palmer he joked that Palmer's dominance over him forced him to finish his career in Japan, conveniently ignoring his career .198 average in 394 at-bats over parts of six seasons with the Los Angeles Dodgers and Minnesota Twins, and the fact he faced Palmer just four times (he went 0 for 4 with two strikeouts).

"I used to pinch-hit off him and know what he was going to do," Manuel said. "I would say I wasn't going to swing at it. Harmon [Killebrew] used to talk to me, 'Don't swing at the high fastball.' I might take one or two, but I'd always swing."

They laughed again.

The conversation eventually turned to pitching. Palmer pitched for the 1971 Baltimore Orioles, the second of only two teams in baseball history to have a foursome of 20-game winners (the 1920 Chicago White Sox were the other). The 2011 Phillies starting pitchers had hoped to enjoy the same level of success as Palmer (20-9, 2.68 ERA), Mike Cueller (20-9, 3.08 ERA), Pat Dobson (20-8, 2.90 ERA), and Dave McNally (21-5, 2.89 ERA). But while it was fun to imagine Roy Halladay, Cliff Lee, Cole Hamels, and Roy Oswalt each winning 20 games, it would be extremely difficult to accomplish.

"It doesn't matter," Palmer said. "They're both great."

"Both are great, but we've got to prove ours," Manuel replied. "They proved it. We've got to prove it. That's how they earned the right to say who they are."

In the end, the Phillies had no 20-game winners. Halladay (19-6, 2.35 ERA) and Lee (17-8, 2.40 ERA) came the closest. Hamels (14-9, 2.79 ERA) missed time because of shoulder stiffness and suffered due to poor run support, which has been a theme in his career. Oswalt (9-10, 3.69 ERA) never had a shot because of back problems.

But that doesn't mean the 2011 Phillies rotation couldn't compete with the 1971 Orioles rotation.

"They might be better," said Washington Nationals manager Davey Johnson, who played second base for the 1971 Orioles, and spent parts of two seasons with the Phillies later in the decade. "We had Cuellar and McNally and they were very good, but I don't know that they were better than Hamels and Lee. And Halladay is as dominant a pitcher as Palmer, if not more. Oswalt and Dobson? It was more of a special year for Dobson, where Oswalt's been special for a long time. The Phillies staff is awful good."

The 2011 Phillies rotation (including starts from Vance Worley, Joe Blanton, and Kyle Kendrick) had a better ERA, WHIP and strikeout-to-walk ratio; averaged more strikeouts per nine innings; averaged fewer walks per nine innings; and struck out 299 more batters despite throwing 107 fewer innings than the 1971 Orioles rotation did.

Of course, the Orioles had a quartet of 20-game winners.

"It's harder to get twenty wins when you take twenty percent of your starts away," Johnson pointed out.

Five-man rotations make sure of that. In theory, each of the four healthy starters in a four-man rotation averages 40.5 starts over a 162-game schedule, while each of the five healthy starters in a five-man rotation averages just 32.4. Cueller made 38 starts in 1971, while Palmer and Dobson each made 37, and McNally made 30.

No pitcher has made at least 37 starts in a single big-league season since Greg Maddux in 1991.

Halladay and Lee led the Phillies with 32 starts. Hamels had 31, and Oswalt had 23.

Despite fewer starts for their aces, the 2011 Phillies rotation thrust themselves into the conversation on what were the best rotations in baseball history by putting up, according to Elias Sports Bureau, some historic numbers:

- 76 wins (tied for 13th since 1989)
- 2.86 ERA (1st since 1985, 12th since 1968)
- 932 strikeouts (1st since 2003, 7th since 1900)
- 1,064⅔ innings (9th since 1989)
- 7.88 strikeouts per nine innings (12th since 1900)

- 1.87 walks per nine innings (2nd since 1933)
- 1.11 WHIP (1st since 1975, tied for 6th since 1945)
- 4.22 strikeout-to-walk ratio (1st since 1900)

The Phillies also became the eighth team in baseball history to have three top-five finishers in their league's Cy Young voting, with Halladay finishing second behind the Dodgers' Clayton Kershaw, Lee taking third, and Hamels placing fifth.

"No question this year's rotation is historical," Hall of Fame third baseman Mike Schmidt said. "Unfortunately, Blanton and Oswalt were injured, but the Big Three held up their end."

ERA+ is a statistic that measures a pitcher's ERA against the league average and adjusts it for ballpark factors, accounting for a pitcher throwing in pitcher-friendly PETCO Park in the National League vs. hitter-friendly Fenway Park in the American League. A 100 ERA+ is the league average, whether it's 1966, when pitchers owned baseball's landscape, or 1998, when juiced-up hitters ruled the day. A 130 ERA+ means the league's ERA that season was 30 percent higher than the individual pitcher's.

According to Baseball-Reference.com, before the 2011 season there had been just five teams since 1901 with two starters with an ERA+ of at least 130 who also had 200 or more innings pitched and averaged at least eight strikeouts per nine innings:

- 1968 Indians: Sam McDowell and Luis Tiant.
- 2000 Dodgers: Kevin Brown and Chan Ho Park.
- 2001 Diamondbacks: Randy Johnson and Curt Schilling.
- 2002 Diamondbacks: Johnson and Schilling.
- 2003 Cubs: Mark Prior and Kerry Wood.

The 2011 Phillies became the first team ever with three starters (Halladay, Lee, and Hamels) that hit those marks.

"Clearly, you had two guys in Halladay and Lee who weren't just staff Number Ones," said Bob Costas, who has chronicled baseball as a broadcaster for NBC, HBO, and MLB Network. "They each were a potential Cy Young Award winner—each guy with a certain sort of throwback toughness, where they weren't looking to just give you six good innings and get out of there.

"They're there not just to keep you in the game. They're there to win the game. The kind of guy that you throw the modern book away, where Charlie

DOC, CLIFF, COLE, AND CY

For the first time since the 2005 Houston Astros, the 2011 Phillies had three pitchers finish in the top five in National League Cy Young Award voting.

The voting by the Baseball Writers' Association of America:
1. Clayton Kershaw, Dodgers (27 first-place votes): 207 points
2. Roy Halladay, Phillies (four first-place votes): 133
3. Cliff Lee, Phillies: 90
4. Ian Kennedy, Diamondbacks (one first-place vote): 76
5. Cole Hamels, Phillies: 17
6. Tim Lincecum, Giants: 7
7. Yovani Gallardo, Brewers: 5
8. Matt Cain, Giants: 3
9. John Axford, Brewers: 2
10. Craig Kimbrel, Braves: 2
11. Madison Bumgarner, Giants: 1
12. Ryan Vogelsong, Giants: 1

Kershaw, Halladay, and Lee were the only pitchers named on all 32 ballots. Two voters from every NL city vote for their top five choices. A first-place vote receives seven points followed by four points for second, three for third, two for fourth, and one for fifth. Halladay is the sixth Cy Young winner to finish second the year after winning the award. The others were Warren Spahn (1958), Jim "Catfish" Hunter (1975), Jim Palmer (1977), Tom Glavine (1992), and Brandon Webb (2007).

The Phillies are the eighth team to have three top-five finishers in their league's Cy Young voting. The others include the 1970 Orioles (Dave McNally, Mike Cuellar, and Palmer), 1974 Dodgers (Mike Marshall, Andy Messersmith, and Don Sutton), 1985 Royals (Bret Saberhagen, Dan Quisenberry, and Charlie Liebrandt), 1990 A's (Bob Welch, Dave Stewart, and Dennis Eckersley), 1998 Braves (Tom Glavine, Greg Maddux, and John Smoltz), 1999 Astros (Mike Hampton, Jose Lima, and Billy Wagner) and 2005 Astros (Roger Clemens, Roy Oswalt, and Andy Pettitte).

would let Halladay go into the ninth with a one-run lead, and even stick with him if the first guy got on base, thinking correctly, 'He might be in a little bit of trouble, but even after one hundred and ten pitches, this guy is still better than whoever I bring out of the bullpen.'"

Of course, it is tricky to compare rotations across eras because baseball has changed so much. Old Hoss Radbourn won 59 games for the 1884 Providence Grays, while making 64 percent (73 of 114) of his team's starts. But just because he won 59 games in one season doesn't mean he's a better pitcher than Halladay, who won a career-high 22 games in 2003.

"You're looking at differences in the way the games were pitched," said Freddy Berowski, a librarian at the National Baseball Hall of Fame in Cooperstown, New York. "You're looking at differences from underhand to overhand. You're looking at differences in the distance between the mound and home plate. You're looking at how pitchers were allowed to move around the box and maybe in some years get running starts.

"There were so many different variables. It wasn't just a pitcher like you see today, where they stand on the rubber, take their windups, and throw."

The distance from the mound to home plate changed in the 1800s. It was 45 feet in the 1870s before moving to 50 feet in 1881. In 1893, it moved to 60 feet, 6 inches, where it remains today. Baseball had a rule as late as 1878 that pitchers had to release the ball below their waists, meaning they delivered the ball underhand. In 1884, the rules changed to allow pitchers to throw however they wanted to, allowing them to legally throw overhand for the first time.

In essence, from 1884 to 1892, pitchers were allowed to throw overhand from 50 feet.

Pitching continued to evolve over the years, often with transformations that benefited hitters.

Frank Selee, who managed the Boston Beaneaters in the late 1800s, is known as one of the first managers to employ a four-man rotation, using Kid Nichols, Ted Lewis, Vic Willis, and Fred Klobedanz in 1898. Baseball outlawed the spitball in 1920. In 1969, the pitcher's mound was lowered from 15 inches to 10 inches and the strike zone changed, moving from the top of the shoulder to the bottom of the kneecap, to the armpit to the top of the kneecap. In reality, today the strike zone is smaller than that.

Rotations started to shift from four-man rotations to five-man rotations in the 1970s, when teams began to become more protective of their pitchers' arms. Increased use of the bullpen also meant fewer decisions for starters, and the use of one-inning closers in the 1980s meant fewer complete-game opportunities for pitchers. Ballparks also got smaller and bats and balls got harder, making life even more favorable for hitters.

"It's much harder to win twenty games than it was forty years ago, no doubt about that," Berowski said. "If you look at the peripheral numbers— the ERA, WHIP, strikeouts—the numbers are there for the Phillies. Even complete games for Halladay and Lee in an era when pitchers don't throw that many complete games."

There were 173 complete games in the majors in 2011. Halladay and Lee threw 14 (8.1 percent) of them. The San Diego Padres, Milwaukee Brewers, Kansas City Royals, Houston Astros, Cleveland Indians, Boston Red Sox, and Washington Nationals combined for just 12.

There is no arguing the Phillies rank alongside the great Atlanta Braves rotations of the 1990s and other great rotations like the 1971 Orioles, 1966 Los Angeles Dodgers, and 1954 Indians.

Modern metrics like WAR, ERA+ and FIP- show as much.

WAR (Wins Above Replacement) judges how valuable a player is to his team. For example, Halladay had an 8.2 WAR in 2011, according to FanGraphs, meaning he gives the Phillies an additional 8.2 wins compared to a replacement player.

FIP (Fielding Independent Pitching) research takes into account how pitchers have little control over balls put in play. Take two nearly identical pitchers. One pitches for the best defensive team in baseball, while the other pitches for the worst. The pitcher with the best defense should have a better ERA than the one with the worst defense, even though they have the same skills. FIP removes the randomness of balls in play and looks at things pitchers can control: strikeouts, walks, hit by pitches, and home runs. FIP accounts for the differences in value of home runs, walks, and strikeouts, and comes up with a number that is better at predicting a pitcher's future success than ERA.

In 2011, Halladay had a 2.20 FIP, the best in baseball.

FIP- simply takes a pitcher's FIP and shows how that pitcher compared to the league average. Halladay had a 56 FIP- in 2011, meaning he performed 44 percent better than the league average.

The 2011 Phillies rotation had a combined 25.8 WAR, which is the second best in baseball since 1974, according to FanGraphs. Only the 1997 Braves (26.4) were better.

The Phillies had a 77 FIP-, which is the best in baseball in the World Series era (1903–present). They also had a 126 ERA+, which tied for ninth in that span. Since 1939, they ranked tied for third with the 1944 Cardinals, behind only the 1997 Braves (127) and 1998 Braves (127).

"It would seem obvious this was probably the best rotation since the Braves of the mid-1990s," said Bill James, baseball historian and godfather of sabermetrics. "There are comparisons with Greg Maddux, John Smoltz, and Tom Glavine. And that fourth starter with the Braves was pretty good, too. That Braves rotation is the greatest starting rotation of all time. But I don't have any doubt the Phillies are an all-time great rotation. I don't have any doubt about that."

Costas agreed.

"The mere fact that the Phillies bear comparison—and this is not a comprehensive list—to the '54 Indians, the great Orioles staffs of the late '60s and early '70s, to the Atlanta staffs of the '90s, right there that makes them among the all-time best," he said. "There's statistically good and then there's a good-chance-of-winning-the-game good. These guys were both of those things."

The Rotation could really cement its legacy with a World Series championship parade down Broad Street.

"[Sandy] Koufax and [Don] Drysdale are locked in people's minds because the Dodgers won the World Series in '59, '63 and '65 and went to the World Series in '66," Costas said. "No knock on Claude Osteen or Johnny Podres, who were very good pitchers, but that Number Three isn't as good as Cole Hamels. But it's still more locked in people's minds because it's that ultimate idea of walking off with the title. Or unless you just go there so often like the Braves did, even though they only won it once, they were on the big stage so often as a group, whereas this group has only been together a short period of time."

That is where James issued a caution.

"All-time great pitching rotations don't have a great record in postseason play," he said.

James recalled the 1954 Indians, who boasted Hall of Fame pitchers Early Wynn, Bob Lemon, and Bob Feller, and All-Star Mike Garcia. The Indians finished the regular season 111-43 for the best winning percentage (.721) in American League history, but the New York Giants swept them in the World Series.

The 1971 Orioles finished 101-57 for the best record in baseball, but lost in seven games to the Pittsburgh Pirates in the World Series. The 1966 Dodgers finished 95-67, but the Orioles swept them in the World Series. The Braves won 14 consecutive division championships from 1991 to 2005, but made the World Series just four times and won just one of them.

"I don't think there's something about great pitching staffs that makes them doomed in the postseason," James said. "But I also don't think having a great pitching staff means you're going to roll through the postseason. Sometimes people convince themselves that this team can't be beaten in the postseason because the pitching is good. History has shown that's not the way it works. You've still got to have some good things happen."

Would good things happen to The Rotation in October?

Would it find postseason success?

That's what it was looking for from Day One of spring training, back when Cliff Lee admitted that, sure, The Rotation had a chance to make history, but a World Series title was what it was really thirsting for.

OCTOBER

The late-night flight home from Atlanta was a happy one. The Phillies had set a club record with their 102nd win and lifted a toast to Charlie Manuel for becoming the team's all-time leader in managerial wins. The skipper rewarded his players with a well-deserved day off.

Their long regular-season journey had produced the most wins in the majors and now it was time to start the validation process, a month-long quest for the 11 postseason wins that would make them World Series champions. Anything short of that would be a disappointment that made those 102 wins a conversation piece, and not much more.

The Phillies entered the eight-team postseason tournament as favorites to win it all, but in the days leading up to the playoffs, more than a few folks had pointed out that being the favorite doesn't guarantee a parade.

"They're the best team around," Washington Manager Davey Johnson said as his club was beating the Phils four straight times during the final week of the season. "Their pitching is dominant. But in a short series, anything can happen."

Slowed by injury, the Phils' offense sputtered in the final weeks of the regular season. Johnson's Nationals held the Phils to just nine runs in sweeping that four-game series. People around baseball were starting to notice the offensive problems and wonder if this club would be a quick out in October.

"If Philadelphia's bats don't wake up, then they are not going to win," said David Wells, the former big-league pitcher who was part of the TBS postseason broadcast team. "It's as simple as that. I don't care how good their pitching is. You can't win if you don't score."

The Phillies learned that—painfully—when they were knocked out of the NLCS by San Francisco a year earlier. The Phils were denied the chance to become the first NL team since the 1942–44 Cardinals to make three straight World Series, largely because they hit just .178 (8 for 45) with runners in scoring position in the NLCS.

Would it happen again?

Would the bats go soft and deny this team and its great pitching staff the corona-tion it had sought for months?

Shane Victorino was leaving nothing to chance.

After that day off, September 29, he showed up at Citizens Bank Park for the team's workout the day before Game 1 of the NLDS. The day before the postseason opener feels like the first day of the season all over again, and this was no exception. Stadium workers hung red, white, and blue bunting from the second deck and painted the NLDS logo on the grass in front of each dugout. Players wore crisp, new, red sweatshirts—postseason merchandise is big business and the players are human mannequins—emblazoned with the postseason logo. As the Phillies came out of the clubhouse to stretch and begin batting practice on this cool autumn day, a representative from the famed Louisville Slugger bat company took orders from players. A trip to the World Series isn't complete without a dozen new bats, right? But what happens if you fail to make the World Series?

Anyone want some kindling wood for the long winter?

"Put some extra hits in them," Victorino shouted good-naturedly to the Louisville Slugger man.

Oh, that it were that easy.

---------------------- K ----------------------

So, who's your Game 1 starter?

Charlie Manuel heard that question several times in the days that fol-lowed the Phillies' clinching of the NL East.

For reporters, the question represented due diligence.

But they knew it was a dumb question. Having Roy Halladay in your starting rotation is like having John Wayne in your movie. He would get the ball in Game 1.

Why?

"Everything about him," Manuel said. "He's the most prepared guy I've ever seen. He works harder than anyone I've ever seen. He's more determined than anyone I've ever seen. He's got four pitches, maybe five, and he com-mands them all. I've seen him load the bases with no outs and work right out of it. He's got a tremendous feel for pitching."

Halladay had also earned the ball for Game 1 of the 2010 NLDS and, in the first postseason start of his life, became the first pitcher in 54 years to pitch a postseason no-hitter.

What would he have up his red sleeve this time?

Halladay wasn't sure, but as he sat at the dais for a news conference the day before Game 1 of the 2011 NLDS, he echoed some familiar personal sentiments. He said he intended to enjoy the ride, the process, the journey. For as much as he wanted that World Series ring, a decade of missing the postseason in Toronto had taught him that this was a special time and it had to be embraced.

"You really have to put things into perspective and understand what this game ultimately means," Halladay said. "You play this game because you love it and you play it because you enjoy the competition. I think that's what, at this point, is most important. I think if you go in with a mentality of this being the end-all and be-all, you're putting a lot of extra things on your plate that you really don't need."

Did Halladay's philosophical view of the situation mean his competitive furnace had lost some heat?

Hardly.

"Believe me," he said, looking at a pack of reporters. "We want to win bad."

To illustrate that, he quoted Shakespeare—even though he probably didn't know the Bard from Josh Bard.

"I heard a quote a long time ago, 'I came here to bury Caesar not praise him,' " Halladay said.

Now that's the old Philadelphia spirit.

As Halladay was speaking, the St. Louis Cardinals' charter flight was approaching Philadelphia International Airport. It was a flight few anticipated on August 25, when the Cards were 10½ games out of the wild-card race. The trip might have seemed far-fetched even back in February, when the Cardinals suffered a devastating blow, as their ace right-hander, Adam Wainwright, grabbed his right elbow in pain and walked off the field to season-ending Tommy John surgery.

But the Cardinals, led by veterans Chris Carpenter, Albert Pujols, Matt Holliday, and Lance Berkman, proved to be baseball's most resilient club. Even without Wainwright, the always resolute Tony La Russa kept his personal GPS locked on the postseason and stressed that his players compete every game, every pitch, every at-bat. General Manager John Mozeliak rebuilt a leaky bullpen and fortified the infield with the acquisition of shortstop Rafael Furcal before the July 31 trade deadline.

All of this, coupled with some help from the stumbling Atlanta Braves, put the Cardinals in position for a late surge that saw them go 23-9 down the stretch to win the NL wild card in Houston on the final day of the season.

While oddsmakers liked the Phillies to reach the World Series, the Cardinals didn't plan on stopping at the wild card. During their champagne celebration in Houston, catcher Yadier Molina stood up and made a proclamation to his teammates.

"We're happy to make it," he told them, "but our job is not done."

Game 1 pitcher Kyle Lohse concurred as he related the anecdote.

"That's the mentality of our team," he said. "We're thrilled to be here, but the work is not done yet."

For some Phillies fans the Cardinals represented a less than desirable matchup. The Cardinals went 6-3 against the Phillies during the regular season, including 3-1 in September, and were the hot team. But the Phillies players were undaunted.

"We're all well aware of how good they are," Halladay said. "We obviously have respect for what they've done and how they've played, but you have to be confident going in that you're going to be able to beat them. You have to be confident the guys around you feel the same way. We don't take them lightly. But at the same time, I feel like, without an arrogant tone to it, we believe we have a team that can go out and get the job done."

Charlie Manuel also believed he had a team that could get the job done. His faith could be traced to the pitcher's mound, where Halladay, Cliff Lee, and Roy Oswalt were hungry to lift the World Series trophy, just as Cole Hamels had done in 2008.

"I like that we have three guys this good who have never won a World Series," Manuel said. "I think they're really looking forward to it and really want to win. They love to pitch—and when they get beat, they're not very happy campers. We're here because of our pitching. I don't think they get enough credit. Every night this season they gave us a chance to win. We had a hard time scoring runs at times, but they usually took us to a point in the game where we could win if we scored, and they pitched over mistakes when our defense was not good. They did a hell of a job for us and I'm excited."

———————————— K ————————————

Citizens Bank Park pulsated with enough electricity before Game 1 to light up the Philadelphia skyline for a month.

This was the Phillies' time.

This was why they spent those seven weeks in spring training, why they won those 102 games. This was why fans sold out every game, why they made those March pilgrimages to Clearwater. It was all for the postseason, the 11 October wins that would lead to confetti flying. This was the most talented, most expensive, and most hyped team in franchise history. Anything short of those 11 wins would result in an emptiness never felt in Philadelphia sports.

Halladay threw his first pitch to a huge, accompanying roar of the crowd. The decibel level cooled when Furcal singled on the second pitch Halladay threw. Halladay got the first out of the inning, and then walked Pujols on four pitches. Three batters into the game, the Phillies' ace was faced with his first jam, and it turned into early damage when Berkman smacked a three-run homer into the right-field seats on the first pitch he saw.

It was an almost surreal beginning. The Phillies had been gearing toward this moment for months and now they were behind, 3-0, just four batters into the game. The crowd was silent. Halladay looked stunned as he waited for umpire Chris Guccione to toss him a new ball.

"I couldn't think of a worse way to start, really, than putting your team in a hole like that," Halladay said.

Once upon a time, Halladay might have been cooked after allowing a three-run home run in the first inning. Once upon a time, his world might have caved in right there on the pitcher's mound. Of course, those were the days before Harvey Dorfman got hold of Halladay and helped transform him from near washout to perennial All-Star. The famed sports psychologist had died in February, but Halladay still lived and worked by the principles he learned from his mentor. Heck, he still had the guy's emails in his computer. So as the Cardinals poured it on in the first inning, Halladay remained calm and focused. In his mind, he could hear Dorfman's voice:

Don't worry about what's already done.

Control your emotions.

Stick to your plan.

Move on.

Breathe.

Execute the next pitch.

Eventually the Phillies' offense thawed and Ryan Howard and Raul Ibanez hit home runs to lead an 11-6 win.

The crowd of 46,480 left Citizens Bank Park with a smile on its collective face that night.

Somewhere, Harvey Dorfman was smiling, too. Halladay's work that night was a tribute to his guru of the mind. After giving up those three first-inning runs, he allowed just one hit and no runs over his next seven innings. He walked just one, struck out eight, and finished his night by retiring 21 straight Cardinals.

"You just really have to avoid trying to make up for what already happened," said Halladay, explaining his key to surviving what could have been a fatal first inning. "I can't go out and subtract runs. You have your moment of frustration and you've got to move on. I'm not going to pack it in. I've got to stick to my plan.

"It took a long time for me to be able to learn that," Halladay added. "You have to put things behind you and move on. You can't lose your aggressiveness and the feeling that you still have a chance to win."

Thanks to Halladay, the Phils were off and running. But there were still miles to go, as Spanish-speaking catcher Carlos Ruiz reminded his mates when he wrote "10 Mas" on the clubhouse white board.

———————— K ————————

The Phillies were winning this series. There was no doubt about that.

When Cliff Lee jogged to the mound in the top of the fourth inning in Game 2, the Phils had a commanding 4-0 lead. They were 72-13 when they scored four or more runs in 2011. Lee was 96-7 in his career when his team scored four or more runs with him on the mound, including 10-1 as a Phillie in 2011.

"When you've got Cliff out there you definitely have a great feeling," Ibanez said.

The first three innings could not have gone any better for the largest crowd (46,579) in Citizens Bank Park history. Cardinals Manager Tony La Russa appeared to outsmart himself by pitching Chris Carpenter on short rest for the first time in his career. Carpenter bombed, allowing five hits and four runs in just three innings. Howard struck first with a two-run single in the first inning to give the Phillies a 2-0 lead. Ibanez knocked in the third run of the inning to make it 3-0, and Hunter Pence knocked in the game's fourth run in the second to make it 4-0. Meanwhile, the Cardinals couldn't cash in on a leadoff triple in the first or a leadoff double in the second.

Lee looked primed for another dominant postseason performance. He went 4-0 with a 1.56 ERA in five postseason starts with the Phillies in 2009, and everybody in the ballpark envisioned more of the same in October 2011. Lee had dominated the National League for weeks. He was 7-1 with a 0.93 ERA in his last 10 regular-season starts. He was a Cy Young candidate. There was no *whatever* about it—he was on his game.

But as Lee jogged off the mound with runners at the corners and nobody out in the seventh inning, the Cardinals had taken a one-run lead. The lefty allowed three runs in the fourth inning and one in the sixth as the Cardinals tied the game. Then in the seventh, he allowed a leadoff triple to Allen Craig, who scored on Pujols' single to left-center to make it 5-4.

The huge crowd, so loud and excited in the early innings, fell silent as Craig crossed home plate with the go-ahead run. Phillies fans were sickened.

What happened? Four-nuttin' lead? Cliff Lee on the mound? This series was over, wasn't it?

Lee blew a big lead in a shocking loss. He allowed a career-high 12 hits and five runs in six-plus innings. He had the Cardinals in a choke hold, but let them get away.

"I take full responsibility," he said after the game. "I had a 4-0 lead and I let it slip away."

There were other factors in the Game 2 loss. Charlie Manuel pointed out the Phillies had just one hit after Carpenter left the game. Umpire Jerry Meals had a questionable strike zone throughout the night, prompting La Russa to rip him during his in-game interview on TBS. La Russa was fined by Major League Baseball for his actions, but it was money well spent. The strike zone was much more to the Cardinals' liking for the remainder of the series.

But when it came down to it, this was Lee's game and he blew it. "I somehow squandered it away," he said.

The Cardinals didn't need an airplane to fly home after that game. They were sky-high, feeling great about their chances to win the short series. They had beaten a man they should not have beaten, not with the lead he had.

"It doesn't happen very often," Lance Berkman said. "But neither does coming from eight and a half back with a month to play."

— K —

Lee's catch and release in Game 2 made a lot of people in the Phillies' camp nervous. The series was tied at a game apiece and the Cardinals had the next two on their home turf. Anything can happen in a short series, even to a team favored to win the World Series. Was that *anything* about to be a disaster for the Phillies?

"Is it a colossal failure if we don't make it out of the first round?" one anxious club official asked before Game 3 in St. Louis.

The anxiety was felt in the clubhouse, too. Shane Victorino sensed it in his belly.

"Was there that kind of stomach feeling that this was a big game? Yeah," he said. "We knew there was a lot riding on this."

Victorino's pregame butterflies turned to postgame euphoria, thanks to Ben Francisco's pinch-hit three-run home run in the seventh inning that lifted the Phillies to a tension-easing 3-2 win.

Francisco was amused by the size of the pack of reporters that surrounded his locker after the game.

"It's been awhile," he said with a big smile.

In truth, it had been a long time since the man known to teammates as Benny Fresh had done anything worth much attention.

Affable and soft-spoken, Francisco had won the starting right-fielder job with a big spring training, but held that job for just two months and was relegated to the end of the bench by the time Hunter Pence arrived in late July.

In Game 3, the Phillies' offense had been shackled by St. Louis lefty Jaime Garcia. The Phils didn't score a run in the last seven innings of Game 2 and now had gone six innings without a run in Game 3.

Just 27 years old, Cole Hamels made his 13th career postseason start that day. Hamels had battled shoulder inflammation in August and was now quietly fighting another ailment—loose bodies in his elbow. This may have been why he had trouble commanding the strike zone and keeping his pitch count down. Hamels threw 117 pitches and left the game after sixth innings. He would have liked to have gone longer, but his contribution was immense, nonetheless, as he managed to hold the Cards scoreless before leaving for a pinch hitter.

Francisco was that pinch hitter, and he went to the plate with a good feeling against Garcia. Three weeks earlier, he had faced the left-hander in Philadelphia and sent a high sinker to the warning track. Had he not hit the ball off the end of the bat, Francisco believed he might have had a home run.

Victorino was on second base when La Russa opted to have Garcia walk

Carlos Ruiz intentionally, putting two men on base for Francisco.

"Ruiz has terrorized us in the past," said La Russa, explaining one of the few decisions to backfire on him in the series.

Garcia's first pitch to Francisco was a ball. The second pitch was a high sinker, a pitch nearly identical, Francisco said, to the one he'd seen three weeks earlier. He didn't hit this one off the end of the bat. He got it right on the sweet spot. The ball climbed high over the shortstop as the Busch Stadium crowd fell silent. It jetted over the outfield and toward the Phillies' bullpen.

"Come on, get here, ball, keep coming," Brad Lidge said to himself in the Phillies' bullpen.

It got there, all right. The three-run home run was the big blow, the only blow, really, for the Phillies that night, and it came from an unlikely source.

"It takes twenty-five guys, bro," Victorino said.

Francisco spoke to waves of reporters as he described what the greatest moment of his career felt like.

"Excitement, joy, a big adrenaline rush," he said. "We won the game and getting a big home run means a lot to my family and friends who've supported me through kind of a tough year.

"I came to spring training trying to help us win a World Series and I can still do that."

The victory put the Phillies one win away from their fourth-straight NLCS, but it wasn't like they didn't have issues. Despite their stress-relieving win in Game 3, a major concern was brewing around the club. The offense was sputtering again. The team had scored in just one of its previous 16 innings, and those runs came on one swing from an end-of-the-bench pinch hitter.

The Phils were ahead in the series, but they weren't going to stay there if they didn't start hitting.

---------------- K ----------------

Roy Oswalt wasn't convincing as he spoke to the pack of reporters surrounding him in a corner of the visitors' clubhouse at Busch Stadium.

"The pressure is back on them," he said defiantly.

How so? The Cardinals beat the Phillies, 5-3, in Game 4 to even the series and send it back to Philadelphia for a deciding fifth game. The Phillies, who had been World Series favorites since Cliff Lee's signing in December, suddenly found themselves one loss from elimination in the first round of the playoffs.

The Cardinals were the unlikely participants in this postseason tournament, the club that had little to lose, the club that was playing with the house's money after being 10½ games out of the playoff chase in late August and 8½ back at the start of September.

The Phillies were the team that had carried heavy World Series expectations since there had been snow on the ground. The pressure would be squarely on them in Game 5.

Oswalt could have prevented all this, but he gave up five runs in six innings to take the loss in Game 4. He allowed a run in the first inning and two runs in the fourth inning when he walked Lance Berkman, hit Matt Holliday with a pitch, and gave up a double to David Freese to give St. Louis a 3-2 lead. Freese got Oswalt one final time when he hit a two-run homer in the sixth to make it 5-2.

"Two pitches, I guess," Oswalt said. "I don't know. I thought I had pretty good stuff."

But pretty good doesn't get it done in the postseason.

For 162 games, starting pitching had been this team's great strength, the weapon that was going to carry the Phillies to the World Series. But in two of the first four games of the postseason, the starting pitching was lackluster, as Lee and Oswalt allowed 10 runs in 12 innings in their two starts

Not that the offense was shining. In Game 4, the Phils scored two runs in the first inning, but failed to build much after that as Cardinals righthander Edwin Jackson retired 17 of the final 20 batters he faced. The Phillies ended that game having been held scoreless in 22 of the previous 25 innings, conjuring up nightmares of the previous October. It looked ugly, too. While Cardinals hitters put on a clinic, working counts and having quality, grinding at-bats, Phillies hitters showed poor plate discipline, and it drove Charlie Manuel, not to mention the folks up in the executive suite, crazy.

"What's that saying?" Manuel said before the game. "I could have missed the pain, but I'd have to miss the dance?"

The agony of those poor Phillies' at-bats would be forgotten if they could win Game 5 at home. History had already proven that. The Phils had just one hit in their first 32 at-bats with runners in scoring position in the 2008 World Series, but few remembered because it all ended with a parade.

"It's a pressure situation," said Jimmy Rollins, looking ahead at Game 5.

"This is what we play for. This is also what we get paid for—to play in these situations. I don't think anyone in here is afraid of it."

Rollins spoke those words in an almost empty clubhouse in St. Louis. Most of the Phillies, including Roy Halladay, had already made their way to the bus for the ride to the airport and flight back to Philadelphia. Halladay would get the ball in Game 5 against his old friend and Toronto teammate Chris Carpenter. Suddenly, it didn't look as if Tony La Russa had outsmarted himself. His decision to use Carpenter on short rest in Game 2 allowed the right-hander to be ready for the decisive fifth game—on full rest.

The thought of Halladay taking the mound was comforting for Rollins.

"You get your big boy on the bump," he said. "This was the reason why he was brought there, for games like this, for him to come out and be the man. Be Doc. Go out there and perform a little surgery."

———————————— K ————————————

Charlie Manuel scheduled a light workout at Citizens Bank Park for the off day between Game 4 and Game 5. The players would have shown up for a workout even if Manuel had given them the day off. The season was on the line and no player wanted to sit around the house stressing about a do-or-die game. Better to get on the field and work up a sweat.

Outwardly, the Phillies appeared loose. Rollins reached back in time and kept it Philly by blasting some Hall and Oates in the clubhouse before the workout. During batting practice, the stadium sound system prophetically blared Lady Gaga's "Edge of Glory."

One team was indeed on the edge of glory.

But which one?

Despite proclamations they were loose and relaxed before one of the biggest games in franchise history, there were signs that the Phillies were anything but.

A few years earlier, Manuel had said that learning to finally stay relaxed in pressure situations was one of the keys to the Phillies' winning the World Series in 2008.

"We got tight," he said in February 2009, referring to the team's maturation in 2006, 2007, and part of 2008. "We'd get in a good position, but it was hard for us to take advantage of it because we got tight. I call it fear of failing. When you have never been through it before, fear of failing enters your mind. The fact of the matter was we had never been there before."

Chase Utley sensed the tightness during the 2008 season and famously told teammates and the coaching staff to "get the rubber duck out of your ass." Everyone had a good laugh whenever Utley said it. Manuel loved the expression so much that he bought a bunch of rubber ducks and placed one in each player's locker before Game 1 of the 2008 World Series, his reminder to everyone to stay loose. A few rubber ducks had resided in Manuel's office at Citizens Bank Park since. Sensing the weight on his team before Game 5 of the 2011 NLDS, the manager reached for some of the 2008 magic and left a few of the rubber ducks on the counter in the clubhouse. Players reacted with laughs and smiles.

But they were still tighter than hell.

At least that's how they looked on the field.

The Cardinals, meanwhile, continued to play like a band of wedding crashers. Rafael Furcal opened the game with a triple against Halladay and the next batter, Skip Schumaker, grinded out a classic Cardinals 10-pitch at-bat that resulted in an RBI double.

Halladay settled down and pitched out of trouble in the inning, pitched like an ace. That first-inning run would prove to be the only one he'd allow in eight innings of brilliance that saw him allow just six hits while walking one and striking out seven.

As good as Halladay was, his old pal Carpenter was better. He pitched a three-hit shutout and did not walk a batter. The Phillies averaged 4.80 runs per game from July 1 through the end of the regular season, tops in the NL. All they had to do was score two runs for Halladay and they would have lived to have seen the second round of the playoffs. But Carpenter, a tough-minded right-hander who battled years of arm trouble before winning the NL Cy Young Award in 2005, gave the Phils nothing. With each zero he put on the scoreboard, tension in the Phillies' dugout grew. With each scoreless inning, Phillies hitters squeezed their bat handles tighter and tighter until there was no more season.

The Phils lost, 1-0, and were eliminated.

The *what ifs* started almost immediately.

What if Halladay hadn't been victimized by a familiar bugaboo? (Leadoff men were 16 for 33 with a walk against him for the season.) What if Victorino had hit the cutoff man and given the infield a chance to cut down Furcal on that triple? What if Raul Ibanez's drive to the right-field warning track with two men on in the fourth had been greeted by a friendly October tailwind and landed in the seats? What if Utley's ninth-inning drive to the warning track in center had traveled a few more feet?

What if . . .

What if . . .

What if . . .

What if management hadn't put together the best starting rotation in baseball?

What if all the hype never followed?

What if the expectations never soared as high as they did, so high that they'd only be reached with a World Series title?

Would it have hurt any less had none of this happened?

Maybe.

But for now, it hurt. A lot. Especially for Roy Halladay, who pitched his ass off but received no run support.

———————————— K ————————————

The end had come, all too shockingly soon, and, now, where there was once great hope, only numbness remained.

The last sellout crowd of the season walked quietly out of the ballpark, heads down and hearts broken.

The Cardinals—talented, resilient, and looking kissed by destiny—danced in triumph on the infield grass.

A few feet away, a wounded Ryan Howard flopped on the first-base line and writhed in pain after his Achilles' tendon ruptured like the Phillies' dream as he made the final out of the game.

In his postgame news conference, a shaken Charlie Manuel searched for the right words, only to finally speak for an entire organization, an entire team, and an entire city.

"I feel very empty right now," he said.

As Manuel spoke, Roy Halladay was down the corridor in the clubhouse. He sat alone, in uniform, and stared frozenly into his locker for 25 minutes after the last out.

For an hour after the game ended, players showered, dressed, and spoke to reporters about their unfulfilled season.

"I'm shocked that we lost," said Brad Lidge, lingering in front of his locker.

Shane Victorino was one of the last players in the room. After dressing in the clubhouse for the final time in 2011, he rummaged through some belongings in his locker. He reached in and pulled out a sheet of World Series tickets marked for games in Philadelphia. He looked at them wistfully, and then slowly tore them into pieces and dropped them into the trash bin as he headed for the door.

Victorino did not speak to reporters.

He didn't have to.

Thirty-four years earlier, to the day, the Phillies suffered their infamous Black Friday loss to the Dodgers in Game 3 of the 1977 NLCS. For a whole new generation of Phillies fans and a whole new group of players, this was the new Black Friday. Even a major-league-best 102 wins would not soothe this wound. So much more was expected from these Phillies.

Disappointing year or disappointing ending?

"Disappointing year," Cliff Lee said. "We had higher expectations than this. It's not over until it's over and for us, it's over now."

Never had a loss hurt the Phillies in so many ways. Another year had ticked off the biological clock of the team's nucleus. A number of key players would become free agents. And from a financial standpoint, the early playoff exit cost the franchise millions of dollars in revenues.

For the second season in a row, the Phillies bowed out of the playoffs with their bats turning feeble. They scored 21 runs in five games against the Cardinals, but 11 came in the first game of the series. The Phils scored just 10 runs over the final four games and pushed runs across the plate in just three of their final 34 innings. As a team, they hit just .226 in the series. Howard was 2 for 19 and hitless in his last 15 at-bats. Placido Polanco was also 2 for 19. Carlos Ruiz was 1 for 17. The Cardinals did not tear the cover off the ball; they hit .259 for the series and were actually outscored, 21 to 19. They were there for the taking, but the Phillies never took them.

The Phillies ran out of gas.

They began to sputter in the final weeks of the season when they struggled to score runs. But through the offensive drought, the starting pitching was always there. That changed in Game 2 of the NLDS when Lee, the man whose December arrival fueled World Series hysteria, couldn't protect a lead at home.

"I take a lot of responsibility for this," Lee said after the Game 5 loss. "I had a 4-0 lead and wasn't able to keep it. If I did, we would have swept the series."

Regret also filled Cole Hamels' voice.

"You only get to play this game for so long," he said. "So it's kind of tough to see it slide through your fingertips."

Roy Oswalt moved on quickly. The contents of his locker were already packed and ready to go by the time reporters entered the clubhouse 20 minutes after the last out. Oswalt had the most difficult season of any of the team's Big Four starters and at times seemed as if his thoughts were elsewhere. On the night it all ended, he looked like a guy who was either double-parked on South Broad Street or couldn't wait to get home. Oswalt was the first one to exit the funereal clubhouse, leaving while many of his teammates were still in uniform coping with the loss.

Disappointed and drained, Halladay lingered in front of his locker and seemed to replay the loss over and over in his mind. He finally took off his uniform, threw on some gym shorts, and met with reporters in the middle of the clubhouse. He had pushed for a trade to Philadelphia because he thought it was the place his World Series dreams would come true. After two seasons and 40 regular-season wins, he was still looking for that ring.

"We came up short," he said. "Obviously winning the World Series was the ultimate goal for us, so this is tough.

"The hard part is you think about all the work you put in over the year, you think about the game today and how big it was going to be, and then all of a sudden that just kind of dissipates. It's hard to have it end like this. You always want to finish happy. It's hard to finish the season losing."

And so, nearly eight months after it began on a warm and sunny morning in Clearwater, it all ended on a cool and dark night in Philadelphia.

The 2011 Phillies headed home for the longest winter of their lives.

EPILOGUE

F our days after the season ended, the Game 5 line score remained hauntingly frozen on the Citizens Bank Park scoreboard:

CARDINALS	1	0	0	0	0	0	0	0	1	6	1
PHILLIES	0	0	0	0	0	0	0	0	0	3	2

In the basement of the ballpark, Ruben Amaro Jr. sat in the same room he had welcomed Roy Halladay and Cliff Lee to the club in the previous two off-seasons. This news conference wasn't nearly as pleasant. Like the city's sports fans, the general manager was still smarting from his team's quick exit. His displeasure with the team's offense was as clear as the goose egg on the scoreboard and he challenged Manager Charlie Manuel and Hitting Coach Greg Gross to rectify the situation in 2012.

"We don't have the same offensive team we had in 2008," Amaro said. "We don't have nearly as much power. We need to realize that and work with what we have. We need to make adjustments, work counts better, have better two-strike at-bats. We should have more .300 hitters, or close to it. We really should.

"There's no question in my mind this is a championship-caliber lineup. We just have to go about it in a different way. What we've done is not working. It's not worked well enough to get to the World Series and win."

As if the pain of early elimination wasn't enough, a number of players, including Ryan Howard and Cole Hamels, quickly had surgical procedures to fix injuries.

Meanwhile in St. Louis, the Cardinals, kissed by destiny, continued their late-season romp. They beat the Milwaukee Brewers in the National League Championship Series and won the World Series in a tense, seven-game battle with the Texas Rangers. It was a difficult series for Phillies fans to watch. One called Mike Missanelli's radio show on FM 97.5 The Fanatic and equated the experience to watching his wife appear in an adult film. "You don't want to watch, but you do because you want to believe the other guy isn't as good as you," the caller said.

Game 6 of the World Series was a classic, with the Cardinals coming from behind five times to win, 10-9, in 11 innings, and send the series to a seventh game. The Cards were down to their last strike in the ninth and 10th innings. David Freese twice delivered big hits—a game-tying triple in the ninth inning and a game-winning homer in the 11th—on his way to winning MVP honors. Freese and Howard were three years apart at Lafayette High School in suburban St. Louis. During his time in college, Freese became frustrated with the game and Howard was one of the people who helped talk him out of quitting. All these years later, Freese helped slay Howard's favored Phillies and went on to win World Series MVP honors.

And, of course, that Chris Carpenter fellow got the win in Game 7.

While the Phillies were two weeks into hunting and fishing season, the Cardinals rolled through the streets of St. Louis in a victory parade.

The next day, Tony La Russa retired after 33 years as a big-league skipper and three World Series titles.

At 67, La Russa went out on top.

Gradually, the sting of defeat eased on the executive level of Citizens Bank Park. The Phillies declined 2012 contract options on Roy Oswalt and Brad Lidge, making them free agents. Jimmy Rollins, Ryan Madson, and Raul Ibanez also became free agents, maybe to return, maybe to move on.

Before the leaves were completely off the trees, Amaro and his lieutenants completely turned their attention to the season ahead and signed free agent Jim Thome, the man whose arrival nine years earlier had signaled a baseball rebirth in Philadelphia.

All those years later, Thome was still looking for that elusive World Series ring, which gave him a kinship with Halladay and Lee.

Maybe 2012 would bring them what they were looking for.

INDEX